Hybridity

SUNY series

EXPLORATIONS

in

POSTCOLONIAL STUDIES

Emmanuel C. Eze and Arif Dirlik, Editors

A complete listing of books in this series can be found at the end of this volume.

Hybridity

Limits, Transformations, Prospects

ANJALI PRABHU

STATE UNIVERSITY OF NEW YORK PRESS

Published by
STATE UNIVERSITY OF NEW YORK PRESS, ALBANY

© 2007 State University of New York

All rights reserved

Printed in the United States of America

No part of this book may be used or reproduced in any manner whatsoever without written permission. No part of this book may be stored in a retrieval system or transmitted in any form or by any means including electronic, electrostatic, magnetic tape, mechanical, photocopying, recording, or otherwise without the prior permission in writing of the publisher.

For information, address State University of New York Press,
194 Washington Avenue, Suite 305, Albany, NY 12210-2384

Production by Diane Ganeles
Marketing by Anne M. Valentine

Library of Congress Cataloging-in-Publication Data

Prabhu, Anjali
  Hybridity : limits, transformations, prospects / Anjali Prabhu.
    p. cm. — (SUNY series, explorations in postcolonial studies)
  Includes bibliographical references and index.
  ISBN-13: 978-0-7914-7041-1 (hardcover : alk. paper)
  ISBN-13: 978-0-7914-7042-8 (pbk. : alk. paper)
 1. Reunionese literature (French)—History and criticism. 2. Réunion—Civilization.
3. Mauritius—Civilization. 4. Racially mixed people in literature. 5. Racially mixed people—Psychology. 6. Miscegenation. I. Title. II. Series.

PQ3988.5.R4P73 2007
840.9'96981—dc22

2006013431

10 9 8 7 6 5 4 3 2 1

For Keshav

Contents

Preface		ix
Acknowledgments		xvii
Chapter One	Introduction: Hybridity in Contemporary Postcolonial Theory: Examining Agency	1
Chapter Two	Hybridity in La Réunion: Monique Boyer's *Métisse* and the Nation as Necessity	19
Chapter Three	Theorizing Hybridity: Colonial and Postcolonial La Réunion	35
Chapter Four	On the Difficulty of Articulating Hybridity: Africanness in Mauritius	51
Chapter Five	Ethnicity and the Fate of the Nation: Reading Mauritius	85
Chapter Six	Interrogating Hybridity: Subaltern Agency and Totality through Edouard Glissant's *Poétique de la Relation*	105
Chapter Seven	Narration in Frantz Fanon's *Peau noire masques blancs:* Some Reconsiderations for Hybridity	123
Afterword:	Why Hybridity Now?	147
Notes		151
Works Cited		165
Index		175
SUNY series, Explorations in Postcolonial Studies		186

[Der Mensch] ist ein freier und gesicherter Bürger der Erde, denn er ist an eine Kette gelegt, die lang genug ist, um ihm alle irdischen Räume frei zu geben, und doch nur so lang, dass nichts ihn über die Grenzen der Erde reisen kann. Gleichzeitig aber ist er auch ein freier und gesicherter Bürger des Himmels, denn er ist auch an eine änlich berechnete Himmelskette gelegt. Will er nun auf die Erde, drosselt ihn das Halsband des Himmels, will er in der Himmel, jenes der Erde. Und trotzdem hat er alle Möglichkeiten und fühlt es; ja, er weigert sich sogar, das Ganze auf einen Fehler bei der ersten Fesselung zurückzuführen.
—Franz Kafka (Das Paradies, 1947)

[Man] is a free citizen of the world, for he is fettered to a chain which is long enough to give him the freedom of all earthly space, and yet only so long that nothing can drag him past the frontiers of the world. But simultaneously he is a free and secure citizen of Heaven as well, for he is also fettered by a similarly designed heavenly chain. So that if he heads, say, for the earth, his heavenly collar throttles him, and if he heads for Heaven, his earthly one does the same. And yet all the possibilities are his, and he feels it; more, he actually refuses to account for the deadlock by an error in the original fettering.

Preface

From the minute I set foot on Mauritian soil in August of 1997 to research my dissertation, I was forced to reconsider my Indianness, and to do so repeatedly. At my preliminary exam before this, when Fredric Jameson asked me how my Indianness was going to play out on my trip to Mauritius, I was puzzled—even vaguely annoyed. I arrived with my four-month old son in a carrier on my back, a huge suitcase full of baby things and a few changes of clothes for myself, another full of books and papers, and all the enthusiasm of discovering what one of my mentors called the "exceptionalism" of her native Mauritius (Lionnet "Créolité in the Indian Ocean" 107).

Several people at the Seewoosagar Ramgoolam International airport seemed curious about my arrival. Almost all the passengers waiting for their luggage appeared to know each other. It was mostly (Mauritian) Indians who started up conversation with me, asking where I was going, what I was doing, but mostly where I was *from*. All were horrified that I was unaccompanied except for my child, some disbelieving that I was not Mauritian and, therefore, even angry that I did not speak Creole, others nodding that I must be from Réunion even though I said I was Indian and lived in the U.S. In the midst of all this they watched censoriously as I hauled the heavy suitcases off the ramp, declined help, hoisted the baby carrier onto my back, and made my way out of the terminal. One driver, whom I later came to know as Mr. Saubourah, literally ordered me into his cab as I made my way uncertainly through the crowd of people outside. I remain grateful to him and Mme Saubourah who, between them, became my babysitter, buffer, chaperone, solver-of-problems. Although disapproving of many things I did and said, he took me under his wing and saw me through various unusual and sometimes startling situations I will not have the opportunity to recount here.

My Indianness became an issue for many Mauritian Indians I encountered: at the Mauritius archives, at the Mahatma Gandhi Institute, in interacting with students at the university, when I wanted to rent an apartment, or when people met me casually. I was chastised for wearing cotton saris (rather than the synthetic ones judged to be fashionable), for wearing jeans, for not having a clear Indian ethnicity and "mother-tongue" (Are you "tamoul"? Not at all, then why do you speak Tamil? Only half Konkan? What is Konkan? Malayali also? Grandmother speaking French?), for being married to a German, for arriving without him. I was repeatedly told that India was full of poverty and in Mauritius poverty did not exist. Nor did the diseases that India was riddled with. Yet, the very obvious fascination with some "authentic" Indianness that I could not uphold was brought home to me on these occasions. People looked askance at me for speaking French and not Creole, for not having a properly recognizable accent (to them) in French or English and thus followed up any conversation with numerous questions to ascertain my identity. I was somewhat forgiven because I could speak, read, and write Tamil and particularly Hindi. (It was the one time I was grateful to the Indian government for having made Hindi a compulsory subject and the national language despite the agitation from Tamil Nadu, where I am from, before and through the time I worked my way through the Indian Certificate of Secondary Education system.) Matters were somewhat toned down for the two weeks when my "Indian" father, arrived to meet his grandson, much to the approval of the same Mauritians I had met. He was respectably from India and clearly and unambiguously Konkan to them (and himself!).

Mauritian Indians were consistently interested in knowing if I was "Brahman," some prefacing it with the fact that they were "practicing Brahmans." They wanted to know how my parents had reacted to my marrying a "white" man. On occasion, I wept angry tears after neighbors or even passersby stopped in or brought others to see my son—whom by now I saw consciously as half-white, half-Indian—at odd times of day or night, when I was just managing to sit down and catch up on my day's notes or other chores because he was asleep. I could not turn them away because they always proffered some sort of "gift," making sure to reiterate that they remained "Indian" and remembered the "Indian way of hospitality." While it is now more common to see new unions (as opposed to the colonially created "Anglo-Indian" population) between whites and Indians in India, racial intermarriage is still certainly an issue there as well, even if in a different way.

In retrospect, however, the source of my tears was less the obvious frustration of being interrupted than the shattering of my utopian idea of what hybridity might mean in the real world. No doubt, attitudes have changed even since this recent sojourn in Mauritius, with even greater contact with India and the presence of Indians working within the Mauritian economy. Perhaps the presence of other whites, who become less connected to colonial whiteness in Mauritius, also deflects some of the loaded meaning of being white there. And it is, undoubtedly, more common to see Mauritian Indians linked to other groups in different ways. But the enduring nature of the categories that French and British colonialism used in administering this colony becomes apparent in the ways in which people understand their interactions with others in this postcolonial nation, even as it is "being hailed as a superb example of successful mediations of the uncertain relationship between nationhood and ethnic or cultural identity" (Lionnet "Créolité in the Indian Ocean" 106). The relationship between Mauritian Indianness and Mauritianness is a fascinating one that I encountered as an Indian visiting Mauritius. It is recorded in very interesting ways in the public culture of this hybrid nation and is explored in some detail in this book.

Hybridity is a seductive idea, which, it is claimed by prominent theories in postcolonial studies, can lead us out of various constraints in conceiving agency. In its most politically articulated guises, hybridity is believed to reveal, or even provide, a politics of liberation for the subaltern constituencies in whose name postcolonial studies as a discipline emerged. In this book, I test these claims with reference to a set of theorists whose work forms the core informing the renewed interest in hybridity in contemporary theory. But I also conduct this investigation by way of a social frame of reference, which will be the overtly "hybrid" and "postcolonial" societies of the Indian Ocean Creole islands of Mauritius and La Réunion.

Mauritius and La Réunion, two small islands of the Indian Ocean, having known, among others, both British and French colonialism, quite easily speak to the theorists of the different theoretical derivatives of hybridity considered. These prominent theorists draw from both the generality of the postcolonial as well as, in some cases, the realities particular to a Creole specificity. Rather than setting up a relationship where society "answers" or even "questions" theory, my reading will privilege a range of texts of differing provenance from these islands. These texts are seen as "theorizing" in situ what I identify as the central question in theories on hybridity in recent postcolonial studies, namely that of agency.

At the same time, let me state early on that this book is not an exhaustive study "about" either or both of these islands. The complexity of focusing on a relatively unknown area of Francophone culture might bring certain expectations for the project, such as a copious introduction to the region, demonstration of where the creativity of particular writers fits into the postcolonial canon, and so forth. These might translate into a pressure, felt by the author, to anthologize compulsively in order to show that there is a vast range of texts that are not being referenced. It is a pressure that I resist actively. Instead, each of the texts selected from these islands will be treated as the eloquent, fully developed creations I judge them to be and for which, precisely, they have been chosen. What I hope emerges also is the richness of the space that generated these texts and the significance of its particular engagement with hybridity and postcoloniality. Readers are referred to pertinent sources for more information on Indian Ocean literary creation, history, and context. What I propose here is a consequential point from which a dialogue can begin on the notion of hybridity as it has entered recent postcolonial studies. And I am persuaded that this dialogue necessarily brings about a restructuring of this notion, indicating a different derivative that I illustrate specifically in the reframing suggested in the culminating chapters. In these later chapters, I propose a different way of allying the thought of two thinkers of global hybridity, Edouard Glissant and Frantz Fanon, both of whom happen to be from the Caribbean Creole context and who have entered and occupied rather different spaces in postcolonial hybridity.

The hybrid is a colonial concept. This is not just to say that the term was coined during the period of high colonialism, but that it served certain interests, which were central to the colonial enterprise. Hybridity, then, is first and foremost a "racial" term. Hybrid individuals in the colonies testified to real encounters between the white colonizer and the native (most often slave) and subsequently required an active inscription in the laws and policies that managed and oversaw colonial activity. The superiority of the white race was, of course, a founding principle upon which colonialism was based—whether of the French style of so-called assimilatory policies or of what is often considered the more distant British form of rule in the colonies. The presence of hybrids directly called into question the clean division between these two groups and required the colonists to engage with this mixed section of the population with regard to inheritance, education, burials, marriage, and the notion of citizenship. In a comparable manner, postcolonial hybridity intervenes in the form of a theoretical argument against the homogenizing tendencies of global capitalism. It presents, one might say, the optimistic view of the effects of capitalism.

The prominence of the notion of hybridity in postcolonial studies should be reexamined with reference to two possible developments. Either the colonial context in which it was conceived is ever as pertinent to the postcolonial world, and therefore, the notion of hybridity retains its centrality in the ongoing, if modified, tensions between white people and people of color; or the radical changes that frame the interactions between these two groups (also recognizable as ex-colonizer and ex-colonized), and the changes within them have modified this notion of hybridity into something quite different from what it was during colonialism.

An examination of prominent theoretical versions of postcolonial hybridity will reveal that, more and more, the tendency in theory is to move away from the original entanglement of this idea with the notion of race. Instead questions of a hybrid culture, of hybridity in reading and in the very notion of identity are shown to exist. These instances of hybridity, it is proposed in these theories, should be recognized and promoted in a step that enables subaltern agency. That is, postcolonial theories of hybridity do away with the old dichotomy of colonizer/colonized, which is substituted by ideas of multiplicity, plurality, and difference in a less specifiable way. We will see that postcolonial texts of different kinds, which are closer to a "social ground," tend to take up and engage with this racial aspect much more explicitly as it is entangled with specific historical circumstances of racial categories and their changing significance associated with the history of that ground.

Postcolonial theories of hybridity can be seen to share some basic Marxian preoccupations and impulses, which are explored in the next chapter. Nevertheless, despite this and the fact that they all aim to privilege agency in the struggle against assimilation or homogenization, we will see that at the same time most of these recent theories work explicitly and implicitly against some concepts that are central to a Marxian account of agency. What then emerges, as I will show, is that an explosive theorist of struggle against colonization such as Frantz Fanon, when read within the framing of this version of postcolonial theoretical hybridity, has to be maneuvered into speaking a discourse that goes against the more basic ideas that inform his entire work. The critique of a "postcolonial Fanon" itself has been ongoing. Here, however, I take a new look at a part of Fanon's text of *Black Skin, White Masks*, which has been canonized within this prominent trend of hybridity in postcolonial criticism. I will argue that it is not that Fanon's dialectic of white and black fails to acknowledge and exploit hybridity fully by lapsing into universalism or humanism as Homi K. Bhabha has claimed, but rather, that the definition and preoccupations of this new derivative of hybridity are themselves at odds with what can be identified as hybridity in Fanon. Fanon's hybridity (particularly with reference to the notion of agency within it) has greater credibility even as a theoretical construct not just because it is anchored in a recognizable context but because it is tied to a politics of action of subaltern subjects. I will show that an idea of totality, which Fanon's work posits as essential for holding up agency, is lacking in the prominent version of hybridity in postcolonial studies. This notion is, however, found as a necessity within the fully ripened conception of thinkers whose intellectual processes and emotional impulses are conditioned by hybridity and an essentially Marxian informed vision of agency.

As in Fanon's case, I will argue that Edouard Glissant's conception of *Relation* explicates such a notion of totality while also activating many impulses central to Marxian thinking. Totality also emerges as a necessary condition for radical politics in the hybrid societies from the postcolonial world that are examined in this book. Derivatives of hybridity in postcolonial theories tend to obscure the conflictual aspect in hybridity, which remains of interest to a Marxian account of social change and is inscribed in societal processes in postcolonial locations. Hybridity as it can be identified in Fanon is tied to revolutionary social change, as we will see, while most postcolonial theories of hybridity, in their wish to be revolutionary, tend to overstate the ability of hybridity to dismantle power structures. Glissant's hybridity brings together reality and thought and challenges Marxian informed thinking to engage more consequentially with the idea of "difference." In this way, hybridity, as it can be gleaned from the thought of Frantz Fanon and Edouard Glissant—particularly through close reading and a Marxian framing offered in the chapters devoted to these two theorists—reconnects more credibly to the impulse for the formation of postcolonial studies as a discipline. The last two chapters provide a reading of each of these theorists in this particular way and are informed by the analyses of postcolonial Mauritius and La Réunion in the chapters preceding them.

Prominent theories of postcolonial hybridity recuperate the notion of agency while somehow eliding the very conditions within which hybridity as a concept emerged: the stunning inequality of two groups of people locked into a relationship of domination that is upheld and perpetuated by a system that operates in the sphere of the psychological and the symbolic as much as in the economic and the structural. My contention is that it is questionable to have recourse to such a disembodied notion of hybridity in an attempt to resolve conflicting situations where the inequalities of the colonial period continue to play out, even if modified or radically transformed through newer forces. The argument, then, is that if the overarching totality of colonialism, which gave hybridity its meaning and necessity has not been dismantled but rather reinvented, using hybridity to dismantle today's inequalities is a questionable gesture unless it is sufficiently retooled and reinvented itself particularly with regard to a new conception of totality in which struggle can be inscribed. If inequalities are no longer so clearly identifiable between this and that group, the area in which the hybrid is produced is still to be properly accounted for in these new theories. Françoise Vergès, whose work on métissage in La Réunion is a historically attentive one, has dry criticism for the proliferation of overly positive and exuberant notions of the hybrid, where an ideal has more currency than reality: "The idea of humanity is more appealing than the actual 'disappointing' human beings. I prefer 'disappointing human beings and their demystifying acts'" ("Post-Scriptum" 357). In the new theories of hybridity it becomes hard to accommodate the stark realities of specific subaltern populations of the world and their versions of hybridity. My critique of new theories of hybridity targets the way in which agency is privileged in them without accounting for totality and contradiction. This critique is implicit in the following analyses that focus on the contours and details of hybridity as a social phenomenon as well as a complex political strategy in Mauritius and La Réunion, and emerges more explicitly later when hybridity in Fanon and Glissant is examined.

Tracking the notion of hybridity in the plural, multiracial societies of Mauritius and La Réunion reveals from the outset that hybridity can only be understood through a proper historical understanding of its connection to colonial administration. Both the colonial and the postcolonial (here referring quite simply to two eras in chronology) versions of hybridity in these islands are dependent upon a particular totality within which hybridity as a concept has been sustained. In the earlier version, colonial culture is instantiated in every hybrid occurrence, while in postcolonial hybridity, it is the post-colony as nation or possible nation (within a system of global capitalism) that informs and even necessitates the claim to hybridity. The will to transcend the nation, to make transnational connections, is in no way precluded as it will become evident particularly in the study of Mauritian politics in chapter 4.

Taking stock of such a situation should not in any way be construed as a defeatist or pessimistic view that foretells doom. That has not been the driving affect of this work. Instead, it is inspired by the place in both Fanon and Glissant of utopia that is ever in the future and ever, necessarily, out of reach. But in resolutely striving toward it, there is no room for complacency, no room even for a lapse in energy. Garnering all the exuberance of contemporary postcolonial theories of hybridity, I suggest that the energies contained within the concept of hybridity and in every identifiable hybrid location be released through an approach that can only be satisfied if its own movement joins up explicitly with the agency of those who occupy these locations. To do so, as I argue in this book, is to render indispensable the concepts of contradiction and totality, the latter being creatively linked to utopia.

Acknowledgments

The intellectual and personal debts to be acknowledged by the author of this book are too numerous to list. A look at the index and bibliography will tell some of this story. Still, I am deeply grateful for encouragement and intellectual stimulation at different points of time in my life from the following teachers, mentors, friends, students, and colleagues: Elisabeth Mudimbé-Boyi, Fredric Jameson, Linda Orr, Walter D. Mignolo, Françoise Lionnet, Ariel Dorfman, Mireille Rosello, Dominic Thomas, H. Adlai Murdoch, Anne Donadey, Ambroise Kom, V. Y. Mudimbé, the late Marcel Tétel, Jeanette Beer, Floyd Merrell, Paul Benhamou, Erdmute White, Selvyn Jussy, Amitabh Mattoo, Shubha Pandey, Sudha Ramachandran, Shibhesh Singh, Rakesh Kumar, C. Jeewan, Rachna Negi, Neela Bhattacharjee, Nandini Sen, Zenobia Irani, R.K. Singh, Aparajita Sagar, Dawn Fulton, Ifeoma Nwanko, Jon Beasley-Murray, Geeta Paray-Clark, Danielle Marx-Scouras, Dorian Addison, Joan McNay, John Erikson, Robert Damoiseau, YoonSun Lee, YuJin Ko, Tim Watson, Sheela Nambiar, Priya Kurian, the late Lisa Mauney, Ayda Sarikaya, Nandita Gulvady, Anujee Matthew, the late M. R. Prabhu, Ralf Schlosser, Ato Quayson, Robert Young, David Washbrook, Rajeswari Sunderrajan, David Chioni Moore, Madhu Dubey, N.S. Yamuna, Nirmala Jairaj, Achille Giacometti, Raphaël Confiant, Dev Virahsawmy, Vinesh Hookoomsing, Elizabeth Daniel, Colleen Murphy, Ashley Coale, and Jenifer Clapp. I wish to thank my colleagues at the Wellesley College French Department in whose company this book was completed.

I benefited from a Mellon Grant for work with the GEREC group in Martinique. To Raphaël Confiant, in particular, I offer thanks for superb company and great perspective. Thanks to the University of Oxford's St. Antony's College for hosting me the year this book was written, African Studies at the University of Cambridge for housing me several summers of my research at the University Library, where I consulted the Royal Commonwealth Society Collections for historical documents on Mauritius as well as the Parliamentary debates. Thanks to Rachel Rowe and her crew for their support and help. Other institutions that supported my research in various ways are the University of Mauritius, Université de Paris VII, Duke University, and Wellesley College. I wish to extend my heartfelt thanks to: Jane Bunker, Larin McLaughlin, Diane Ganeles, and Anne Valentine, all at SUNY Press, as well as the series editors and anonymous reviewers.

Elisabeth Boyi has been a mentor, friend, and supporter on so many levels and with such good humor and balance, it would be impossible to describe. N. S. Yamuna somehow inspires everything I do. Others whose friendship and support I have relied upon are Linda Orr, Adlai Murdoch, Dominic Thomas, Mireille Rosello, Jim Petterson, and Priya Kurian. Special thanks to Mary Kate McGowan for friendship and frequent doses of sanity. For inimitable friendship, fierce debate, and every conceivable type of support, I have turned to Ato Quayson, who responded with the immense energy, enthusiasm, and generosity of spirit that are only his.

To Kairav Tobias: the experience of your meteoric arrival and brilliant energy continue to restore my sometimes-waning internal resources.

To Ralf: in admiration of the example of your work, in gratitude for the unwaveringness of your presence, and in humility before the vastness of your love.

This book is dedicated to Keshav Raphaël for roughing it out with me on the many journeys it took to write this book, and for your stylish sporting of hybridity: in wondrous anticipation of the unpredictable places to which you will take it or where you will abandon it.

Part of chapter 4 was published in the *International Journal of Francophone Studies*. I thank Intellect Publishers for granting copyright to use it here. A different version of chapter 6 was published in *Research in African Literatures*. Thanks to Indiana University Press for granting copyright to use it here. A slightly different version of chapter 5 has appeared in *Diacritics*. Thanks to Johns Hopkins University Press for granting permission to use it here.

CHAPTER ONE

Introduction: Hybridity in Contemporary Postcolonial Theory

Examining Agency

This book represents an attempt to align more closely the notion of hybridity in postcolonial studies with the exigencies that led to the founding of this academic discipline itself. Such exigencies arose from recognizing and studying situations of stark inequalities, which were held in place and legitimated by the various machinations of, or inherited from, colonialism. That is, in unpacking and examining hybridity today in some of its theoretical versions as well as specific societal configurations, this book attends to the ways in which such inequalities might inform current derivatives of hybridity.

Hybridity is an enticing idea in current postcolonial studies.[1] In its dominant form, it is claimed that it can provide a way out of binary thinking, allow the inscription of the agency of the subaltern, and even permit a restructuring and destabilizing of power. These assertions need to be tested and this is precisely what I propose to do in this book. This book evaluates central claims regarding agency in postcolonial theories of hybridity and investigates the avatars of hybridity to be found in the realities of the Indian Ocean "Creole" islands of La Réunion, which remains a French department, and Mauritius, independent from Britain since 1968.

In theoretical discourse, hybridity has spawned a variegated vocabulary, including terms such as diaspora, métissage, creolization, transculturation. Although skeptical about the validity of an exuberant type of hybridity that, it is claimed, poses an effective challenge to oppressive forces of the increasingly globalized world, I am interested in exploring what, if any, benefice hybridity holds for a radical conception of agency. The term "radical" means quite simply here that agency, in this conception, must be tied to social change in which some inequality or injustice is addressed. I therefore think it important to provisionally, but clearly, distinguish between hybridity as a theoretical concept and a political stance that we can argue, and hybridity as a social reality with historical specificity. The collusion of these two domains (of theory/politics and social reality) with regard to the hybrid will become significant to the analyses that follow. For me, the most productive theories of hybridity are those that effectively balance the task of inscribing a functional-instrumental version of the relation between culture and society with that of enabling the more utopian/collective image of society. Privileging what is hybrid in today's world cannot, even parenthetically, leave out the moment of capitalism in which such a view is offered—a moment that invites and, indeed, celebrates the hybrid through heterogeneity, multiplicity, and difference. On this view, a critical stance toward capitalism introduces skepticism into the idea that agency of the subaltern is thriving. The critique of capitalism comes from recognizing the unequal access to enabling processes, positions, and different kinds of capital for larger portions of the world's population.

Politics of Hybridity

I wish to suggest, at the outset, some simple reconsiderations to demonstrate the importance of a more careful attention to the varied vocabulary that is employed in referring to hybridity in contemporary theory. Throughout this book I will work between vocabularies generated in the relationship of Francophone studies to the more general field of (anglophone) postcolonial studies. Part of the reasoning for this is purely circumstantial in that my training has been in French and Francophone literature and culture and French theories of culture especially as they relate to postcolonial studies. Also, the rapid movement of French theory into postcolonial studies has occurred in various ways, not insignificantly and apart from the many translations, through more and more theorists who are conversant in these two idioms and who activate these channels.

It is my contention that there has been, in the proliferation of recent and disparate work on hybridity, a rather loose set of related terms that have not been problematized. It is no longer clear what is being suggested when referring to processes that are understood to be hybridizing. Some terms one frequently encounters are, for example: diaspora, créolité, creolization, intercultural interaction, transculturation, métissage, or syncretism. I am not undertaking the task of sorting through each and every one of these terms.[2] Rather, I wish to demonstrate by way of a brief investigation, the comparatively different politics that specific versions of hybridity can presuppose and engender. Therefore, it follows that it is important to be able to identify what politics are implicated by the use of a specific term born within a particular theory, especially if a different term carries with it an opposing signification. We should then reconsider using them interchangeably as is often the case.

I show the significance of such a gesture by investigating two avatars of hybridity under the provisional terminology of "diaspora" and "creolization" (or postdiaspora hybridity).[3] My choice of these two terms for the following discussion is based on my reading of them as incarnating two salient and opposed types of politics in the discourse of hybridity.

We can begin by deliberately separating these two terms for analytical purposes even while considering the arguable usefulness of keeping them distinct. Of course, the difficulty of doing this does not just follow from the fact that these terms are linked conceptually in fundamental ways and that they perhaps even share common meanings—or at least connotations—but also because they are entangled with a host of other terms such as those mentioned above. Still, the merit of the following exercise will become evident: it is to demonstrate first that in contemporary discourses of theoretical hybridity, there are some shared politics that differ from those of a prior moment, which I shall specify; also, while contemporary derivatives of hybridity seem to ally quite easily with a version of Marxism in promoting the agency of subaltern subjects, they are actually antagonistic to some basic Marxian notions, which are central to a conception of agency.

Diaspora as an enterprise obviously has deeply political foundations. Speaking of the African diaspora, we could agree that it became a project in response to racist ideologies developed in tandem with colonial exploitation in essentialist and biological terms. In this context, the idea of the African diaspora might be said to really take root at a particular historical moment: that of Pan-Africanism of the nations of the African continent as well as of pan-Africanism as the connection of all peoples of African descent, who were disadvantaged due to white supremacy, colonialism, slavery, and forced migration. Diasporic discourses, inasmuch as we are able to identify them today, tend to continue to function in the same mode of solidarity as they grapple with negative representations (and their very real consequences) of peoples seen as African in origin, in considering this diaspora.[4]

However, positing the idea of an African diaspora in this manner has been questioned because of a certain fixedness that it imposes, consequentially aggravating the pigeonholing, in particular ways, of "Africans" in different national and transnational contexts. The bases for solidarity within emancipatory movements also proved to be skewed toward a particular male subjectivity.[5] Creolization, then, as a theoretical stratagem was seen to release notions of diaspora from this essentialist one. Stuart Hall explains the new vision of diaspora, which I qualify here for clarity as creolization, implicitly opposing it to the previous one: "[. . .] diaspora does not refer us to those scattered tribes whose identity can only be secured in relation to some sacred homeland to which they must at all cost return, even if it means pushing other people into the sea" ("Cultural Identity and Diaspora" 401). The most evident example of the creolization versus diaspora dialogue in the Francophone context came with the publication of Bernabé, Chamoiseau, and Confiant's *Eloge de la Créolité*, which took a quite specifically antagonistic stance toward négritude, and Aimé Césaire in particular, despite problems within their own theory and the homage paid to Césaire himself in this manifesto.[6] Creolization, when viewed as a theoretical formulation postdiaspora, is tuned in to the present of diasporic populations away from the homeland. It addresses their concerns about advancement without blind assimilation but rather by preserving difference, allying around particular causes, connecting with the motherland in a way that is practical and practicable, and connecting with other diasporics. Hall explicitly places himself as theorizing about this second moment, when he explains that "[t]here are at least two different ways of thinking about 'cultural identity'" ("Cultural Identity and Diaspora" 393). The first posits a oneness and shared culture, while the "second position recognises that, as well as the many points of similarity, there are also critical points of deep and significant difference . . ." ("Cultural Identity and Diaspora" 394).

Viewed in this diachronic manner, we can identify in theoretical and political discourses dealing with the idea of minority constituencies, various changes that transform diaspora into creolization. This has to do with diaspora discourse having to encounter and accommodate itself to other experiences of minority status or new immigrations. It has to do with different generations having to maneuver their desires within the framework of this diaspora. It also has to do with the need for mobility in the new setting and the opportunities that are not equally available across this population for numerous reasons. The vigorous interest in this general concept of hybridity in postcolonial studies cannot be explained away as just a trendy thing. The fact that Bhabha's hybridity has come to have such vast applicability can be seen, in part, as fulfilling an urgent theoretical need. It is not the case that all theoreticians investigating the broad question of hybridity as creolization, intercultural interaction or any of its other forms, are necessarily creating responses to the notion of diaspora as were the créolité critics against négritude or in, say, the way Paul Gilroy does.[7] But together they create an influential discourse (postdiaspora) that I have put under the umbrella term of creolization for the moment.

Creolization Post Diaspora: A Marxian Take On Hybridity?

Theorists of hybridity such as Homi K. Bhabha, Françoise Lionnet, Paul Gilroy, and Stuart Hall employ this discourse of creolization, with a very varied vocabulary, as a way to combat the domination of one voice, one canon, one mode of thought, singular identities, linear history, and so forth. This is evident when Hall writes, regarding the new cinema, that it "allow[s] us to see and recognise the different parts and histories of ourselves, to construct those points of identification, those positionalities we call in retrospect our 'cultural identities.'" ("Cultural Identity and Diaspora" 402). Lionnet also writes similarly, for example: "The global mongrelization or métissage of cultural forms creates complex identities and interrelated, if not overlapping, spaces" (*Postcolonial Representations* 7).[8] Further, hybridity, in whatever guise, is linked to contingency and is time-bound. That is, the analysis of hybridity (and of specific instances of it) is obliged to account for a historicity, while at the same time the impulses of this process are to valorize synchrony over diachrony. In fact, the impulse of hybridity (as creolization as opposed to diaspora) has much in common with the communist one. The analogy I shall proceed to make between these two discourses is linked to a particular type of politics that they seem to share and that I wish to privilege in reexamining our interest in hybridity. The analogy also serves to bring into sharp focus the distinction between discourses of creolization and those of diaspora.

The Communist Manifesto claims that bourgeois society is dominated by the past while in communist society the present dominates the past (Marx and Engels 485). Similarly, a dialectic between diaspora and creolization is identifiable with diasporic discourses relying on a past trauma that justifies a present affiliation and solidarity, whereas creolizing discourses, even if not concerned with an actual erasure of the past trauma, direct their energies toward interaction and new connections in the present.[9] Diaspora discourses must distinguish, for example, between African or Indian or Chinese or even Islamic diasporas. Discourses of creolization sound like this notorious proclamation: "Neither African, nor European, nor Asian, we proclaim ourselves Créole" (Bernabé et al.).[10] Therefore, just as the Manifesto claims that "Communists do not form a separate party opposed to other working class parties (483), the créolistes' manifesto does not emphasize the different diasporic affiliations. Just as the bourgeoisie, in the terms of the Manifesto, "produces its own grave-diggers" (483), so too diaspora eventually saw creolization announce its practical demise in giving up a "sacred homeland" (Hall "Cultural Identity and Diaspora" 401). If "the essential condition for the existence, and for the sway of the bourgeois class" (Marx and Engels 483) is the formation and augmentation of capital, the essential formation of diaspora rests on the capital of the idea of the mother country. If capital's condition is wage labor and the competition between laborers, then diaspora is also historically linked to quantifiable labor, where the competition or at least the comparison of, for example, African slave labor versus Indian indentured labor, is identifiable.

I have used this analogy to show how in our own recent theoretical history in postcolonial studies from diaspora to creolization, we are inevitably speaking of periodization. The idea of periodization in postcolonial studies is linked to a critique of modernization and development within the colony-metropolis relationship. Periodization is repudiated and hybridity intervenes as a way out of this kind of sustained historicity because it privileges the here and now. Such a political relationship to history, for Hall, is "[n]ot an essence, but a positioning" ("Cultural identity and Diaspora" 395). Marxism, on the contrary, ends up undervaluing much of the formerly colonized world in its comparison to the "developed" world, comprised of the imperial nations. In postcolonial hybridity, the long view of history is usually given up in favor of focusing on a synchronic reality that can privilege the present engagement of those who comprise these societies. Bhabha and Lionnet, who invokes Bhabha, use hybridity as a way of valorizing the struggles of subaltern subjectivities within History. In Lionnet's reading of postcolonial women writers, "[t]he postcolonial subject [. . .] becomes quite adept at braiding all the traditions at its disposal" (*Postcolonial Representations* 5). Bhabha's "purpose in specifying the enunciative present in the articulation of culture is to provide a process by which objectified others may be turned into subjects of their history and experience" (*Location* 178). Development, on an historical view, emerges in terms of the technological advancement and modernization visible in culture accomplished by the developed world and, not in small measure, we might add, due to the latter's long enterprise in the various colonies. Domination is seen as inevitable and all encompassing. These theorists suggest a valuable reconsideration of such a unitary view of historical domination and in this way join up with the essential raison d'être of anthropological discourse. As suggested by Marcus and Fischer, this view, in the twentieth century, "has stood for the refusal to accept this conventional perception of homogenization toward a dominant Western model" (1; see also 67). For these latter, anthropology's mission is to show how difference exists, to explicate this difference, and then use this difference as a counter point to critique your own culture (1 and 20, for example).[11] In this way, as Bart Moore-Gilbert has noted, evoking Tangiers in Barthes' *Pleasure of the Text* and China in Julia Kristeva's work, while "the East may function as a means by which to deconstruct the authority of the West [. . .] it is still being appropriated [. . .] as a solution to 'internal' Western cultural problematics" (128). In these prominent theories of hybridity, metropolitan marginalization or marginalized theoretical positioning within the academy provides much of the impulse to undo the authority of assimilation. I am interested in bringing together hybridity that derives from the metropolitan (epistemological) encounter of these theorists with authoritative readings of culture (even when the matter these theorists analyze is not necessarily canonical), and hybridity in postcolonial regions (former colonial holdings where the political apparatus has been strongly marked by their colonial history). I am also interested in testing the viability of agency as it is conceived in these new theories of hybridity by examining readable claims to agency in overtly "hybrid" postcolonial locations.

It is possible to trace among these theories (provisionally grouped under creolization) an intellectual "solidarity," to borrow a term from Ian Baucom's article on what he calls Frantz Fanon's radio. In this more generous view, we can follow Baucom's explanation (where he is speaking specifically of the affiliation of Gilroy and Fanon) that:

> . . . it is a form of solidarity which does not insist that Gilroy say again what Fanon has said before. It is the discursive enactment of a solidarity which does not imply that intellectual solidarity demands a community of those who speak and think the 'same.' Rather, intellectual affiliation here constitutes itself in much the same fashion that Fanon indicates a subaltern collectivity produces itself—through listening and re-creating, paying attention and remaking. Solidarity, thus understood, demands both a 'common' narrative, canon of experience, or object of attachment and a set of differentiated reproductions of that common thing; a common consent to listen and a collective dissent of interpretation; not so much an identity in difference as a differencing in identity. To my mind, this sort of performative solidarity provides a model (if an admittedly paradoxical 'model') for the ways in which intellectual workers might construct their critical 'solidarity' with one another. (p 35)

In privileging subaltern agency, these theories simultaneously suggest that hybridity is a positive, resistive force to cultural hegemony. What is less obvious is the ways in which such cultural resistance is tied to other types of social resistance to economic oppression. It is unclear as to how immediate opposition that can be identified in texts, art, and theory participates in restructuring what supports and enables cultural hegemony. Also, the promotion of hybridity by capitalism's bringing together different parts of the globe is not accompanied by a theoretical evaluation of this contradiction.

Hybridity in Theory

While sharing this concern for the agency of subaltern subjects, each of these theories focuses on quite particular aspects of hybridity.[12] Françoise Lionnet's métissage is presented as a methodology of intertextuality and interdisciplinarity in analyzing postcolonial realities. In citing Glissant's writing, Lionnet preserves the French term "métissage" rather than the preferred "creolization," employed by his translator Michael Dash in order to refer "to the racial context" (*Autobiographical Voices* 4, note 6). However, the term métissage more generally in her writing refers to an enabling "reading practice," described as follows:

> *Métissage* is a form of *bricolage*, in the sense used by Claude Lévi-Strauss, but as an aesthetic concept it encompasses far more: it brings together biology and history, anthropology and philosophy, linguistics and literature. Above all it is a reading practice that allows me to bring out the interreferential nature of a particular set of texts, which I believe to be of fundamental importance for the understanding of many postcolonial cultures. If, as Teresa de Lauretis has pointed out, identity is a strategy, then *métissage* is the fertile ground of our heterogeneous and heteronomous identities as postcolonial subjects. (*Autobiographical Voices* 8)[13]

Métissage is the way to "think *otherwise*" [italics in original], and is "a concept and a practice: it is the site of indecidability and indeterminacy, where solidarity becomes the fundamental principle of political action against hegemonic languages" (*Autobiographical Voices* 6). This solid grounding in solidarity leads to the conviction that in this practice, "[t]o establish nonhierarchical connections is to encourage lateral relations: instead of living within the bounds created by a linear view of history and society, we become free to interact on an equal footing with all the traditions that determine our present predicament" (*Autobiographical Voices* 7). Such an ideal informs Lionnet's method of métissage and is the innovation of her first book where she "chooses[s] authors across time and space and read[s] them together for new insights" (*Autobiographical Voices* 7–8). My interest in pursuing hybridity is to pause further at the way in which we can conceive how such innovation plays out in social locations and how these nonhierarchical connections are attempted across recognizable social groups and generalized from literary texts to other social texts.[14] Lionnet allies her work with poststructuralist epistemologies, stating that: "If métissage and indeterminacy are indeed synonymous metaphors for our postmodern condition, then the fundamental conservatism of those who fight against both should be obvious" (*Autobiographical Voices* 17). To question the ways in which reliance upon particular instances of indeterminacy and métissage might also imply an acceptance of capitalism as a central structural feature of the current world, which promotes these very aspects, need not necessarily be representative of any kind of "conservatism." Neither does questioning the limits of capitalism in supporting the efforts of marginalized groups to eschew indeterminacy and make claims for their constituents.[15]

When Stuart Hall uses the term "diasporization," which he coins, it actually encompasses the sense of creolization (as postdiaspora) we have been discussing: the process he describes involves improvisation by black jazz musicians, rappers, etc., and "the process of unsettling, recombination, hybridization and 'cut-and-mix' arising out of 'diaspora experience'" (Hall "Deviance" 293). He sees art as being able to constitute peoples as "new kinds of subjects" (Hall "Cultural Identity and Diaspora" 403). In both these descriptions, what is emphasized is movement across boundaries in an aesthetic and/or theoretical quest. Bhabha's hybridity is more concerned with an assessment of the unitariness of dominating discourses, which are then revealed to be fractured, doubled, and unstable. But he also believes in the remedial power of a new conception in which he makes a "shift from the cultural as an epistemological object to culture as an enactive, enunciatory site" (*Location* 178). In this form, culture is revealed to be hybrid, and this hybridity provides the space from which subaltern agency can be enabled. Hybridity is generated by dominating discourses:

> If the effect of colonial power is seen to be the *production* [emphasis in original] of hybridization rather than the noisy command of colonialist authority or the silent repression of native traditions, then an important change of perspective occurs. It reveals *the ambivalence at the source of traditional discourses on authority* and enables a form of subversion founded on that uncertainty, that turns the discursive conditions of dominance into the grounds of intervention." [my emphases] (Bhabha *Location* 173)

So, for Bhabha, even if the hybrid arises from contact, it is hybridity within what was (seen to be) coherent and a unity that he calls up. In this way, his version of hybridity gestures more directly to the unequal position of power within which hybridity is created.

In the case of all the theorists mentioned, the material they consider, or at least the lens that informs their analyses, is anchored in a moment or a period that follows either colonial contact (Bhabha on India) or the shunting of populations to new lands under colonialism (Gilroy and Lionnet) or immigration to the metropolis (Hall or Bhabha). The analogy with communist discourse made earlier serves to foreground the positioning of this later discourse of what I grouped as creolization against an earlier moment of diaspora by its renouncing of the trauma that was central to diaspora. Instead these theories focus on the notion of difference.[16] The similarity with anthropological discourse brings into sharp focus the stake in hybridity and difference in an age that has been increasingly, or at least more overtly, marked by economic and cultural interconnectedness, most often on unequal terms.

In more specifically diasporic discourses, the bases of solidarity, as Ian Baucom remarks with Freud, is trauma. Trauma is heard rather than seen, and is that which was even "overheard." If trauma is the "tradition" of diaspora, then, we are tracking, with Freud, its transmission over generations. Diaspora is thus held up by trauma. That is, it is the memory of shared trauma that assures diasporic cohesion in the present.

If there is the possibility for diasporic discourses to inscribe a return—even mythical—it is perhaps not so much to the mother country as to trauma itself. The ground or space from which diaspora discourse transmits itself, the space also that its listening communities occupy or create in this act of listening, is trauma. Discourses of creolization when theoretically positioned postdiaspora renounce trauma as a space from which to speak. I want to clarify that this move refers to theories growing out of what we call the New World experience that is based on imported slave labor, as well as new immigrations to various metropolises for their beginnings. In this way, it is evident that I am placing Bhabha's theory of hybridity as having its theoretical framework develop from this history as much as, or even more than, simply from the history of the British in India. The already shaky, unseen space of the mothercountry can only be felt into being by passing through trauma for the diasporic imagination. This base is pulled from under the feet of diaspora to project creolization into the ungrounded, unstable, and ambiguous terrain that we chart through theorists such as Bhabha. My point, in having separated these terms, is that the different politics implied by them, each of which equally, but differentially, claims the hybrid is worth noting.

In reality, though, I want to suggest that if we might designate this theoretical distinction by relentlessly reinscribing time and space in order to distinguish between diaspora and creolization, most postcolonial discourses have claims to both spaces. This is evident in Paul Gilroy's efforts to extend the notion of "diaspora" to the sense of creolization we have been discussing. For him,

> [t]he value of the term 'diaspora' increases as its essentially symbolic character is understood. It points emphatically to the fact that there can be no pure, uncontaminated or essential blackness anchored in an unsullied originary moment. It suggests that a myth of shared origins is neither a talisman which can suspend political antagonisms nor a deity invoked to cement a pastoral view of black life that can answer the multiple pathologies of contemporary racism. (*Small Acts* 99)

Through his study of black music, Gilroy seeks to "comprehen[d] the lines of affiliation and association which take the idea of diaspora beyond its symbolic status as the fragmentary opposite of an imputed racial essence" (*Small Acts* 141). Still, his writing is essentially concerned with "the discontinuous histories of black populations" (*Small Acts* 98) all over the world or the exploration of what a "black aesthetic" might be (*Small Acts* 116) rather than that of different populations within the same space. This tension shows the ways in which both tendencies are essential to forging an effective discourse of postcolonial hybridity. It is therefore probably useful, if we wish to preserve the distinctions that these terms allow, to employ them as analytical tools that allow us to track these two opposite forces as they speak through the same voice. One might even say that it is their simultaneous but precarious presence within the same voice or narrative that actually permits current postcolonial discourses to *be* that Third Space celebrated by Homi Bhabha.

The significance of this terminology to our realities today is evident when we consider, for example, R. Radhakrishnan's recent book, entitled, *Diasporic Mediations: Between Home and Location*. In this book, among other things, he considers the delicate difference in the relationship to India between two individuals (himself and his son) living away from India, but separated from each other by the relative histories of two different generations. In his concluding chapter, entitled, "Is the Ethnic 'Authentic' in the Diaspora?" he asks: "If a minority group were left in peace with itself and not dominated or forced into a relationship with the dominant world or national order, would the group still find the term 'authentic' meaningful or necessary?" (211). In my view, such a conception of a minority group without a specifiable relationship in which it is a minority does not allow further theorization regarding authenticity or anything else. It is the forging of a consciousness of subalternity or minority status by means of a contradiction within an identifiable totality that can make such a group recognizable. Totality becomes an essential factor in thinking hybridity in this book.

We can identify, with regard to hybridity, the following three broad positions:

1. Hybridity is everywhere. It represents in many instances the triumph of the postcolonial or the subaltern over the hegemonic. The resistant always appropriates the cultural onslaught and modifies its products or processes for its own purposes. This position is most prominently associated with Bhabha, but also held by Hall and Lionnet, for example.
2. Hybridity is not everywhere. It is only the elite who can afford to talk about hybridity. For others, there is no investment in such a concept. It applies more to metropolitan elite emigrés and far less to migrant diasporas and even less to those who have "stayed behind" in the (ex)colony. This position can be associated with critics of Bhabha's textuality, such as Benita Parry.
3. Hybridity, when carefully considered in its material reality, will reveal itself to actually be a history of slavery, colonialism, and rape, inherited in terms of race. It is a difficult and painful history of interracial identity. It joins up with issues of choosing one's affiliations or having one's affiliations thrust upon one. Today, any account of hybridity must contend with this history. Vergès provides a powerful demonstration of this in *Monsters and Revolutionaries*. My analyses of Indian Ocean discourses of hybridity suggest that social engagement with hybridity calls up this signification.

Taking seriously a critic such as Françoise Vergès, I will activate Raymond Williams's notion of structure of feeling to validate the deep connections of hybridity to culture and material history in chapter 2. In this way, hybridity is intimately linked to the question of resistance to homogenization or assimilation and it thus implies an engagement with what we might broadly call subaltern agency.[17]

It is suggestive, indeed, to show how postcolonial thought and creative energies participate in and structure Modernity so as to prove that the "rest" also has claims to what has been seen as the prerogative of the "West."[18] In chapter 6, devoted to Edouard Glissant, I will be interested in a more direct reading of Glissant through a Marxian lens. I am interested, eventually, in reconnecting the thought of this influential thinker to the more explosive, and more obviously Marxian, thought of his compatriot Frantz Fanon. When I use the term Marxian, I refer directly to the ultimate desire underlying any Marxian praxis, which is revolution for social change that collapses particular inequalities. Therefore, the gesture in this book of allying more closely than has been done before, the thought of Glissant and that of Fanon is less about a categorization as Marxian or Caribbean and even less about a stake in Modernity. Instead, it is linked to my belief that the affect and politics that issue from the life and work of Fanon offers, more than any other strategy I can identify, something to the urgency with which the differential inequalities in what we call the "postcolonial world" demand to be addressed. A world, as Achille Mbemebe has shown in the African context, bruised by colonialism, ridden with contradiction from internal leadership, and, ultimately, savagely undermined by capitalism.

Fairly recently, Fredric Jameson declared, in what has become a sentence structure rather notoriously his own, that: "[a]ll cultural politics necessarily confronts this rhetorical alternation between an overweening pride in the affirmation of the cultural group's strength, and a strategic demeaning of it: and this for political reasons" ("Globalization and Political" 53).[19] If "diaspora" in the paradigm I specified makes a strategic return to trauma in petitioning for Africans, for example, then creolization can be seen to display an overweening pride in hybrid agency. It is in negotiating the reality and myth of victims and heroes that I want to propose the theories of Fanon and Glissant as the most successful in making a bid for agency.

If, as we generally acknowledge, it is no longer tenable to consider areas of postcoloniality in isolation, it logically follows that our theoretical engagements that arise from the consideration of different zones of contact also urgently demand not to be generated in isolation. Such isolation in the field of theory can be seen despite the commonalities highlighted here within the proliferation of writing on hybridity.[20] I believe such isolation in fact puts us further away from a postcolonial project of critical understanding and of enabling the agency of less powerful constituencies. What follows in this book can be seen as a first step in working to remedy it by carefully bringing into dialogue hitherto separately developed versions of hybridity.

Within postcolonial studies, it is no longer clear what is being implied with the use of terms such as diaspora (when Stuart Hall uses the term diasporization it is quite close to what Glissant might mean by creolization), hybridity (when used by Bhabha has a variety of particular meanings that are often not clearly specified in many critical appropriations of his work), métissage (means entirely different things for Françoise Lionnet, Edouard Glissant, and Françoise Vergès), intercultural interaction, or even multiculturalism.

As we have seen, creolization is closely concerned with a certain synchronic consideration of a people, is forward-looking, and concerned with interaction, while diaspora is premised on a past (and shared) trauma that constitutes and links the members of a group. I have suggested that these contrary impulses should be analytically separable but that, in reality, most postcolonial discourses, through historical and political necessity, engage in both stances within the same narrative. It is when this negotiation is more successful that postcolonial discourses (and here I include discourses from postcolonial locations as well as those on them) are able to become an alternative and productive site for staging or at least thinking resistance to hegemonic forces of colonial and other oppressive provenance. When creolization, in the particular way I have described it for analytical purposes, dominates, there is a disregard for history and a utopianism that is, in the end, unrealizable within current realities; when diaspora dominates, there is a tendency to fall into a discourse of victimhood and/or of narrow ethnicities. Both impulses are, however, crucial to the forging of a discourse adequate to the multiple tactics required for a successful postcolonial praxis. In Jameson's terms, the rhetorical alternation between heroism (in the first case) and victimhood (in the latter) is one that takes center stage in constructing discourses of hybridity in the postcolonial context.

It is the precariousness of balancing the two tendencies (within the same voice, the same narrative, the same political intervention, the same discourse) that gives much postcolonial discourse its productive tautness. I will show that it is by concern with, and the urgency of, the double task of representation in the two senses (darstellen and vertreten, to which Spivak attends in her engagement with Marx's German text) that these impulses are also driven. We will observe how an anthropological account of hybridity requires closer attention to the political/historical story of its manifestation in society. Further, how does one put forth a narrative of one voice to incarnate desires that are in themselves hybrid, but that also come from multiple sources. How can the speaking (unitary) subject convey and perform the multiple, which can also include contraries? How, also, do we make the moment of representation (of) *count*—that is, how do we put it to work, and in this sense enable it to intervene, thus calling up its second meaning (of representation by)? These are some questions that emerge in postcolonial theories of hybridity and to which I provide if not authoritative, then practical, answers based on this critical study of hybridity: considering the various theories, the politics of their application, and an examination of the scope and limits of a practicable discourse of hybridity in "real" hybrid locations.

All of reality is, and always has been, hybrid as most theories indicate. For example: "It is only when we understand that all cultural statements and systems are constructed in this contradictory and ambivalent space of enunciation, that we begin to understand why hierarchical claims to the inherent originality or 'purity' of cultures are untenable, even before we resort to empirical historical instances that demonstrate their [particular] hybridity" (Bhabha *Location* 37). In this case, the usefulness of *indicating* hybridity in particular instances must have some basis. It is thus a political gesture whose particular political valence can only have an impact if we are willing to depart from, and specify, these bases. In this way, we demarcate a particular framework or closing-off of an historical moment, action, or geographical space *as* hybrid by also specifying the terms between or among which such hybridity occurs or is called up. I will argue, following from this, that both history and a notion of totality are essential to a coherent and politically viable conception of hybridity. It seems that this question of specification in the case of the hybrid encounters an instinctive resistance from within the theoretical positioning of hybridity in its various recent derivatives. The vexing complexity of this situation is that such specification is inherently contrary to sophisticated cultural analyses, which rightly hesitate to impute political intent and *explain* aesthetics as a critique of a corresponding outside reality opening up the whole question of "engaged" criticism. My method, or the one I shall strive to achieve here, is to test the suppleness of the derivatives of hybridity as a politics and a mode of understanding in both the theoretical writing as well as other discourses such as literary texts and political speeches.[21] My aim is to not abandon aesthetics at the moment when it is required to "answer" reality, but rather to valorize this moment as one from where the mode of such a relationship between them is to be forged and understood.

While Vergès has shown what métissage meant for the Réunionese anti-abolitionist movement (*Monsters and Revolutionaries*), I move to a more contemporary assessment of the politics of métissage in La Réunion. Chapter 2 is a study of what Raymond Williams calls a "structure of feeling" that is traced outward from a contemporary autobiographical novel in late-twentieth-century La Réunion. Organized around my reading of the Réunionese author, Monique Boyer's *Métisse*, chapter 2 indicates how the continued importance of métissage for La Réunion is linked to its racial history and tied to a feeling of nationalism that is inextricably linked to Creole language. Totality emerges as a necessary element to conceive of agency against French nationalism. Contradiction emerges as necessarily privileged in adopting the particular version of hybridity that is Réunionese métissage.

Chapter 3 provides an historical reaching back by showing the origins of métissage as a novelistic trope in Réunionese literature. Métissage in the colonial novel exposes the intricate relationship of hybridity in culture to the colonial enterprise. The jump from colonial hybridity to postcolonial hybridity in examining métissage is seen historically and proves to be at odds with postcolonial theories of hybridity. Chapters 2 and 3 are best read together and in sequence. Chapter 4 moves from La Réunion to the neighboring island of Mauritius. In studying the difficulty of articulating Africanness in Mauritius in the public speeches of the first prime minister, this specific study of Mauritius attends to the differences in the development of a discourse of hybridity in the case of this proximate island. In this way, we are seeing how the use to which hybridity is put makes of it a different derivative and it is for this reason that my previous discussion of the implicit politics of different theories remains crucial to a larger postcolonial context. It emerges that the concept of "ethnicity" in its particular variation here is closely tied to any derivative of hybridity in the Creole islands. It is also similarly linked to any articulation of hybridity related to the political advancement of a group (be it for recognition, action, or political representation). Multiculturalism (based on cultural difference or ethnicity) has, in the second half of the twentieth century been the subject of various debates around the world in different forms, from affirmative action in the United States to "quotas" in India. Given that the discourse of difference has shifted its vocabulary from that of "race" to "ethnicity," I turn to the field in which ethnicity is most coherently theorized, indeed from which it is generated.

In chapter 5, I evaluate the anthropological approach to ethnicity in a region that has been held up as the exemplary, successful nation for multiculturalism. Mauritius offers, as seen in anthropology and even economics, a model for multicultural efficaciousness. According to this literature, various groups, bound by cultural ties that are signaled by religious or ethnic categories (Hindu, Muslim, Christian, and Buddhist, or Indian, Chinese, Creole, and White) all live harmoniously and build a strong economy and a plural culture without bloody conflict. Although there have been, in the fairly recent past, some incidents of violence in Mauritius, on the whole, its history has been spared such happenings. I read the anthropologist Thomas Hylland Eriksen's authoritative study of ethnicity in Mauritius along with the observations of a British colonial administrator on the island regarding the categorizing of the different populations who arrived in Mauritius. I show the ways in which the colonial idiom of race/ethnicity was articulated by individuals situated high within the colonial structure. Such vocabulary and conceptualization were incumbent upon the conditions of settlement, slavery, and indenture, as well as upon the position of this colony within the larger framework of the colonial enterprise historically. Contemporary novels show how a picture of articulating difference in the hybrid nation must contend with different aspects of history: immigration, colonialism, slavery, emancipation, indenture, economic globalism, all of which inform the collective forging of a functioning idiom that posits hybridity and upon which literary authors rely. It is only when seen in such a complex manner that a more full meaning of hybridity in its social occurrence and activation can be suggested.

In anthropology, ethnography as method functions to challenge the notion of a successful homogenization operated by globalization. Through the study of distinct cultures, even if they cannot be considered isolated today, anthropology reveals how these cultures renew their own views of the world or personhood, which are not commensurate with a rejuvenated and modified universalizing discourse that accompanies globalization. Thus, if the globe is hybrid rather than homogenous, hybridity challenges globalization. Yet, at the same time, the argument turns out to suggest that the encounter of different cultures does not mitigate difference even when there are unequal relations of power in such an encounter. Rather, when properly observed, such encounters can be seen to create a proliferation of difference through resistance or strategic adaptation. In this case, hybridity relies upon globalization. In fact, like globalization itself, the hybrid has developed with and in many aspects even through colonialism and its official demise. For these reasons, I present in this work views of the hybrid that call up different engagements with colonialism and its ongoing legacies and with globalization itself.

La Réunion and Mauritius have not been central in an academic discussion of postcoloniality, yet they are situated, geographically and theoretically, at the crossroads of the most consequential ruminations in recent postcolonial theory: they are crossed by the most vigorous sources of colonialism (French and British), have known both slavery and indenture, between them imply both a new nation as well as an overseas department, and have been marked by their position on the trade routes, colonial maritime projects, as well as cold-war strategy. I am concerned with the different ways in which the vocabularies and concepts of hybridity have been generated and claimed in these spaces as groups and individuals engage in self-definition and coexistence.

In chapter 6 on Edouard Glissant, I provide a Marxian reading of Glissant's notion of *Relation*. In showing his affinity for Marxian categories and Marxian (Hegelian) impulses, I argue that Glissant's derivative of hybridity that is based on observation and connection to the Caribbean Creole reality of his home, rectifies the two main problems in the aforementioned postcolonial theories of hybridity, which inhere in misrecognition of the importance to agency of totality and contradiction. Chapter 7 is a close reading of part of Frantz Fanon's *Black Skin, White Masks*, a text that is read frequently in postcolonial studies and eminently from within hybridity by Bhabha. In my reading, Fanon emerges as providing some very important insights into hybridity and confirms the importance of totality and contradiction to agency. These two Caribbean theorists are brought together as sharing a common agenda in the entanglement of their thought with both Marxism and hybridity.

A word about the study of literary texts is in order. Most prominently, Aijaz Ahmad has argued in his *In Theory* against considering English-language literature, in the anglophone context, as the "central documents" (76) of the national context in question because this neglects those discourses that stem from the true location of the people while privileging the position of the national bourgeoisie, who, one is to understand, is already coöpted from colonialist to capitalistic concerns. While sympathetic to the impulse behind such a pronouncement, I believe it crucial to study the movement of writing (and symbolic capital) from the hands of the colonizers to a new group of French-educated mass in the Creole islands in question, a movement that threatens the very act of writing and the tradition that writing in French calls up. The engagement of writers with Creole spaces, with concerns that have to do with monolingual Creole speakers, or with Creole culture that is at the center of their writing is of central interest in the following chapters.

This study of hybridity in contemporary theory and specific societies is linked to debates on globalization, multiculturalism, and ethnicity. In examining any of these terms the question of the hybrid becomes implicated. Conversely, the contemporary consideration of hybridity inevitably calls up globalization (and its relation to colonialism/imperialism), multiculturalism (and the older question of assimilation), as well as ethnicity (and the elision of race). Each of the following chapters works through these contemporary issues while investigating both their dominant form and hearing the echo of what they often silence, provided here in parentheses. In this way, the two aspects of diaspora and creolization are dialectically positioned and the pull and push between them in the various theories and social contexts is explored.

CHAPTER TWO

Hybridity in La Réunion

Monique Boyer's *Métisse* and the Nation as Necessity

Métisse (1992), written by the Réunionese Monique Boyer, tells of the coming of age of a young girl on her native island. It is the story of Anne-Marie who "realizes" that she is a mixed-blood or métisse when she is so categorized by her teacher at school. This realization comes, significantly, at the moment of her transition from the space of Creole language at home and outside the school to the official system of colonial education and her encounter with "French French." Written in French with many Creole inflections this text continually problematizes the many avatars of Frenchness in La Réunion: language and culture, education, entry into middle-class Frenchness, and most broadly, French citizenship. As Bourdieu puts it, "linguistic exchanges [] are also relations of symbolic power in which the power relations between speakers or their respective groups are actualized" (38). It is in this encounter with colonial culture (incarnated by the French-trained teacher) in its reality in La Réunion that an individual from a Creole space experientially knows early on the structure of feeling of nationhood that we shall follow.

Réunion, Métissage, and Creole Nationalism

I will show how the idea of nationhood, which enters this text as what Raymond Williams calls a structure of feeling, is the required overarching logic within which the narrator's agency is framed. Stated otherwise, Réunion's departmental status and dependency on France, following from colonialism, forms the totality in which certain racist tendencies occur. The narrator's agency to struggle against these tendencies posits an alternative totality: the utopian idea of Réunionese nationhood. It is also the totality in which hybridity is understood and, in the avatar of métissage, is transformed from a socially accepted reality into a politics of resistance.

Boyer's engagement with métissage involves tracing and confirming a past of slavery, upon whose forgetting the Frenchness of La Réunion is predicated. Simultaneously, it wrenches the protagonist's status as a métisse out of her assimilatory (white) possibilities especially through the agency of her black, working-class father, thus allowing her character to affectively foreshadow a feeling that goes beyond the area of her class. This enlarged area is one that in La Réunion is that of a language: Creole, for, "the area of a culture . . . is usually proportionate to the area of a language rather than to the area of a class" (Williams *Culture and Society* 320). Réunionness as a structure of feeling itself participates in validating a Réunionese *Creole* culture: "une culture métisse" [a hybrid culture]. But, in the context of La Réunion, even though the value of education in Creole has been proven by the intellectual/author/academic/activist, Axel Gauvin, its institution in the area inevitably promotes a two-tier system, given the prestige and power that French *already* enjoys and has historically done.[1]

What interests me is the original way in which this structure is addressed in Boyer's text: through métissage and critical history.[2] These two ways of reaching Réunionness become its substructure and are theoretical consequences of each other. That is, a critical understanding of history leads to a complex picture of creolization proceeding from métissage, while a radical inscription of métissage requires a critical historical method.

Nietzsche's three types of history help in the analyses that follow. To begin with:

> A historical phenomenon, when purely and completely understood and reduced to an intellectual phenomenon, is dead for anyone who understands it, for in it he understands the delusion, the injustice, the blind passion, and in general the whole darkened earthly horizon of that phenomenon, and from this simultaneously its historical power. At this point this power becomes powerless for him as someone who understands it, but perhaps it is not yet powerless for him as someone who lives it." (Nietzsche 95)

One way of knowing oneself through history and history through oneself is by weaving them together structurally, causally, thematically in the text in a repetition of the textuality of the self, which becomes a process of understanding through reliving. It is in the textualizing process of writing or rewriting/reading that conscious living and understanding can come together productively. I show here only how this text, in the pictures it presents of history, is a particular incarnation of a more general structure of feeling that can itself, however, be verified outside of it in powerful forms with reference to late twentieth-century promotion of Creole language, which lies at the heart of this nationalism.

Métissage, Race, and Class

For this reading of *Métisse*, I isolate instances of what Nietzsche calls monumental and antiquarian modes of history being constantly interrupted by the critical mode. Anne-Marie, the narrator, presents the reader, early in her story, with a photograph of her grandmother that has been preserved. The careful description is suggestive of the antiquarian mode being operative:

> [ma grand'mère] tient fièrement mon frère Henri sur ses jambes. Elle porte une grande jupe sombre qui lui recouvre les genoux. Sa taille et ses lunettes rondes au dessus desquelles son regard semble se perdre, lui donnent un air digne. Presque d'intellectuelle. Et mon frère, on dirait une grosse poupée, tant il est blanc et potelé. Derrière elle, un petit rideau de dentelle. Un rayon de soleil entre dans la case. C'était sa case à elle, toute petite, toute en bardeaux que mon père avait achetée à P'tit Serré là-bas en haut, démontée et remontée de toutes pièces à Saint-Pierre là-bas en bas. Au fond d'un grand jardin peuplé de perruches, de poivriers, de jujubiers. (8)

> [my grandmother] is proudly holding my brother Henri on her knees. She is wearing a large dark colored skirt that covers her knees. Her stature and her round glasses beyond which her gaze seems to disappear, give her a solemn air. Almost that of an intellectual. And my brother, one would say he was a big doll, he was so white and chubby. Behind her, a small, lace curtain. A ray of sunlight enters the house. It was her small house of shingles that my father had bought in P'tit Serre, there high up, which he took down and put back up from scratch in Saint-Pierre, there down below. Set back in a large garden full of parakeets, pear trees and jujube trees.[3]

The photograph in all its precision captures the here and now by enumerating the cluster of acquired bourgeois signs (her dress, her glasses, her home, and the garden). It is a synchronic, rather "flat," and static view that is, in Nietzsche's formulation, "antiquarian."[4] It is antiquarian because it seems to want to preserve this beautiful memory: the grandmother who hardly resembles a descendant of slaves and the white doll-like grandson. This excerpt is, however, sandwiched by two passages that rip the antiquarian mode out of its complacency with the happy synthesis it conveys. It is preceded by: "Grand-Mère Ba était une *cafrine*, Oh pas une vraie cafrine, une métisse fille de métisse, et *arrière petite-fille d'esclave*. Mais elle était bien noire. Je n'ai d'elle qu'un coquillage, le souvenir de sa mort—en 1960—et une seule photo prise cinq ans avant: . . ." (8) [Grandmother Ba was a negress. Oh not a real negress, a métisse[,] daughter of a métisse, and *great granddaughter of a slave*. But she was clearly black. All I have left of her is a shell, the memory of her death— in 1960—and one sole photograph taken five years before . . .] [my emphases]. Being and not-being a particular entity constantly interrupt each other in this text. As seen here, the grandmother is first a "negress." Immediately, however, this is undone as the text proclaims that she was not a "real" one. Métissage that denies one color and one origin seems to be presented as an escape from blackness and also from slavery at the beginning of the quotation. But yet again, the text goes on to assert that she *was* black as well as explicitly recalls her ascendance from slavery.

The excerpt above describing the photograph suggested a "forgetting" of this reality. The passage following it, which I shall quote, reestablishes it with the violence of certitude. Vergès writes regarding this autobiographical novel by Boyer that "[s]lavery has become a 'tragic,' traumatic event that it is better to forget for the sake of reconciliation than to remember as a *constitutive* reality. Slavery was the *secret de famille*. Amnesia was the operative word" [all italics in original] (9). Yet, in telling this story of amnesia, the narrator prevents the "flat" reading, suggested by Vergès, of her family's history through a naming that is at once, obviously "racial" (negress, métisse), as well as situational (great granddaughter of a slave), both aspects becoming pertinently historical. Historical, in the sense that the explanation of her métissage as not being truly a negress, requires an examination of this history. The specifics of her "black" heritage are given through the explanation regarding her being the great granddaughter of a slave. Slavery is reestablished through the ironical: "Non personne ne pourrait dire, devant cette photo, que nos ancêtres étaient des esclaves " (8) [No, no one could say, faced with this photograph, that our ancestors were slaves]. While a synchronic view, focusing on the state of hybridity as synthesis (as opposed to its processual, diffracting quality that is privileged in creolization) could "forget" this reality, the entire text works to reconsider it. Even as the novel is an autobiographical reconstruction of the past, there is a sense of recovering this past through a critical mode in order to insert the character in the present of her society. This is accomplished by her coming to terms with her present through a critical reconstruction of history. In this way, Boyer's text disallows a consideration of métissage outside of the context of slavery for La Réunion, and in fact does remember it as a "*constitutive* reality": the character's hybrid identity, and by extension all other such instances, is necessarily tied, directly or indirectly, to the institution of slavery under French colonialism. Such an intuiting awareness of the impossibility of French citizenship renders impossible the amnesia that permitted La Réunion to become a part of the French nation.

The narrator reveals the surprising union between the descendant of the slave and the "real" Chinese merchant:

> [. . .] Soixante ans après [l'abolition], Grand-Mère Na avait épousé un *vrai chinois de Chine*.
>
> Il avait débarqué seul sur ce lointain rocher du bout de la terre. Son bateau était assez léger pour accoster à Saint-Pierre, un joli, un tout petit port. [. . .] Et une fois que son pied eut foulé le quai, les grands champs verts qu'il avait aperçus du large au pied des crêtes, et qui se courbaient comme les vagues contre le vent, lui avaient déjà dit que cette terre voudrait bien de lui. Que les chinois n'étaient plus des mondes étranges, des contre-nations, des mal-fondés. Que son coco rasé ne ferait plus rire. Que personne ne voudrait couper sa natte qui dirait son art inné: l'art du commerce. (8–9)
>
> [. . .] Sixty years after [Abolition], Grandmother Na had married a *real Chinese from China*.
>
> He had disembarked alone on this faraway rock at the end of the earth. His boat was light enough to come up to Saint-Pierre, a beautiful little port. [. . .] And once he had set foot on the quay, the large green fields that he had seen from sea at the foot of the craters, and which curved like waves against the wind, had already told him that this land welcomed him. That the Chinese were no longer strange people, dissidents, renegades. That his shaved coconut head wouldn't provoke laughter. That no one would try and cut off his braid that would tell of his innate art: the art of commerce. [my emphases]

The narrator presents the coming together of her grandparents two generations before her own. If the grandmother was deceptively presented in the antiquarian mode of the photograph as not a "real" negress, as we saw, this is undone textually by the interference of the critical mode. The grandfather's being a "real" "chinois" is asserted in a "monumental" evocation.[5] In the passage above, the struggle of the Chinese, who were seen as outsiders—their large-scale immigration occurring after that of the whites, imported slaves, and then indentured laborers from India—is suggested.[6] The real Chinese grandfather is presented as the inheritor of the fruits of the struggles of earlier immigrants who, upon their arrival on the island, were seen as "strange people, dissidents, renegades," who had been mocked for their "shaved coconuthead[s]," and had threats to have their braids chopped off. Chinese ethnicity is presented historically through the monumental image of the Chinese merchant, an image recognizable to anyone familiar with today's "boutique chinoise" [the Chinese store]. Yet, the monumental is rudely cut short—in this case by death. The grandfather dies even before the birth of her father. I am tempted here to say that the textual effort is to parry any kind of possible purity, even if this has to be suggested through the available (and all pervasive) sign system of race. Still, hybridity in Lucien, his son and the narrator's father, as the ability to pass as white (suggested by the description of the photograph,) is ruptured by an interruption of "blackness" that I shall shortly discuss.

There can be no doubt that in understanding her own "hybrid" identity, Anne-Marie, as a narrator (as artist of history, in Nietzsche's terms), is strong enough (for Nietzche, historically developed enough) to deploy the critical mode.[7] In placing herself as a "mixed-blood" there is no hesitation to demystify the whiteness that can be asserted and to understand racially named categories through their interactions with realities that have to do with class. It is finally a matter of class that brings together Lucien, Grand-Mère Na's son, and Marcelle, the petite blanche [literally: "small" white] from the mountains.[8] These are, of course, the narrator's parents. Lucien was born after his Chinese father left on a boat, never to return since he drowned on a cargo ship. While people wanted to know "s'il [l'enfant] était jaune, s'il était noir [,] [l]e monde vit qu'il était rose, Lucien, celui de Na et de Robert" (10) [if he [the child] was yellow, if he was black[,] the world saw that he was pink, Na and Robert's Lucien"]. First, the element of the unexpected in métissage is thus invoked: he was neither "black" nor "yellow." However, "l'enfant rose, *malgré* ses pommettes saillantes *malgré* ses yeux bridés et sa bouille ronde, devint *il faut dire* noir" (11) [the pink child, *despite* his chubby cheeks, *despite* his "folded" eyes and his round face, became, *it has to be told*, black"] [my emphases]. I read this return of/to blackness in the body of the narrator's father, which literally enacts the differentiating, diffracting quality of creolization, to be emblematic of the betrayal of whiteness (and consequently of "white" citizenship). This move is significant to the problematizing of color and class pursued through this character. Boyer shows how through a radical métissage it becomes eminently clear that blackness functions as the corruption of whiteness, as a glaring presence *in* whiteness, as, in the end, an impossibility of assimilation into Frenchness.

Lucien and Marcelle would never have been married if it were not that Augustine (Marcelle's mother), however white she was, remained "une *petite* blanche" [my emphases] (11). This is important "car si elle avait été de la race des gros blancs [. . .] jamais elle n'aurait laissé sa fille épouser mon père" (11) [because if she had belonged to the race of the "great" whites, she would never have allowed her daughter to marry my father]. While "petit" and "grand" are indicators of class, like the "petite bourgeoisie" and "grande bourgeoisie," the suggestion of *racial* purity is also clearly evoked ("*race* des gros blancs"). This, despite the more encompassing meaning of "race," which can explicitly link the term to a sociological understanding of lineage and community. Whiteness is clear and unambiguous in the beginning as the world "could see [Lucien] was pink." However, the subsequent ironic confession/concession ("it has to be told") following the repeated "despite" is telling: blackness has to be admitted to. There is no escaping its facticity despite other signs of Frenchness. Lucien will go on to secure a place, however low, in the French administration—he will become a government servant (a fonctionnaire). But real Frenchness, for which no apologies are required, can only be whiteness. Next, the slightly accusatory "never would she have allowed . . ." indicates a clearly critical stance toward the concession to her black father made by the impoverished whites of her mother's family. Just as the larger society (le monde /the world) is taken to task for buying into whiteness, so are poor whites, who, *despite* whiteness, are excluded from participatory parity in white citizenship and for whom blackness always remains a stumbling block.

Hybridity as a consequence of racial mixing is posited early in this text; it is impossible to invoke this term in La Réunion (and elsewhere) without also invoking what implicitly precedes this mixing. Yet, in a moment that is subversive to the idea of thinking through racial categories, the class background of Marcelle, which permits the union between the narrator's parents, takes precedence in that it renders possible this métissage within the society. Blackness (and slavery to which it is historically linked in this island's story) intrudes into any complacent bourgeois spaces offering a synthesis or melting pot logic. Simultaneously, the narrator interrupts racial readings through an analysis that requires an understanding through class, and thus to lived experience. Anne-Marie's ability to summon the critical mode consists in her not giving up the analysis at the point when her father is blackened. So, while métissage is still read "racially," its implementation as a process of creolization can only be understood at the point where the concept of class intervenes.

At the same time, one can see the narrator undoing the type of analysis Frantz Fanon makes of Mayotte Capécia's autobiographical *Je suis Martiniquaise* in his *Black Skin, White Masks*. This is done by pursuing an understanding of the gendering and racializing processes that underlie any kind of advancement that can be accounted for economistically.[9] Still, if Mayotte's desires are easily censured by Fanon, Marcelle's attraction to Lucien in *Métisse* is pushed further by pursuing her desires in their entirety, as they may be known to the narrator (specifically Marcelle's desire to escape poverty). If Mayotte is summarily dismissed by Fanon, Marcelle is also dismissed by the narrator, but only after a consideration of her motives and desires, and their subsequent rejection as a viable strategy. Mayotte Capécia's bourgeoisification comes through a movement toward the white world by means of a fairly well-placed white man (André), while Marcelle's comes through a movement away from the poor white world through an upwardly mobile black man (the narrator's father). What weakens Fanon's analyses of Mayotte is his focus on part of Mayotte's desire instead of considering Mayotte and her white lover, André's interaction within colonial culture as the space within which their desires are articulated. In his haste to dismiss Capécia, Fanon falls short of properly positing a totality in considering Mayotte's actions. Such a totality is explicitly reclaimed by him elsewhere in *Black Skin, White Masks* as we will see in chapter 6. In *Métisse*, Marcelle's desires are examined in their knotty engagement with her husband's position as a black man entering the middle class of a fraught postcolonial society still negotiating many colonial structures.

To be sure, "sexual desire in colonial and postcolonial contexts has been a crucial transfer point of power, tangled with racial exclusions in complicated ways" (Stoler 190). The narrator of *Métisse* casts her unflinching gaze on this point between her parents. It is clear that in presenting Lucien and Marcelle as coming from socially quite distinct spaces, the common "brèdes" [leaf of a vegetable plant] eaten during their childhood serves to register that the impoverished whites of La Réunion experienced a similar everyday struggle to that of many nonwhites. Therefore, the idea of contesting Frenchness and what it has meant is, in Williams's terms, thought as a feeling (or felt as a thought) of a necessity by both groups. Williams chooses "feeling" to "emphasize a distinction from more formal concepts of 'world-view' or 'ideology'" (*Marxism* 132). The progeny of these spatially differentiated but experientially united groups must, in following the logic of Anne-Marie's narrative, understand their shared interest. This shared interest, rather than any primordial or essential factor, when made visible, is the "oneness" that is required to think a nation. The exclusion from what Frenchness has symbolized historically is experienced by whites and nonwhites whose exclusion from this definition is apprehended through an affective understanding of radical métissage as being a rejection (in reciprocity) of Frenchness.

Understanding métissage diachronically—as opposed to a simple acceptance or even celebration of it synchronically—itself, in a sense, paves the way to critical history; in other terms, critical history demands a closer scrutiny of métissage as an historical process. Such an understanding of hybridity disallows the more disembodied derivatives in postcolonial theories examined in chapter 1. It brings métissage close to its more fixed social valence as well as its signification as a liberating politics tied to creolization and language in the Réunionese experience of race, slavery and indenture, labor, colonialism, and departmentalization. Here, métissage reclaims specificity, historicity, and an accounting of the constitution in Réunionese society of race. Anne-Marie is able to deliver the criteria Vergès considers essential to "[t]hinking métissage." She brings us in this text "the recognition of a past of rape, violence, slavery, and the recognition of [her] own complicity with the wicked ways of the world" (Verges *Monsters* 11). One might see Boyer's entire text as an excavation and a searching critique of the narrator's possible complicity with white citizenship in French La Réunion. As we have seen, in this historical venture, the narrator of *Métisse* provides monumental and antiquarian images only to inexorably reject them in favor of a stance for action that critical history makes imperative.

There can be no escaping the "fact" of blackness that Fanon so poignantly describes (*Black Skin*). But in this story, if relative wealth has a "pouvoir miraculeux, magique," [a miraculous, magical power] and if to the impoverished whites of his wife's family, Lucien "n'était plus noir. Depuis longtemps il ne l'etait plus," (72) [was no longer black. For a long time now, he had not been black], his daughter dredges up this blackness with resolute and vivid bitterness. The following scene occurs after the divorce of the narrator's parents:

> Ma mère était venue rendre visite à sa sœur Iréna. Elle se retrouva au moment de sortir face à mon père sur le pas de la porte. C'était la première fois qu'ils se revoyaient.
>
> Ma mère alors, fouillant au fond d'elle la plus dure, la plus insupportable des insultes, ma mère lui dit avec rage:
> —"Espèce de cafre!"
> Il s'engouffra dans la maison de ma tante Iréna, s'assit, prit sa tête dans ses mains noires. Tout bruit avait cessé. [. . .]
> Longtemps après il se leva, partit sans avoir ouvert la bouche, retirant enfin sa tête de ses mains. Tandis qu'y résonnaient encore ces mots, ces terribles mots. (128)

[My mother had come to visit her sister, Iréna. She found herself face to face, at the door, with my father as she was leaving. It was the first time they were seeing each other again.

Then, my mother, reaching deep within herself to find the most cruel and unbearable of insults, my mother said to him with rage: "Bloody nigger."

He rushed into my aunt's house, sat down, took his head in his black hands. Everything was quiet [. . .]

Much later he stood up, finally lifting his head up from his hands, and left without having said a word. While those words, those horrible words, continued to resound in the room.]

While the term *cafre* is not necessarily pejorative, the dimension becomes horrific in the mouth of the speaker, given her identity and the circumstance of the word's enunciation. The narrator continues that "[p]endant 31 ans il n'était donc resté qu'un cafre, aux yeux de celle qu'il avait sortie de la misère, la mère de ses enfants" (128) [for 31 years he had thus remained nothing but a nigger in the eyes of the one he had lifted out of poverty, the mother of his children]. The violence of métissage Vergès invokes is recorded differently. It delivers the pain of the interaction between two individuals, which cannot occur outside that of the over-determined sphere of interracial relations whose configurations are inherited from colonial practices; nor can it occur outside the historical imbalance of power between the sexes. With astounding lucidity, the narrator later understands that: "les mots durs que ma mère humiliée, mortifiée par le départ de mon père, avait prononcés, fouillés tout au fond d'elle, *n'étaient pas siens: ils étaient ceux des femmes, des hommes, de tout ce que notre terre avait porté*" (130) ([. . .] the harsh words that my mother, who was humiliated and mortified by my father's leaving, had pronounced, dug up from deep within herself, *these were not her words: they were those of the women and men, of all that our land had borne*) [my emphases]. This understanding is remarkable in that it examines a clearly racist remark as a structural problem within La Réunion (our land), and, in so doing, it checks the momentum of racializing, French colonial logic and undoes bourgeois individual identity as authentic or even functional for the people of La Réunion. It renders responsible (and victimized) "the (gendered) people" (the women, the men) as well as the fabric (all) of the society—of the land. This feeling of Réunionness is subtle in that the land itself—as an isolated island, with its topography of highlands where marooned slaves escaped and poor whites were pushed as wealthier immigrants arrived and took over the land, and with its treacherous harbor where various other immigrant populations arrived—is a participant in the creation of this unaccomplished "nation" from métissage through (still from the above quotation) the "bearing" (carrying as well as birthing) of this relation.

The narrator, Anne-Marie, understands in the negative epithet her mother's gendered claim to whiteness as the only space of rationality that the narrative of (failed) interracial marriage in La Réunion allowed. She uncovers how the colonial idiom and logic continue to have currency even as the hierarchical legacy they left is slowly being undone generation by generation, in individual and collective actions. The epithet underlines the fact that "[t]he specific class element, and the effects upon this of an insecure economy, are parts of the personal choice [of marriage] which is after all a choice primarily of a way to live, of an identity *in* the identification with this or that other person" [emphasis in original] (Williams "Thomas Hardy" 138). Marcelle's way of entering the middle class through her black husband could not, in the end, sustain her *in* the identification with a black man. This is because, for her, his blackness consistently called up her fraudulence in this class due to the unspoken structure in which her middle-class position sought its coherence: French citizenship. Réunionness, here, is "at the very edge of semantic availability" (Williams *Marxism* 134), and in fact not at all available to Marcelle. It becomes the precocity of her daughter to unearth this structure in such a personal and painful space.

It is in this sense that we can note a shift in the totality that particular acts posit. In the racialized language of the narrator's parents, the French nation is the totality that gives them coherence. Sensitive to what race signifies and yet seeking a way out of it through class and nation, Anne-Marie's narrative accesses a new totality in the form of a structure of feeling.

The fact that the narrator's mother could only wish to get out of the oppressive and isolated space of the poor white community by marrying a fonctionnaire is to be read through her gender; the fact that she could not get herself a "good catch" in the white bourgeoisie is to be read through her class. While these two facts are inseparable in the person of Marcelle, it is their particular combination that rendered Lucien not-black to her and her family. Even instinctive proclivity or disinclination of individuals for each other takes place in force fields of these interactions. Only a critical view of the history of the specific interaction and its relation to History helps understand such interactions without complete disingenuousness, or worse, indifference. If Frenchness is always whiteness, then whiteness is not always Frenchness. Therefore, it is evident that the feeling of un-Frenchness is the starting point for the logic of rejecting Frenchness, an understanding that is accessed in Creole language. Métissage, when lived out as the diffractive process of production of non-Frenchness (of differently inflected spaces of non-Frenchness) then moves away from an investment in racial description and precision to indicate a structure of feeling whose desire seeks an alternative, nonsynthesized totality of *Relation* for its limits that the French nation cannot fulfill.[10]

Yet, métissage does not generate a simplistically utopian alternative to departmental status related to French nationhood. From the perspective of the Réunionnese "people," the violent moment in Boyer's text is a devastating reminder of the impossibility for difference to be equally different (and different "equally"); that the famous idealistic cry that "Neither Europeans, nor Africans, nor Asians, we proclaim ourselves Creole" (Bernabé, Chamoiseau, Confiant 75) from another French department is constantly rendered impossible at the level of individual interactions, and therefore, of groups; that the playing out of race is so intricately wound up with questions of gender and class and so pervasive, as we have seen, that disentangling them in each instance becomes a painful surgical process, where each extricated part always connects up through the tissue to another, sometimes surprisingly distant one.

Anne-Marie's father visits his daughter, the narrator, and her newly born child. When some guests arrive, he leaves the house unnoticed. Later, she speaks to him, upset that she was unable to introduce him to her guests, as she wanted. At this time, his answer belies a shocking repetition of her mother's branding strategy. This strategy derives from a process that necessarily leads to working through the ongoing history of colonialism in La Réunion. He answers: "Je ne voulais pas te faire honte! Ne me fréquente plus, ne me dis plus bonjour. Personne ne saura que ton père est un cafre!" (133) [I did not want to humiliate you! Don't socialize with me any more, don't even greet me. Then no one will know that your father is a nigger], thus reverting to the same discourse that his wife uses, for the same historical reasons, only from a differently inflected space within this society. It is such an understanding of the symbolic power of discourse and its connections to points of enunciation that enables their daughter to break out of this infernal inheritance by means of a huge, courageous, and emotional effort of separation. She accomplishes this through a critical historical understanding of her parents' story as a couple, to feel her place within this nation (and to feel it into being) in a "relational" way that is impossible for them to do. Difference is thus held together, fragmented and fragile, through a totality that the "Nation" (which is not [yet?]) provides: "J'aime l'heure où le soleil s'éteint p'tits pas-p'tits pas, après avoir tout le jour durant, arrosé de ses feux *notre bout* de terre de La Réunion" (7) ["I love the hour when the sun disappears step by little step after having watered all day, with its fires, *our patch* of land, La Réunion"] [my emphases] are the opening lines of this "récit réunionnais."

Beyond the Literary Text

If the word "bout" recalls the small size of the island, it also designates this island as an appendage to (and an extremity of) the hexagon politically and to the continents (especially Africa and Asia) geographically. Retracing these connections through a critical, rather than simply the monumental or the antiquarian, mode of history rejects any celebration of a synthesized state (creole*ness*) like the photograph or the happily integrated Chinese merchant evoked earlier. It renders impossible considering métissage at only a cultural level, which does not account for race. It also brings skepticism regarding synthesizing processes that can inscribe multiple and equal differences. If the literary text allows us to identify at the level of subjectivity inscriptions of Réunion's colonial history, it can not become a "substitute for any examination of the broader material and cultural practices of empire building, or the aftermath of the political dissolution of empires" (Kaul 81). The close association of Creole language and the culture of La Réunion as the basis from which the non-French nation is experientially evoked, necessarily links up to the history of the colonial educational system and the simultaneous denigration of Creole language. Quite simply, for Axel Gauvin, to deny the reality of Creole and the reality of its speakers is to deny the reality of the "nation": Les colonialistes nient donc la langue réunionnaise pour mieux nier l'existence de la nation réunionnaise" [The colonialists thus deny the Réunionese language to better deny the existence of the Réunionese nation] (*Du créole opprimé* 65).[11]

The narrator, Anne-Marie's quest in *Métisse*, through a situated historical reading of La Réunion, curiously satisfies, or at least leads to, Said's call to "leave the modest refuge provided by subjectivity and resort instead to the abstractions of mass politics" ("Exile" 359). Indeed, it goes further to show how individual subjectivity cannot provide refuge in a situation where much of what gives this subjectivity coherence actually works to denigrate it. In this case, the narrator accesses her selfhood through Creole. Arriving at school, she understands how she is perceived and "read" in the dominant language (French). Much of what follows in this text is actually a reevaluation of her selfhood through the dominant French model of citizenship that is given to her and us in French.[12] Her reflections are thus intimately tied to her native Réunion's recuperation and attaching of itself to the French nation. If we can consider that this jump from the subjective to the collective is not to be read as an allegory (without entering this debate), then at least it is a necessary theoretical move from the particular to the general. This move is enabled by the text as a structure of feeling whose movement sweeps through and beyond the particular subject position from where it is experienced.

For La Réunion, given that Creole is the mother tongue of the vast majority of its people, one historical reality that has to be urgently and consistently addressed is a persistent attitude that can be traced to a 1930 proclamation that, Creole

"[. . .] est la langue du peuple, la langue des serviteurs, des ouvriers, et, malheureusement de presque tous les jeunes enfants; par l'influence néfaste des bonnes qui les élèvent, une fois que les enfants ont adopté le mauvais pli, il faut souvent combattre des années avant de réussir à extirper de leurs cervaux le vocable grossier qui doit faire place à la langue française"! (Ithier 17)

[is the language of the people, the language of the servants, the workers, and, unfortunately of all our young children; by the dangerous influence of the nannies who bring them up, once the children have adopted this bad habit, it is often the task of years of struggle before we can manage to banish from their minds the vulgar expressions that must give way to the French language].

Ithier's book on the French literature of Mauritius was first published in 1930. While La Réunion and Mauritius had already developed in different ways following the short period of common administration under French colonialism in the early 1800s, this is only the beginning of the entry of "Oriental" languages into the school curriculum in Mauritius.[13] Despite the presence of Bhojpuri speakers in the vast Indian population that replaced slaves after Abolition in Mauritius and the presence of Tamil speakers in La Réunion, the relationship between Creole and French on the two islands was still quite comparable in the public sphere.

As Bourdieu has pointed out:

The educational system [...] no doubt directly helped to devalue popular modes of expression [...] and to impose recognition of the legitimate language. But it was doubtless the dialectical relations between the school system and the labour market—or more precisely, between the unification of the educational (and linguistic) market, linked to the introduction of educational qualifications valid nation-wide, independent (at least officially) of the social or regional characteristic of their bearers and the unification of the labour market (including the development of the state administration and the civil service)—which played the most decisive role in devaluing dialects and establishing the new hierarchy of linguistic practices. (49)

In *Métisse*, the narrator experiences this precise imposition of the legitimate language of French. It is also the relationship between educational qualification and the development of the civil service that established not just a new hierarchy of linguistic practices, but also, as in the case of the narrator's father, a new means of upward mobility. Through this new possibility, her father's blackness was mitigated up to a certain point in allowing the union of her white mother with him, as we saw. In the end, however, his blackness became a stumbling block where the problems of her parents came to reside.

In the silence following her father's assuming of the identity of a "cafre," Anne-Marie writes a letter to her father. Finally, in the last chapter, entitled,

"The Letter," she fails to give it to him, and puts it back in her bag (Boyer 139). Instead, we are told, the letter becomes the narrative we read: "Alors dans mon cœur sont venus les mots pour écrire ce livre: la lettre que n'avais pas su donner" (140) [Then the words came to me (to my heart/spirit) for me to write this book: the letter that I had not been able to give (him)]. This overt invitation to proceed from, and even abandon, the personal subjective relation between the daughter and her father in favor of an enlarged area of readership is one we can not fail to accept. Monique Boyer's Anne-Marie writes a letter to her father but, in the end, delicately side-steps the authority of his response. She understands her hybrid female position as it is generated and as she claims it, giving her narrative, instead, to an audience that goes beyond her gender, her class, and even her posited nation. If Mayotte Capécia wrote too early before any kind of nationalism could welcome her voice in Martinique that she was "Martinican," (*Je suis martiniquaise*) Mariama Bâ wrote her "long letter" post-Senegalese independence, forcing her to demasculinize crystallized, nationalist discourse.[14] It is to the well-timed credit of Monique Boyer to have placed as the locus of a structure of feeling of her possible nation the properly historical female "I."

Whether Bâ's Ramatoulaye, Jamaica Kincaid's Lucy, or Boyer's Anne-Marie, one finds repeatedly in postcolonial women's writing a self-conscious uneasiness in claiming entry and inscription into literary language. Gayatri Chakravorty Spivak remarks following her discussion of *Lucy*: "Is this because women, by historical definition, not essence, relate differently or obliquely to the history of language, especially public language—published literature—which is also singular and unverifiable?" ("Thinking Cultural" 353). In this text, the revelation to the reader that s/he has been reading what was a private letter from the narrator to her father comes at the end (as does the revelation in Bâ's and Kincaid's texts). The reader is thus forced to look back and impute a proper accounting of the specificity of this as a *female* narrative, which is strengthened retroactively. One could claim that in these examples of women's writing, there is also a more definitive hybridizing attempt of the space of the literary text itself. In fact, in the case of Boyer's text we might understand how Anne-Marie's narrative is retroactively feminized by this act: while up to this point, the narrative explicitly problematized the position of her black working class father in Réunionese society, this act seizes the narrative out of any kind of gender neutrality in then questioning the authority of the father from the position of the hybridly situated daughter.

From the space of the personal, the question asked is: "Who are we," a question that Edouard Glissant considers urgent in the context of Martinique, as opposed to what he terms "a question that from the outset is meaningless," that is, "Who am I?" (*Caribbean Discourse* 86).[15] *Métisse* allows us to identify a structure of feeling that goes beyond class, gender, and race, even while properly recognizing them. It asks Glissant's question, "Who are we?" as the essential basis of its own raison d'être ("Who am I?"). And it shows that the answer, "We are French," is dismally inadequate.

What *Métisse* articulates here (and I mean very specifically in the late twentieth century in La Réunion) is a conception of the "nation" as a structure of feeling in the sense that Raymond Williams gives it, by tying it to a specific period within a context (Williams "Film . . ." 33). Williams chooses "feeling" to "emphasize a distinction from more formal concepts of 'world-view' or 'ideology'" (*Marxism* 132). His preference for "feeling" over "experience" indicates synchronicity with lived reality rather than the idea of the past that the term experience conjures up. He is quick to indicate that it is "not feeling against thought, but thought as felt and feeling as thought" (*Marxism* 132), in this way breaking down the division between affect and intellect and also, potentially, exploding boundaries that might make it the prerogative of a very narrow part of the population. It is this development from métissage, then, that is the carrier of the structure of feeling of Réunionness and that marks the area of a shared culture, which is inextricably intertwined with Creole language historically. These thoughts link métissage in La Réunion with the concept of "creolization," while the monumental images of the Chinese merchant and the grandmother examined earlier link it explicitly with "diaspora" as these terms were delimited in chapter 1 of this book. Here, we see the way in which hybridity when examined in connection with an identifiable social ground seeks out a totality and the movement toward such totality is thought through contradiction. More on this follows in chapter 3, when hybridity as presented by *Métisse* is reexamined upon looking at the colonial novel.

I propose for this structure of feeling (of the nation) an inherent hybridity in its being a precarious "sign," still full of possibility for the generation of "meaning," rather than a "signal" as it has become in many new nations.[16] If the (Réunionese) nation has not been actualized through institutions, and that it is "a cultural hypothesis" in Williams's formulation (*Marxism* 132), it is thus linked to utopia as envisioned by the narrator of this text. It provides the framework in which much militancy for change has been conceived in La Réunion.

CHAPTER THREE

Theorizing Hybridity

Colonial and Postcolonial La Réunion

The fairly successful genre of the "roman colonial" [colonial novel], in which colonialism itself becomes part of the aesthetic, implies recognition of the notion of totality in upholding the genre as well as the social conditions of possibility for its conception. At the same time, however, much like in newer theories of hybridity, contradiction must be sidestepped in positing a utopian vision of the mingling of races and cultures. In this way, the colonial context is rendered superior to the original cultures—the lower African, Chinese, or Indian cultures or even that of French culture that is impoverished in comparison to the enriched version of French *colonial* culture.

Métissage: A Novelistic Trope

Miracle de la Race [Miracel of the Race] is a colonial novel written by Marius-Ary Leblond, the pseudonym for the Réunionese cousins Georges Athéna and Aimé Merlo. These colonial authors were prolific writers as well as literary critics. In this novel they go about proving the superiority of the white race in what to them was an informed and sympathetic manner. *Miracle de la Race* is set on île Bourbon, the island of La Réunion, in the late nineteenth century. The authors represent the period following economic crisis due to the severe competition faced by colonial cane sugar from foreign sugar and sugar from beets (mid-century). This crisis questioned the wisdom of monoculture of sugarcane, and encouraged other produce such as spices. In addition, with the opening of the Suez Canal in 1869, Réunion loses its former importance as the first port for ships rounding the Cape of Good Hope heading from the East Indies to metropolises mostly in Britain and France. This period is also marked by the after effects of Abolition (1848) and massive importation of labor from India. At first, the sources for labor were the French "comptoirs" but later indenture on a massive scale was conducted from diverse parts of India with the various agreements the French entered into with the British as well as from China, Mozambique, the Comora islands, even Somalia, Yemen, and Rodrigues (Chane-Kune *Aux origines* 168).

Balzamet, the white protagonist of the novel in question, who is an orphan, experiences a nonvoluntary "déclassement" (demotion of class) due to the loss of his uncle's fortune. This inheritance, which was "rightfully" his, goes to the uncle's Creole mistress. From the prestigious "pension" run by Mme Cébert, Alexis Balzamet goes to the "Ecole des Frères" reserved for all nonwhites. The building itself is in the former palace of the "Compagnie des Indes" (Leblond 35). France's position on the Indian subcontinent by this time is of negligible political importance and, hence, the building's former glory is lost while it is now peopled by children of Indian servants as well. Mme Cébert admonishes Alexis' two aunts who refuse to pay for him to continue at her exclusively white school because they are excluding him from the "droit d'arriver un jour aux postes de considération qui sont destinés aux enfants blancs" (33) [right to one day take up significant positions, which are meant for white children]. In fact, she warns that, instead of the various posts Alexis dreams of, he may end up becoming "*un déclassé* par [leur] faute, petit comptable chez un boutiquier arabe ou commis de quincaillerie" (33) [a "declassed" person because of them, an insignificant accountant in an Arab shop or a clerk in a metal shop].[1] This reiterates the process by which colonial education clearly became the agent that formed the future élite. We have seen, in chapter 2, how the father in *Métisse* enters the middle class through this education. This enables him to become a civil servant, while his move is buttressed by his acquiring a white wife through his new currency.

Here, while Alexis suffers because, "il se retrouvait faible pour résister, lui, *tout seul*, à descendre de plus en plus parmi les noirs" (104) [he was too weak to resist, *all by himself*, from sinking lower and lower amongst the blacks], his struggle is a process of reconsolidating his innate strength, which he inherited from his whiteness.[2] Frère Hyacinthe, of the Ecole des Frères, understands his troubles and correctly guesses that Alexis' fear is for his future and not reflective of any hatred of other races: "Vous souffrez non point tant dans le présent, que par l'appréhension de vous laisser peu à peu dégrader pour l'avenir" (87) [Your suffering is not so much in the present, as it is brought on by the thought of letting yourself be, little by little, degraded in the future]. As the story progresses, others in the colonial administration nurture Alexis' future, and his success is assured.

The genre of the colonial novel, developed by the authors of this text, speaks to a metropolitan audience, which needs to be educated about the colony of the Creoles (here this means the whites of the colony). This genre tells of their struggles and innovation in adapting to conditions seen as very difficult and different compared to those of the metropolis. The colonial novel, quite simply, should exhibit the "miracle" of the white race in the colony. The ambiguity of a certain "progressive" white colonial point of view becomes clear in this text. The vague idea that it is *structural* privilege that affords to the whites such "miraculous" stories as that of Balzamet informs Father Hyacinthe's view. Even in the more recent *Métisse*, as we have seen, from early on one can trace certain "slippages," where the *white race* (most often essentialized in this earlier vocabulary as Creoles, who have acquired the strength over centuries to maintain their purity, innate goodness, and superiority) is seen as the *white class*. Here, too, for example, M. Izabel, a mulatto, who has acquired through hard work and the generosity of some well-placed whites a position in the colonial administration, takes on Balzamet to *repay*, as it were, the generosity of those whites: "M. Izabel, avec la simplicité du devoir, s'empressa d'acquitter sa dette de reconnaissance envers *la classe blanche* qui l'avait aidé à se distinguer" (199) [M. Izabel, from a simple sense of duty, was eager to repay his debt of gratitude toward the *white class*, which had helped him to be successful [distinguish himself][my emphases]. In a reciprocal moment, Alexis himself realizes his debt toward M. Izabel. In his terms, Izabel "a fait pour moi plus qu'aucun de ceux de *ma classe*" (255) [did for me more than anyone from *my class*] [my emphases].

This conflation of white class/race was at the time certainly the broad reality. Its knowledge and implications imbue with ambiguity the so-called progressive discourses arising from sources such as the anti-abolitionists. We will trace some instances of this ambiguity here in this colonial novel.[3] There is a certain uneasiness that it is the structural position of these other groups that renders the whites superior. This is reflected in an almost paranoid desire, exhibited by Fragelle (who is Balzamet's metropolitan friend), for pure whiteness to be preserved: "Eh bien! ces populations arriérées n'admireront et ne chercheront à assimiler nos meilleures qualités que dans la mesure où notre société, quelque restreinte soit-elle pourra maintenir inaltérable le génie européen que nous avons mission de représenter ici" (249) [Well! These backward people will neither admire nor try to assimilate our best qualities unless our society, despite all obstacles, maintains unchanged the European genius that it is our mission to represent here]. So, while there is a suggestion elsewhere in the novel that assimilation of good qualities is to occur on both sides, whiteness itself (here in the guise of Europeanness) must be preserved intact at all costs. M. Vertère, Alexis' mentor, also concurs: "Voici ma formule: les Français, nés ici, n'auront vraiment accompli le miracle de leur race que quand ils se seront assimilé le génie de toutes celles qui peuplent la colonie" (301) [Here is my formula: the French born here will not have truly accomplished the miracle of their race until they have assimilated the genius of all the other races that populate the colony].

If M. Vertère's view mitigates Fragelle's, it still operates under the assumption that the "miracle" is reserved exclusively for the white race. While in the first quotation European genius is to be absorbed by lower races, in the second the French in the colony are to become superior to all other examples of Frenchness by absorbing the best from the other races present in the colony. The impossibility of true cross-cultural exchange and politics in the notion of colonial hybridity resides in reliance upon the *purity* of the dominant race, as in the first quote, or in the superiority of the culturally transformed but still dominant race. It is the *simultaneous* desire for cross-cultural exchange and the maintenance of this superiority that constitutes the ambiguity in the following passages. Frère Hyacinthe explicates the superiority of the white Creoles, born in the colony, to metropolitan whites. He remarks to Balzamet:

> Ayez plus de confiance en votre race [. . .] elle est plus résistante que vous ne croyez. Ah! si vous étiez un petit Français qui, récemment débarqué d'Europe, venait s'égarer au milieu de nos élèves, peut-être risqueriez-vous de compromettre à leur contact vos qualités natives! . . . [sic] Mais vous êtes d'une souche d'émigrés qui, établie depuis deux siècles sous ce climat, a déjà déployé une force considérable pour se conserver sans altération au milieu d'une population arriérée—qu'elle était obligée d'approcher et d'éduquer grossement dans son propre intérêt." (*Miracle* 87)

> Have more confidence in your race [. . .] it is more resistive than you think. Ah! If you were a young French boy, who recently set sail from Europe, and wandered amongst our pupils, upon contacting them, you might have risked compromising your native qualities! . . . But you come from a stock of immigrants who, having established themselves over two centuries in this climate, have already deployed considerable strength to conserve themselves unaltered in the midst of this backward population—that they were obliged to approach and to educate in their own interest.

However, holding up this hierarchy of the hardy Creole, created in the tropical climate of the colony over two centuries, also has to do with their building up of a "resistance" to the degrading possibility through contact with the lower races encountered in the colony.

When M. Vertère gives his idea of the accomplishment of the miracle of the white race through the assimilation of the genius of each of the others, he does not fail to add that Bourbon will make history (in, it is understood, the "History of France"):

> [s]i, nous autres, les blancs, savons du moins dans l'avenir rester leurs supérieurs, tout en les aimant, selon la tradition de nos plus dignes ancêtres. Ah! Dieu de mes pères! si *le créole* tentait un effort intellectuel pour connaître la civilisation originale des populations qui l'entourent, Indiens[,] Chinois, Malgaches, Africains, ces races que par préjugé et par paresse il prétend à jamais inférieures . . . , quelle riche, quelle vaillante expression d'humanité *il* représenterait! (301)
>
> [I]f we others, the whites, know at least how to remain their superiors in the future, even while loving them, according to the tradition of our most admirable ancestors. Ah! God of my fathers, if *the Creole* [white born in the colony] made an intellectual effort to understand the original civilization of these populations that surround him, Indian, Chinese, Malagasy, African, these races that he claims owing to prejudice and laziness are forever inferior . . . , what a rich and valiant expression of humanity *he* would represent! [my emphases both quotes]

Note that it is the *Creole* or the colonial-born white who will be the rich valiant expression of humanity after having absorbed what is best from the other races, and that, at the beginning of the quotation, the white must remain superior. In another passage, Frère Hyacinthe tells Balzamet that he should have faith in his race, in the colonial-born white. He goes on to suggest that the blacks are *equal* to whites and even that *"les noirs soint* [sic] *loin d'être ceux à qui Dieu a départi le moins d'intelligence. Je vous dirai même que bien des petits garçons de nos campagnes, en France, ne sont pas plus doués qu'eux: ils sont en tout cas beaucoup moins désireux de s'élever par l'enseignement!"* [italics in original] (87) [*the blacks are far from being those whom God made the least intelligent.* I will even tell you that many of the little boys of our villages, in France, are not more gifted than them: they are in any case much less desirous of raising themselves up through education!]. He even goes on to say that there is an "égalité naturelle" [natural equality] between the blacks and whites. He wants his school to be a space where children of different races will be "brothers." Still, Frère Hyacinthe sees Alexis as one of the early examples of individuals of the "race des blancs les meilleurs, puisqu'ils auront été obligés de bonne heure d'être des exemples des autres" (88) [best of the white race, because they will have been obliged, early on, to be examples to others]. This sentence debunks the rhetoric of brotherhood and equality because it stems from a textually inscribed awareness that brotherhood would require a renunciation of class privilege; that superiority is only maintained through this structural fixing of the other "races."

In 1908 the Société d'Anthropologie de Paris came up with a questionnaire, which included an entire section on the métis. This document was distributed to colonial administrators and functionaries of all kinds along with instructions to only record observations and refrain from any interpretation (Claude Blanckaert 43). These documents fueled many of the century's positions on *gens de couleur* and their status with regard to citizenship, considering them as quite a specific group within the colony. One of the presumptions of this document was the unquestioned distance between the purely and clearly different races (Blanckaert 42). Prior to this, racial classification of individuals was essential to various processes in the colonies. Adjustment was required in the vocabulary in order to accommodate changes in colonial life. For instance, after Abolition, the term "noir" replaces quite systematically the term "nègre" in documents such as birth registers, marriage records, or death certificates. Laurent Dubois notes that in Guadeloupe, when a certain Cazimir married Marie-Noël, with other soldiers as witnesses, all those present were ex-slaves, but only Marie-Noël was marked racially as a "Citoyenne Noire." Male ex-slaves escaped a racial ascription due to privilege gained by military service, thus highlighting the racial difference of some women (Dubois 99). Dubois's research suggests that plantation workers were consistently called "noir" in these registers, while other male "new citizens" could escape being categorized as "noirs" or "gens de couleur" by proving themselves of value within the republican hierarchy (100).

As is well known, the concept of hybridity was indispensable to discussions, dating from as early as the eighteenth century, of the unity of the human species or its understanding as multiply constituted by mutually exclusive groups. For the monogenists, on one hand, hybrid humans only served to reiterate the unity of the human family, using reproduction across groups that produced the hybrids as part of a natural process. Differences among groups within this family arose from environmental differences such as climate. For the polygenists, on the other hand, the hybrids were of particular interest because the observation of them over time would reveal the impossibility of their propagation due to infertility, thus showing the monstrousness of hybrids and reinforcing the argument that these different groups were naturally incompatible owing to fundamental distinctions that would suggest the division of the human species. Among the polygenists, notorious was, of course, Robert Knox in whose 1850 *Races of Men*, the mulatto was a monstrosity. Paul Broca's 1858 *Mémoires sur l'hybridité* presents a somewhat different argument. Observations of the animal kingdom, he writes, showed that distinct species could produce fecund new métis, and therefore, fecund métis in humans did not automatically signal the unity of the human race. Other polygenists of the era, such as Jean-Baptiste de Bory de Saint-Vincent or Pierre-Nicolas Gerdy, argued that it was no longer possible to maintain the purity of any one of the diverse racial groups in humans (Blanckaert 51–53). Broca's work reinforced the polygenist position but was explicitly positioned against monogenists such as James Cowles Prichard and his followers for their complete espousal of total hybridity. At the same time he also opposed followers of Gobineau, who associated purity of race with a moral purity or lack of this latter when race was corrupted.

The consequences of the "victory," so to speak of the polygenists resulted in many interesting maneuvers in science, culture, and politics in the twentieth century. Even if Darwin's research put forth the thesis of the unity of the human species, nothing in it contradicted the prevalence of permanent varieties. Knox would seize upon this point. Still, whether monogenist or polygenist, whether the argument was used for or against slavery, race subordination remained a constant across the different positions. To take a prominent historical milestone, the Exposition coloniale internationale de Paris of 1931 (and the objections to it) is only one of the examples we can cite of events that exemplified how the plurally inflected discourses on race came together to reinstate the hierarchy long established through colonialism. Although the main intent of the exposition was to celebrate Empire (and from France's dominance at this event, particularly the French Empire), it also served to educate the French about the importance of their colonies and to recruit French youth to participate more actively in the colonial venture. The underlying logic of the exposition held up the long-established "superiority" of French culture and civilization over those of France's colonies and, implicitly, recalled the opposition to such an idea. In the following decades, this opposition would lead to revolutionary change across the colonial world.

In thinking through hybridity from the colonial novel, it becomes evident that the racial articulation of hybridity that caused certain upsets in maneuvering the clear superiority of the white race was elided in favor of concentrating on a cultural definition of it. Therefore, it is all the more important to be able to properly and quite specifically articulate what is meant by total cross-cultural interaction and transformation that postcolonial theories of hybridity envisage. If, through colonial hybridity, racial hierarchies became explicitly or implicitly reiterated, what are the terms in which postcolonial hybridity escapes or at least deals with hierarchy in difference? As is evident also from the above citations from the colonial novel, explicit engagement with hybridity from what we might term a "progressive" colonialist perspective elides the question of racial hybridity and focuses on a cultural concept. This adoption of cultural hybridity is also evident in postcolonial theories of hybridity as noted in the introduction. In the first case, the conflictual situation in which racial métissage occurred is elided in the colonial novel, while in postcolonial theories, along with this, the ways in which conflicts between the groups among which hybridity is created become obscured in the wish for free cultural exchange among them. The relationship of postcolonial hybridity to colonial hybridity necessarily brings into the dialogue colonialism, slavery, indenture, and other forms of labor under colonialism, racial métissage, immigration, and the administration of colonial peoples. It links more consequentially hybridity in the metropolises to hybridity in the ex-colonies with and through global capitalism. In terms of the distinction made in the introduction, it brings to the forefront both diaspora and its connection to history, homeland, and racial unity as well as creolization and its insistence on immediacy and solidarity across boundaries.

Hybridity as Métissage in La Réunion

When read against the backdrop of this notion of cross-cultural interaction, it is evident that cultural hybridity was promoted as a way in which the white race would assimilate all the positive qualities of the other races to make the white Creole (born in the colony) population superior not only to the various immigrants that French colonialism brought to sustain its island colony, but also to metropolitan Frenchmen in the colonial period. It is thus easy to see why there has been, in progressive discourse in La Réunion, a much more consequential anchoring of class and shared interests than we will find even in neighboring Mauritius. The discourse of hybridity more particular to Mauritius will be discussed in chapter 4. In colonial La Réunion, culture and other traits historically seen to be intrinsic to specific groups of peoples only functioned in colonial thinking as a way of funneling these aspects to a small group of whites, who would lead and develop this colony. These observations help identify the limits of French assimilation offered to "other" populations.

Vergès' study of anticolonialist discourse and strategy in La Réunion (*Monsters and Revolutionaries*) suggests that the notion of hybridity has often worked to the detriment of those not privileged in La Réunion's history: all forms of labor brought in by the French colonial system. In chapter 2, following the more contemporary *Métisse*, it became evident that in the narrator's analyses hybridity calls up the history of slavery, of the meeting of underprivileged units in La Réunion's history, and a recognition that the differences upon which La Réunion's Frenchness was predicated have historically been of no political value to those who are called on to bear these differences. As cross-cultural encounter, hybridity could only speak through the voice of the inherited racial and racist signs that, even as they are rethought, give credence to the colonial idiom. The power of this idiom was demonstrated in the adoption by both the narrator's white mother and her black father of the degraded version of blackness that was to be insulted and shunned.

Degradation of whiteness from contact that is suggested in the colonial novel is reclaimed and rethought in the title of *Métisse* and takes the form of its speaking subject itself. Métissage emerges as a form of politics enabled by Creole language and which posits the nation. At this point I want to pause to reconsider some of the theoretical underpinnings of hybridity, drawing from chapter 1. On this reading, any theoretical account of the production of hybridity becomes saturated with the conceptual and historical framework of racially marked exploitation making it increasingly difficult to evoke the hybrid as the ambiguous point, privileged in postcolonial theories, at which we encounter hegemony, resistance, and agency. Bhabha's attempt to do so involves what Stuart Hall calls "intervening ideologically" (qtd. in Bhabha *Location* 22). In arguing against the artificial separation between politics and theory, Bhabha comments that a movement between them "is initiated if we see that relation as determined by the rule of repeatable materiality, which Foucault describes as the process by which statements from one institution can be transcribed in the discourse of another" (*Location* 22). What he sees as the movement of statements across this divide doing is that "any alteration of its field of experience or verification, or indeed any difference in the problems to be solved, can lead to the emergence of a new statement: the difference of the same" (*Location* 22). So, it is in "hybrid forms" that Bhabha wants to articulate "a politics of the theoretical statement" (*Location* 22). In his terms, deriving from Foucault, "the theoretical enterprise has to represent the adversarial authority (of power and / or knowledge), which in a doubly inscribed move, it simultaneously seeks to subvert and replace" (*Location* 22). Following a semiotic mode (although he calls this "reading Mill against the grain") Bhabha states that "politics can only become representative, a truly public discourse, through a splitting in the signification of the subject of representation; through an ambivalence at the point of the enunciation of a politics" (24). But, as we have seen, moving "hybridity" as a notion between two spaces is not such an easy task. Here, we have seen the move from the colonial to the postcolonial novel. In this case, the movement did not so easily "lead to the emergence of a new statement." What it necessitated is a move beyond the literary text that the narrator explicitly suggests and that is evidenced in late twentieth century Réunionese society in Creole nationalist politics. The difficulties of making hybridity a politics from the concept and reality of colonial hybridity was explored briefly in chapter 1.

It becomes evident, then, that it is not possible to evoke the hybrid outside of this racially charged or over-determined conceptual space. Here, it is not in the "moment of enunciation" that in Bhabha's terms, "objectified others [are] turned into subjects of their history" (*Location* 178). Instead, it occurs through the long view by which a "métisse" is able to become the enoncé in her own énonciation. Such a reading questions, also, Bhabha's insistence on the divided will and the challenge it presents for representation in that it offers that the differentially situated subjectivities and desires must all come to terms with the objective reality of the colonial idiom within which their "selves" are available. It is only a strategic unity of will, activated through some kind of collective consciousness of shared interest or suffering, that a path can be forged toward representation or action. The common experience incarnated in the vegetable "brèdes" eaten by poor whites and blacks alike is, however, insufficient to forge the relationship between Anne-Marie's white mother and black father. Neither is able to come up with the ethical engagement at the level of the individual that will be explored in discussing Glissant in chapter 6. Instead, they allow their experience to lapse into the idiom directly inherited from colonialism. Difference is not supported within the objective structure of the department. From these remarks, it becomes clear that postcolonial hybridity needs to account for the way in which such inheritance is worked through. The movement we examined of the concept of hybridity from the colonial to the postcolonial novel, which proposed a change in the structure surrounding the enunciation, participates in the "perpetual cultural revolution, [which] can be apprehended and read as the deeper and more permanent constitutive structure in which the empirical textual objects know intelligibility" (Jameson *Political Unconscious* 97).

Further, *Métisse* refuses Bhabha's "Third Space" that "represents both the general conditions of language and the specific implication of the utterance in a performative and institutional strategy," because it disallows such a split between the two. The term "cafre," for example, brought together effectively these two spaces by resolutely denying there was any understanding for it as a general and then a particular. The only implication, its only coherence, for *both* the white mother *and* the black father was the general signification of the uncivilized negro, slave in history, who is culturally and developmentally inferior to the French settler (Creole). Colonial hybridity, as the colonial novel demonstrates, does not undo this hierarchy. If we were to ask for specifications of the process of interpretation and signification, following from Bhabha's version of hybridity, we could say that the meaning of the utterance has to be specified in a Réunionese idiom. In so doing, it is impossible, following this text, to impute ambiguity to these particular usages of the term "cafre" as anything other than a negative enunciation of "nègre." The term does not give the historically objectified black man agency in the moment of its utterance—neither by his wife, nor even by himself. Neither was able to implement a significant change to the colonial suggestions within this term, in a moment of ethical agency.

For Jameson, the choice in artistic representation between victims and heroes has to do with the strategy at work:

> For such a politics can foreground the heroic, and embody forth stirring images of the heroism of the subaltern—strong women, black heroes, fanonian resistance of the colonized—in order to encourage the public in question; or it can insist on that group's miseries, the oppression of women, or of black people, or the colonized.
>
> These portrayals of suffering may be necessary—to arouse indignation, to make the situation of the oppressed more widely known, even to convert sections of the ruling class to their cause. But the risk is that the more you insist on this misery and powerlessness, the more its subjects come to seem like weak and passive victims, easily dominated, in what can then be taken as offensive images that can even be said to disempower those they concern. Both these strategies of representation are necessary in political art, and they are not reconcilable. But it is impossible to resolve this particular antimony of political correctness unless one thinks about them in that political and strategic way. ("Globalization" 53–54)[4]

In *Métisse*, the negative image of the father as a victim of racism—that goes beyond his control, even beyond his understanding because he also shares this negative perception of himself that his wife's instinct belies—has a corrective. Although this may arouse indignation for potential readers of the text, it creates a moment of ethical possibility for his daughter within the text itself. In Jameson's terms, she does not try to reconcile this image of her father with some monumental one she erects in its place nor does she buy into the victimized interpretation. Instead, she activates her own agency in an act of distancing and autonomy whereby she does not seek her father's validation for her own purpose. Instead of giving him the letter, the narrator "leaves" the text to coincide with the author and gives readership the opportunity to understand what métissage has meant in La Réunion. In her terms, it has meant a strong Creole consciousness through Creole language as a counter-hegemonic force (against French departmentalization); it has meant demystification of what aspirations to whiteness mean for La Réunion: her mother's validation as a legitimate white woman came from movement away from poverty and into middle-class respectability. But as the narrator understands, such an understanding of the move had to come at the cost of ignoring the commonality between whites and nonwhites that was evident before her move. The irony, of course, is that this occurred even though her move was made with and through her association with a black man. But this irony serves to highlight even further the impossibility of believing in French middle-class identity and culture, in French departmentalization, in French citizenship.

This interaction between the narrator's parents occurs, in Lacan's terms, in a "transindividual" space where the image of the slave remains in the unconscious, as it were, and furnishes the violent scene between the parents as well as the retreat of the father from his daughter's life, based on this image of himself. The restructuring of the subject occurs in the teller of the story—the narrator who witnessed the different enunciations of "cafre." The only way that there is any retroactive imputing of meaning to these prior events is through a restructuring of the idea of hybridity and through a long view of history. The meaning of "métissage" within the colonial novel and its support system of colonialism cannot just be altered: from meaning, in the colonial novel, the absorption of the positive traits of other races for the fortification and perfection of the white race to, in the more recent representative apparatus, a mingling of the positive traits within the entire culture. The only way that this term can be rehabilitated is through a restructuring of the entire colonially created and sustained system that gives it coherence, implicating an ethical investment in its enunciation. In this way, *Métisse* demonstrates intuitively the way in which a new totality must alter the terms of métissage through the structure of feeling of nation.

If the Réunionese nation is a cultural hypothesis, as suggested in its evocation as a structure of feeling, textually, it comes as a *jouissance* because it is necessarily linked to a desire that opposes the Law—the law of French nationhood. The idea of interdiction is textually articulated in the constant presence, even threat, of Creole in the French text. The fact that Creole language is linked to Réunionese nationhood, as we have seen, makes of it a forbidden idiom whose appearance records this desire that opposes the French status of La Réunion. In the history of La Réunion, the strong desire for otherness is what métissage testifies to (as the product of this attraction) at the most obvious, yet available and readable, level of racial identification. One might then say, following from this, that focusing on a legitimate position for the métis(se) and a legitimization of the discourse of métissage in the narrator's story in her relationship with her parents is the sublimation of this desire. The urgency for sublimating this desire for otherness can be explained, at least in part, by the fact that the terms in which otherness is available in departmental La Réunion are only the grotesque racialist colonial terms that render the narrator's father a nigger. Paradoxically, the naturalization of this negative image of the father through the historical process of colonization also becomes the Law of the Father, which the narrator explicitly rejects. Recognition of this coincidence of the Law with that of the Other (her parents)—even as this Law is what renders a mutual satisfaction of her parents' desire impossible—makes the narrator's ethical intervention into the Real or History radical. Postcolonial theories of hybridity seem to jump quickly from one stage to the other without any evidence of the intellectual and practical effort required to enable the new meaning they wish to attribute to hybridity.

Bhabha asks from within his conception of hybridity: "[. . .] [H]ow do we fix the counter-image of socialist hegemony to reflect the divided will, the fragmented population? [. . .] [H]ow does the collective will stabilize and unify its address as an agency of *representation*, as representative of a people?" (*Location* 30). These texts, when read to shed light on the postcolonial, show that language is an important place to begin such a representation—not just as the actual language in which this will is to be represented, but as the place where histories and agency can be understood and thought through by a people. In the quotation above, it is implicit that it is easier to succumb to a singular voice that does not succeed in representing all its constituencies. While such a risk is run in any type of real world situation involving plural spaces, building of a strategic unity of will does not mean to lapse into simplistic consensus; rather a strategic unity of will presupposes dialogue, thought, ethical decisions, and intelligent creative process in provisional collectivities. Such collectivity must be forged in engaging with the "social ground" in question. Hybridity, then, demands perhaps more than any other concept specifications in its use, because engaging it as a politics can have very different consequences and presuppositions in each instance. In La Réunion, it is more useful to think in terms of language rather than a language metaphor for the purposes of using hybridity as an emancipatory concept.

In the early 1960s some Réunionese students of the AGERF (Asociation générale des étudiants réunionnais en France) refused to join the general outcry against French aggression in Algeria. This prompted a split and the formation of the UGECR (Union générale des étudiants créoles en France), which for its part openly affirmed its desire to emancipate the island from French colonialism (see Armand and Chopinet 150). Although their journal *Rideau de cannes* had a short life (1961–63), several of the members continued the cause in France and upon their return to La Réunion (for example Axel Gauvin and Roger Théodora).

The 1970s are characterized by the discernable split between the *créolie* and *créolité* movements. The former, with Jean-François Samlong, Jean-Claude Thing Leoh, and some of Jean Albany's writing define themselves as "apolitical." Their insouciance when it comes to the necessity to standardize in any way written Creole, and their admission and acceptance of the minority position of Creole characterize this trend. Creole is used as the language of intimacy, familiarity, love, and family, and is not seen in a conflictual relationship with French, which is naturally viewed as the language of logic and reason. Most of these writers produce their major creation in French and their use of Creole was more a capitulation to what they saw as a "trend" (Armand and Chopinet 291). The Mauritian critic, Jean-Georges Prosper, in what I see as a problematic article in the special issue of the journal *Notre Librairie*, tries to situate Mauritius with regard to the *créolie* of the Indian Ocean. One must first question why he chooses the term "créolie" and not "créolité" for the title, but this is not the place to explore that. In this same article, he claims that "la créolie [est un] synonyme de réunionnité" ("La place" 83) [créolie (is a) synonym for reunionness], thus either conflating the two movements of créolie (described above) and créolité, or totally disregarding the more militant, nationalist movement in favor of the bland, apolitical one that is rather condescending to Creole language.

Armand and Chopinet note that despite the boom in the construction of schools on the island, the results were catastrophic and showed no promise of improvement (229). Axel Gauvin's *Du créole opprimé au créole libéré* presents the problematic of Creole as first an issue of literacy. His work with teaching adults a Creole script (there are eight recognized graphic systems proposed on La Réunion) for the language they already speak with fluency leads him to conclude that it would be an easy task to make a vast majority of so-called illiterates literate. To defend this project in a Francophone context, he shows how, through various examples, Creole speakers do not understand French, even if they seem to on the surface. In fact, this situation is even worse than the one Bourdieu proposes where, due to the educational system, "social mechanisms of cultural transmission tend to reproduce the structural disparity between the very unequal *knowledge* of the legitimate language and the much more uniform *recognition* of this language" [emphases in the original] (62). The constant misunderstandings in the educational context, and the simultaneous outlawing of Creole in the classroom, result in an educational system, which produces students who can not function in French. Gauvin cites a student who sums up the result:

—si ou-i koz an kréol i bous a-ou
—si ou-i koz an franssé ou-i fé fo't sï fo't, i ri d-ou
—si ou-i koz pas, i di ou lé timid, sinon sa ou-i rèv, daouar ou-i anfou d-lékol, i fé in don't èk sa pou fé mon't a-ou d'kla's. (*Du créole opprimé* 10)

If you speak in Creole, they tell you to be quiet. If you speak in French, you make mistakes one after the other, they laugh at you. If you don't speak, they say you are timid, that you are dreaming, that you probably don't care about school, and they keep track of that for promotion to the next class.

In fact, he gives various examples of how in the classroom as well as outside it, simple information is not understood when communicated in French (see for example 89), thus questioning even the recognition of French. However, clearly, for Gauvin as for many other members of the créolité movement, the status of Creole language is related to the status of the people of La Réunion. Showing where (with respect to classes and strata) in Réunionese society (bilingual and sometimes) monolingual Creole speakers and those who speak ["possèdent"] (*Du créole opprimé* 68) French and thus consolidate "linguistic capital" (see Bourdieu 51) are located, he remarks that the latter group is made up of "les classes et couches sociales favorisées par le système colonial" (68) [the classes and strata favored by the colonial system].[6]

In chapter 4 on the neighboring island of Mauritius we will see a very different articulation of hybridity in the context of the official political and nationalist discourse close to the time of Mauritian independence.

CHAPTER FOUR

On the Difficulty of Articulating Hybridity

Africanness in Mauritius

[Mauritius] has succeeded to a remarkable degree in evolving a distinct Mauritian way of life. The visitor to Mauritius is impressed by the fact that on the whole, Mauritians have more in common with each other than with the native inhabitants of the lands of their [forefathers].
—Seewoosagar Ramgoolam, First Mauritian Prime Minister in a speech at the United Nations

In the previous chapters, it became evident that in La Réunion, the concept of mixedness has been employed to call up the not-yet accomplished nation. While hybridity and ambiguity were acknowledged, there was a certain underlying strategy that reactivated the racial meaning of the French term métissage in its historical specificity of the encounter of racially marked bodies after the advent of colonialism. The racial component being reactivated, the colonial history of this French department was reconsidered along with a simultaneous rejection of Frenchness. This can be identified in a "feeling" of Réunionese nationhood as against the imposed French nation. The referent of the term "métisse," in the novel we considered located the protagonist while the play of this vocabulary of race with that of class and gender became significant in the observations the narrator made of her parents and their history on the island of La Réunion as traced through their ancestors. If these observations about the collusion of race, class, and gender have become commonplace, and even come back as a kind of litany in postcolonial studies, their intersections with regard to hybridity have not always been so evident.

In this chapter, the term Creole will become significant to the recent history of Mauritius, an explicitly hybrid nation, where articulating the hybrid moment becomes complicated. The idea of a dominant culture shifts in this consideration from a postcolony—metropolitan dialectic to one that has to do with an internal relation of the specifically ethnic to a national context. Here, in trying to privilege culture as enunciation, in Bhabha's terms, it becomes necessary to then examine the impossibility of other enunciations: in this case, the impossibility for Africanness to appear in Mauritian society. Specifically, in this chapter I am considering public discourse from the period immediately preceding to the several decades following Mauritian independence as I examine parts of speeches made by the (now deceased) first Mauritian prime minister, Sir Seewoosagar Ramgoolam. The second part of the chapter focuses on contemporary Mauritian politics.

Hybridity here involves troubled and difficult mythical as well as concrete ties to the lands seen as the "origin" of various groups, thus drawing attention to what I referred to as diasporic positioning in chapter 1. In addition, relationality refers to the positioning of these groups vis-à-vis other groups within the Mauritian national space, opening our discussion to preoccupations central to the notion identified as creolization. In this chapter I will consider social antagonism through language as a crucial element of culture itself. Cultural difference becomes an event that is actualized through language and in speech. I wish to show how politics, viewed here primarily through the symbolic use of language, eschews the articulation in what is "distinctly Mauritian" (see Ramgoolam's quotation above) of anything "African." I argue that the prime minister's discourse is emblematic of the inability of Mauritian society to come to terms with the issue of slavery and with its historical ties to the African continent and Madagascar. If Vergès has pointed out how, for the French department of La Réunion, any talk of métissage should in fact lead to a history of slavery, this kind of discourse has proven even more difficult in Mauritius, an independent nation. While in chapter 3, the salient term from which hybridity was considered was "métis," here, the term "Creole" will become our focus.[1] I discuss language as an ethnic marker that disallows a legitimate configuration of Africanness and/ blackness, resulting in an eternal elision of this "part" of the Mauritian "mosaic." All future references to "Africanness" in this chapter point to qualities or aspects that might be associated with both the African continent and Madagascar.

Historical Considerations

Mauritius is 550 miles east of Madagascar and about 2,300 miles from the Cape of Good Hope. It is a small island that measures thirty-six miles in length and twenty-three miles in width. The Arabs are considered the earliest visitors to the area, which was never known to have been populated by indigenous people. The Portuguese were the next to arrive (Vasco da Gama rounded the Cape in 1498; Goa was captured in 1510, Malacca in 1511) as they pushed eastward toward the Malabar (western) coast of India. Neither the Arabs nor the Portuguese used these islands as anything more than crucial docking and resting places in their commercial ventures. Soon the Dutch and English were to follow and the East India Companies were established.

The Dutch took possession of Mauritius in 1598, naming it after Prince Maurice of Nassau. No attempt was made to settle or colonize the island at this time. English, French, and Dutch ships used the island as a halt on their way toward India. Although the English, French, and Portuguese were driven out of Java in 1619 when it was taken over by the Dutch (who were later defeated in India in the Anglo-Dutch war 1665–67), they all continued to trade simultaneously in India. The inner route, through the Moçambique channel, was used onward to Bombay, Goa, Cochin, or Ceylon. The outer route, East of Madagascar via the Mascarenes, usually led to Madras, Pondichéry, or Calcutta. The subsequent settlement and establishment of full-fledged colonies on the island, and the latter's destiny were closely tied to the expansion of the French and British Empires in India. The area was also affected in various ways by the developments and changes occurring at the Cape of Good Hope, which was a source of supply to the French bases of Bourbon (La Réunion) and Ile de France (Mauritius) since the early 1780s, and considered the "Gibralter of India" (Graham 25).

Gradually, though, the British preferred the safer harbour of Mauritius as compared to the "vicious currents [. . .] and the violent winter storms" around the Cape (see Graham 50). In 1810, Bourbon (July) and subsequently Ile de France (December) were taken from the French by the British. The strategic importance of Mauritius for the British Empire in India is evident. The British *Quarterly Review* reported that "were we, by any unforseen event, compelled to abandon the peninsula of India, we verily believe that no power on earth would hold it to any advantage, or in any state of tranquillity while the Cape of Good Hope, the Mauritius, and Ceylon remained in our possession" (qtd. in Graham 52). In fact, the Mauritian author Loys Masson reminds us of her ensign "stella clavisque maris indici," in his novel *Etoile et la clef* (1941). In 1869, the opening of the Suez, of course, changed this status of the "star and key" of the Indian Ocean. The significance of Mauritius is linked to the struggle between the French and British in India that culminated in the seven years war (1756–63). The key to the control of the Bay of Bengal depended on the strip of the Coromandel coast near Madras. Consequently, the nearest French base to this east coast of India was Mauritius. Following the impossibility of a French India, Bourbon and Ile de France gained economic attention: populations doubled, agriculture and the harbors were developed. Mauritius became a British possession in 1810.

The Emancipation Act was passed in 1833 and the official abolition of slavery in Mauritius is dated at 1835. Owners received a grant of 2 million pounds as compensation for the freed slaves (see Graham 71). Patrick Beaton, the minister of St. Andrew's Church and secretary of the Bible society of Mauritius writes that "[i]t was a master-stroke of Mauritius genius, still looked back to with unqualified admiration, first to introduce some 15,000 slaves in defiance of the laws of Great Britain, and then to make Great Britain pay half-a-million of a compensation for the slaves thus illegally introduced" (65). It was at this time that the introduction of "coolie" labor from India was made large scale. Chinese merchants migrated to the area in the late nineteenth century, although a very small number of the *engagés* laborers from the earlier period were also Chinese. It was around the same time (1860s) that Muslim merchants, primarily from Gujarat in India, also came to Mauritius and on to La Réunion. These last two groups were completely outside of the experience of labor in the cane fields (see Chane-Kune *Aux origines*).[2]

The political becomes a site where these multiple, contesting histories play out in interesting and sometimes unexpected ways. Discourses around the language question have always been highly charged in the Mauritian context. There have been great efforts, with renewed vigor since independence, to include ancestral languages in the curriculum. While the various Indian languages such as Hindi, Urdu, Bhojpuri, Tamil, Telugu, and Gujarati as well as Chinese are represented in the educational system, no African language enjoys this status.[3] There are no imprints of African languages in the way Indian languages and Chinese as well as the more prestigious French and English are inscribed. Creole, the language whose origins can be traced to the interaction of Europeans and African slaves, while clearly implicated in everyday life for all groups of Mauritians, often has a discordant relationship to other languages. This position of Creole language will be explored further.[4]

A Prime Minister Speaks

On 7 December 1943, Sir Seewoosagar Ramgoolam, then a nominated member of the Legislative Council and who was later to become the first Prime Minister of the Republic of Mauritius, spoke thus regarding Indian languages:

> *My section* of the community wishes to see that Indian languages such as Hindi, Urdu and Tamil are taught to our children as a matter of right. Any change that will bring about the suppression of one language or another is undesirable and will have a detrimental effect *on that section* of the community.
>
> I do not see why. . . . Hindi or Urdu or Tamil should not be made optional *for Indian students*. By that I do not mean that they should take either French or one Indian language. I think they should have the option to take both of them, as is done in other parts of the world, like India. [my emphases] (101)

Here, Ramgoolam does several things. First, he clearly allies himself with the general Indian community ("my section of the community")—racially or culturally, as one would have it—and, in his role as representative, speaks for them. Second, he divides the community along linguistic or ethnic lines, and makes specific languages the "property" of particular sections (". . . that section . . ."). It is significant that Indian languages become the property of Indians, even if they don't (yet/anymore) speak them. It seems inconceivable that there may be other links, apart from the "ancestral," to Indian languages and therefore, according to his speech, that, for example, non-Indian Mauritian children should want to learn Indian languages. Ramgoolam also holds up his ancestral country (not-yet-independent India) as the example. Following Mauritian independence and the clear Indian majority for the electorate, the Indianness of Mauritius has been exalted and celebrated to an even greater degree.

Although the presence of various languages in Mauritius is indubitable, their actual use and the competence of their speakers can be examined. The one language that is understood and spoken quasi universally, with perhaps different degrees of frequency, is unquestionably Creole. Yet Creole is the only language that no constituent wants to claim. I shall briefly explain what I mean by "claim." In Mauritius, especially after the institutionalization of statistical surveys from the 1930s onward as well as the subsequent inclusion of "Oriental Languages" in the curriculum, the language/ethnic marker has greater reality.[5] British records of Indians arriving in Mauritius categorized them according to their ethnic belonging, which inscribed what would generations later be claimed as language affiliation. Even if newly formed families were not able to sustain the language brought from India (except notably Bhojpuri), China, the African continent, or Madagascar, Indian languages and Chinese later entered the Mauritian linguistic scene through the educational system. In this way, links with the land seen as the origin of the various groups were reaffirmed. Government census questions included "what is your mother tongue?" which was later changed to "what is your ancestral language?" This change registers the functioning of languages more as markers of claimed identity and supposed cultural affiliation than as the competence of one's means of expression. To mark on the census form as one's ancestral language, say, Tamil, Telegu or Chinese is not necessarily to say one speaks it, but rather to affirm that one identifies with that community.

Yet, as Robillard has noted, studies show how the government has consistently avoided making any statement regarding Creole, notwithstanding its recognized use even in the Supreme Court. In fact, here, interpreters are available for almost any other language except Creole, implicitly pointing to its universality in Mauritius. In addition, it is stipulated that if a language other than English is spoken by all parties concerned, it may be used in the case in question as the language of communication. This "other language," likely to be spoken by all parties, is Creole; still, it is not indicated by name (Robillard 124). Despite tacit recognition of the *reality* of Creole and its universality on the island, no official position exists on its usage.

Another important point involves the introduction of "Oriental languages" in the school curriculum and its instigation of further competition among groups (and classes). English has been accepted as the official language, yet there is no particular group that comes together around this language in the manner in which it has occurred with, say, Bhojpuri or Chinese. One might suggest that the Indian population's preference for English be seen in the light of its use in India and in the light of the possibilities for educational as well as other exchanges through this language. These possibilities include going to the U.K. and India for education, and also to the more recent mecca of education, the U.S.A. The preference of many Indo-Mauritians for English can also be read as a move to counteract the hegemony of the "white" French population and the "Creoles" who have historically allied with them, an important uniting factor between these latter two groups being identification through, and the use and/or command of, French.

The term "Creole" is loosely used to indicate those in the so-called "General Population," who are "not white." The term "mulâtres" colloquially specifies those in this population with perceived lighter skin color, thereby capacitating the complete avoidance of the use of the term "black" or even

"African." Although this might not necessarily be significant in itself, it becomes so, given the widely used terminology that specifies individuals as "Indo-Mauritian" or "Sino-Mauritian," or even quite simply as "indien" or "chinois."

The argument against introducing Indian languages into the curriculum was based on the "threat" ("menace") that it presented to French (see Rughoonundun "Créolophonie"). Lionnet also notes an interesting point regarding the promotion of English from an unlikely quarter.

> Mauritians want to hold on to English as their official language because of its economic and international usefulness; the French-speaking minority, who tended to defend French against the British administration during the colonial period, is now in favor of the linguistic *status quo* because they feel that Hindi—the most widely spoken language of the Indian majority—would most probably become the 'official' language should English be abandoned. (Lionnet "Créolité" 105)

One might consider the entry of English—which, while being a language of power, is also "neutral' with respect to the language-ethnic relationship in Mauritius—as the medium of education to have moved French from being the official and "legitimate" language in the direction of becoming one of the "ethnic" signifiers, just as Indian languages and Chinese have historically been. Evidently, though, in the case of French, its prestige remains intact as its legitimate speakers include the most financially and symbolically powerful group: the former colonizers, sugar-barons, and, often, controllers of major financial institutions and capital.

Historically, the arrival of each (immigrant) group on this island was tied to a function the group would fulfill. The French arrived and established a colony, once authorization from the King was received. British administrators were not numerous following the British takeover of Mauritius. Also, Britain's colonial interest in Mauritius being strategic rather than anything else, there is no statistically significant British population that is traced over generations in Mauritius. According to the reverend Patrick Beaton's account, which was written in the middle of the nineteenth century, "apart from the military, not more than a thousand of the two hundred and thirty thousand inhabitants can speak English or identify themselves with England as their mother country" (24). He writes regarding the English who came to Mauritius seeking a fortune, that "their object is to make a certain sum of money, and when that object is attained, they betake themselves to other lands, where money is more valuable and life more enjoyable than in Mauritius" (26). The African and Malagasy slaves were imported to plant and harvest the cane as well as provide domestic labor to the colonists. Early Indian immigration was for the purpose of providing skilled labor and household labor, while massive Indian immigration was deployed to continue sugarcane cultivation and sugar manufacture after the abolition of slavery. Early Chinese immigration is linked to labor, while later, Indian and Chinese merchants were primarily associated with trade. To be sure, other groups can be conceived, and members of the groups that have been named above operated outside these prescribed functions, for example, Indian slaves prior to the massive Indian immigration postslavery.[6] Yet, in the Mauritian context, one can speak of the Indian indentured laborers or the Chinese merchants, for example, and appeal to a set of common images, even if the attitudes and emotions in recalling these images vary widely. What I am trying to establish here is that the Indian laborer, as well as the white colonist, are emblematic figures in the national memory. One can speak of common memories (in terms of content), even if the attitude or sentiment (recalling Ernest Gellner's terminology) toward them is vastly different, depending on the situation of the person(s) "remembering."

The rigidity of these groups and a lack of a proper class-consciousness based on the experience of exploitation make other forms of alliances very difficult to accomplish. In the Mauritian novelist Marie-Thérèse Humbert's *A L'autre bout de moi*, the metropolitan French visitor, Paul Roux, remarks: "Ici la classe sociale n'existe pas, on peut être pauvre comme Job, si on a la peau claire, on se sent solidaire des Blancs riches, on vote avec eux en croyant de bonne foi défendre ses propres intérêts . . . La richesse ou la pauvreté du Mauricien, c'est la couleur de sa peau, voilà le mensonge qu'il faut démasquer" (242–43). [Here social class does not exist, one can be as poor as Job, if one is light-skinned, one feels a solidarity with the wealthy whites, one votes with them and truly believes to be defending one's interests. Richness and poverty in Mauritius are measured by the color of one's skin, this is what has to be revealed]. Colonial and even postindependence statistics group under "general population" whites and Creoles, that is, all parts of the population except Indians and Chinese. It goes without saying that such a strategy has traditionally found these groups voting along the same lines, despite what are quite obviously different interests. Boisson and Louit, in their study of the 1976 legislative elections on Mauritius write about this "general population":

> L'hétérogénéité se trouve surtout dans les statuts socio-économiques puisqu'on y trouve aussi bien le sommet de l'économie sucrière, encore solidement tenu par les franco-mauriciens, que les catégories socio-économiques les plus modestes: pêcheurs, manœuvres et dockers "créoles." Entre les deux extrêmes s'étend une succession quasi-continue de statuts sociaux, avec cependant une partie importante, proportion-

nellement, de membres de la fonction publique, à tous les échelons et en concurrence assez directe avec les membres de la communauté hindoue, plus rarement jusqu'ici, de la communauté musulmane. La population générale fournit le gros de l'électorat du Parti mauricien. *L'évolution économique, l'hétérogénéité des statuts économiques remettent en cause cependant cette orientation assez conservatrice.* [my emphases] (17)

[Heterogeneity is found in socioeconomic status because one finds the height of the sugar economy still firmly in the hands of the Franco-Mauritians, than in the more modest socioeconomic categories: Creole fishermen, laborers, and dockers. Between these extremes there is an almost continuous succession of social statuses, albeit with an important part, proportionally, of members of the public service, at all levels and in direct correlation with members of the Hindu community, and more rarely until now, with the Muslim community. The general population provides the majority of the electorate of the Parti mauricien. *Economic development, the heterogeneity of economic standing, however, does question this rather conservative orientation*].

For Etienne Balibar "[t]he category of immigration structures discourses and behaviours, but also, and this is no less important, it provides the racist—the individual and the group as racist—with the *illusion of a style of thinking, an "object" that is to be known* and explored, which is a fundamental factor of 'self-consciousness'" [emphasis in original] (221). While Balibar is referring to hexagonal France, I extend this point to the group identities, which are formed alongside categories generated by immigration controls by the colonial administration in Mauritius. Arriving immigrants were constantly categorized based on origin. Subsequently, colonial and then postcolonial government statistics generated adhesion along these lines in postindependent Mauritius. Political representation continues to be viewed through such categories (Indian, Hindu/Muslim, White or French allies under General Population, and Chinese). A "racist" approach pervades the very thought about identity: by providing, in Balibar's terms, certain "objects" such as Chinese, Indian, etc., to be "known and explored" especially during colonialism—and later reclaimed by groups and individuals themselves. Balibar continues to note, however, that an ambiguity arises because "what we have here is not the illusion of thinking, but rather *effective* thinking upon an *illusory* object. Whoever classifies thinks, and whoever thinks exists. As it happens here, whoever classifies exists collectively. Or rather—and here again we must make a correction—causes to exist in practice that illusion that is collectivity based on the similitude of its members" [emphasis in original] (Balibar 221).

The various colonial, and then national, ethnic and racial categorisations generated—or at least participated in the generation of—these groups, which have an effective presence today. The "illusion" of ethnic collectivities was enabled by well over a century's worth of constant classification and lived on in quotas in the representational system of government. How can one begin to articulate a vocabulary of radical hybridity when the entire society is pervaded with one that is structured and universally understood along racial lines? Such an understanding is a legacy of the colonial history of the region. Note, for example, a 1929 University of Paris doctoral dissertation by a Réunionese student:

> Les Africains sont très robustes, mais livrés à eux-mêmes, ils ne rendent pas les services qu'on pouvait attendre [. . .] [ils] se mêlent volontiers à la population du pays [. . .]
>
> Les Indiens constituent une bonne main-d'œuvre; souples et plus intelligents que les nègres [. . .], mais ils n'ont pas la force de l'Africain; [ils] ne se mêlent qu'au bout d'un certain nombre d'années à la population.
>
> Les Chinois [. . .], ont un tempérament essentiellement mercantile, ils s'adonnent plutôt au commerce de détail; les Malgaches eux, font preuve avant tout d'un grand esprit d'indépendance. (Champdemerle 39–40)
>
> The Africans are very robust, but left to themselves, they don't carry out the services that one could expect [. . .] [they] mingle freely with the population of the country [. . .]
>
> The Indians constitute a good labor power; they are supple and more intelligent than the Negroes [. . .], but they don't have the strength of the African; [they] only mingle with the population after a certain number of years.
>
> The Chinese [. . .] have an essentially mercantile temperament, they devote themselves to small business; as for the Malagasies, they display a strong spirit of independence.

Speakers of French endowed with legitimacy are those who can also claim "whiteness." At the same time Creole language became *symbolically* linked on the scene of Mauritian politics to the so-called Creole population, that is, those who can be "racially" traced to African origins, in some "blood ratio," however small. Although this is the description of the "Creole" group derived by elimination within the General Population as defined officially, it should be remembered that early Indian immigrants (especially Tamils) also sometimes form part of this group. The amorphous "Creole" group, however, has historically rejected this link and allied with the French cause. Likewise the Indian population constantly seeks to distinguish itself from and posit itself as superior to Creoles. The Creole population is less likely to reclaim

Creole (language), preferring to use French as its language of identity, while in general considering itself superior to Indians. The actual use of Creole, paradoxically, has little to do with these language/identity "claims."

In Carl de Souza's novel *La Maison qui marchait vers le large*, which tackles the interactions of the various groups in Mauritius with humor, warmth, and severity at once, Mme Céline, one of the elderly M. Daronville's early Creole maids who could not put up with him (and eventually quits) explains: "En plus d'être un malade anormalement exigeant, il la chargeait de tâches humiliantes *'qu'une Indienne refuserait de faire'*" (37) [my emphases]. [On top of being an extraordinarily demanding invalid, he gave her humiliating tasks *that even an Indian (maid) would refuse to do*]. First, this puts Indians below Creoles in the hierarchy; but more importantly, it *excludes* Indians from the Creole population. This is how things function for the most part, by a disavowal (from both the Creole and the Indian sides) of any possible overlap, real or symbolic, between these groups. All this while there is a simultaneous denial of the real existence of the Creole group itself; their distinction from Indians (and Chinese) is suggestive of an inclusion with the "French"—or, at least a desire for it. The relationship of those of identifiable mixed-blood with the whites has evolved since the time of Patrick Beaton, who was mentioned earlier. This man of the church, who was stationed in Mauritius for five years under the British government, notes the animosity between Creoles and whites. According to him, the local government and the press constantly exacerbated the poor relations between them. His remark that "the coloured population are far more ambitious of social than of political equality" (see 99) uncannily echoes the study, about a century later, by Boisson and Louit, as we have seen earlier, who come to the conclusion that Creoles align themselves to the voting patterns of whites (that they aspire to be) rather than the majority of Indians (with whom they share real interests).

Telling the story of early Indian immigration to Mauritius, K. Hazareesingh, director of the Mahatma Gandhi Institute (MGI), longtime prominent member of the influential Indian Cultural Association, as well as an active member of Ramgoolam's government of the newly independent Mauritius during his lifetime, writes: "Labourdonnais [the Goverrner of Mauritius 1735–47] imported slaves from Madagascar for agricultural work, but they proved to be temperamentally unsuited to it, and he looked to India [. . .]." The Indian artisans are described by Baron Grant, and cited by Hazareesingh, as having "features of Europeans" (Hazareesingh 2). Even though this is a citation (of Grant) by Hazareesingh, the statement about the closeness of Indians to Europeans juxtaposed with the one regarding the unsuitability of Malagasy slaves, clearly attempts to set the Indian community in a superior position in comparison with the Malagasies. This functions in the same way as Nathalie Melas' description, in her discussion of Frantz Fanon's *Black Skin, White Masks*, of how identity in nationalist discourse is often presented as a "difference from difference": a distancing from the rest in the space of the nation, through a closer resemblance to the colonial ideal.[7] Here, Indians are different from what is different from the white/French (i.e., here, Malagasies)—they are thus closer to the white/French. This general preoccupation with comparative superiority between groups is also noted, in a rather harsh moment, by the Mauritian literary critic, Jean-Georges Prosper, who characterizes the Mauritian as being more interested in appearances than in being (see *Histoire* 11).

Admiration for the African slave "as ancestor" becomes impossible in any kind of official discourse. Mauritius became an independent nation in 1968. Now the prime minister of independent Mauritius, Sir Seewoosagar Ramgoolam, speaking on this historic occasion of independence, pronounced:

> As we open a new chapter of our history we shall always remember that we are the inheritors of a great tradition which is vested in the very history of our land. The daring and valour of our seamen, the creative imagination of the early colonisers, who included men and women from all continents, the hardy patience of those legions of workers whose efforts have enabled us to reach our present position, the respect which we have always shown for democratic principles, our love for justice and liberty, these will be the guiding lights of our national policy. (129)

In this quotation, he is at pains to give recognition to the different groups on the island and suggests their harmonious implication in the new nation through shared ideals (democracy, justice, and liberty). In presenting the new nation as the canvas on which different histories have been drawn, the prime minister evokes the workers (the image in Mauritius becomes, indisputably, that of the quintessential Indian), the seamen (a rather vague idea that could suggest the precolonial European traders, or even those Arabs who passed by before settlement and colony had been established), and he even includes the "creative imagination of the early colonisers." Silenced here are clearly the *later* colonizers under whom full-fledged slavery became an institution, and the slaves themselves. Talk of slavery is repressed as far as possible on this island, where the current majority of the population is the far from homogenous group of Indian origin (well over 60 percent) from where various strategically positioned claims of Indianness have come.

The figure of the Indian worker as the ideal symbol for "Mauritianism" slips very easily into political rhetoric. In 1970, Indira Gandhi (then Prime Minister of India) laid the foundation stone for the Mahatma Gandhi Institute in Moka, Mauritius. This institute received funds from India, and Indira Gandhi returned in 1976 to inaugurate its opening. Mahatma Gandhi himself becomes the perfect symbol in the Indo-Mauritian prime minister's political rhetoric, for he is seen, in the manner of this new nation itself, as the link between Africa and Asia. Like the Indian, Gandhi, Ramgoolam would have us believe, Mauritian Indianness is truly a "thatness," which can encompass *all* oppressed sections of the society:

> It is a historical fact that the foundations of Gandhiji's work were laid in Africa when he took up the cause not only of overseas Indians but of all who suffered the indignities of oppression and servitude. It is pleasant to be able to recall this morning that in his first and perhaps greatest campaign of Satyagraha in South Africa, Gandhiji was supported by many of our own people who had gone to South Africa from Mauritius. It was surely in keeping with his universal outlook of brotherhood that he received the cooperation of Africans, Chinese and Europeans. Satyagraha was made possible by the efforts and collaboration of people of several different races, all of them represented so harmoniously in our island society.
>
> The philosophy Gandhiji took back to India was enriched by the experience he had of suffering and hardship in the pursuit of truth. He came to represent not only his fellow Indians but all those who laboured under the yoke of oppression and injustice.... (123–24)

In this way, it seems that, in keeping with other types of visible nationalist discourses from Mauritius, the prime minister's speech makes a comparison between the new Mauritian nation and that most recognizable emblematic Indian freedom fighter. Like Gandhi, Ramgoolam suggests, Mauritius draws together Africa and Asia; like Gandhi, the Indian symbol truly embodies the efforts of struggle for independence carried out by the different peoples of Mauritius.

Yet, it would be unfair to say that the prime minister completely neglects Africa as an entity. He clearly understood the importance of the African continent and the implication of Mauritius as one of the new nations in the region (he even served as president of the Organisation of African Unity). At the ceremony to lay the foundation stone of the School for Mauritian, African and Asian Studies, which is part of the Mahatma Gandhi Institute, he is at pains to emphasize this task:

> In our quest for the discovery of Africa we will have no preconceived ideas and our object will be to find the basic values, the glorious achievements of the newly independent states. We are interested in the past as

well as the present. We wish to know all that has gone into the making of their great civilizations. We wish to know what ancient Egypt and ancient Ghana and other civilisations of Africa have given to the world in the development of astronomy. The arts and the skills of social organisation. Also we wish to discover contemporary Africa, virile and ready to embark upon new programmes of economic expansion and of experiment in new forms of government and new forms of artistic expression. (120)

Still, delving into an African past would thus involve, as we see from the above quotation, learning about the civilizations of *Africa*'s past much more than a retracing of the path that brought Africans to Mauritius and thus an examination of this aspect of Mauritius's past. There is scant place for an articulation of slavery in most discourses that engage the question of a "Mauritianism."

In 1965, shortly before independence, the Mauritian writer, Marcel Cabon published a short novel entitled *Namasté*. The title, which is a discernibly Indian salutation, and the name of the protagonist, Ram, conjure up Indianness with unsurpassable authority. The novel, among other things, describes the daily life of a primarily "Indian" Mauritian village. Indianness, invoked as we saw by Ramgoolam through the figure of the Mahatma (who, incidentally, visited Mauritius in 1901), also figures prominently in the presentation of this text by a visibly Creole author, whose engagement with Indians goes beyond an interest in the "people." Marcel Cabon, according to Aslakha Callikan-Proag, a researcher at the Mahatma Gandhi institute who wrote the preface to the 1981 edition of his book, was "un des pionniers d'un mauricianisme authentique" [one of the pioneers of an authentic Mauritianism]. His work, she continues, "indique la voie à suivre pour sortir des sentiers battus et atteindre le but suprême: une Entité Mauricienne" [shows the path to be followed if we want to escape from the beaten track and attain the supreme goal: a Mauritian Entity]. This follows from the possibility for Indians, or Indianness, to somehow convey Mauritianness. However, Callikan-Proag does concede that spaces assumed to be "Indian" often include other groups: "Le potentiel de poésie que renferment ces villages mauriciens—dits "indiens" mais où se côtoient malgré tout différentes communautés—va de pair avec la dure réalité de leurs souffrances" (1) [The poetic potential contained in these Mauritian villages—that are termed "Indian," but where, in reality, all the different communities rub shoulders—is inseparable from the stark reality of their suffering].

In a move that is strikingly similar to the prime minister's comparison of Gandhi and Mauritius itself, the author of the preface likens this author of

Namasté, Marcel Cabon (of Malagasy origin), to Abhimanyu Unnuth, the contemporary and recognizably Indo-Mauritian author who has published in Hindi and who has been edited with success in India:

> Dans la même lignée se présente à notre esprit un autre écrivain mauricien au plein sens du terme: Abhimanyu Unnuth. D'expression hindi, lui aussi vit les problèmes qu'il pose dans son œuvre; il les vit même plus intensément que Cabon en ce qui concerne les indiens vu sa propre origine.... Tous deux ... ont porté et portent toujours le flambeau *d'un vrai mauricianisme*, incarnant en même temps la lutte et les aspirations des classes labourieuses. [my emphases] (2)

> [In the same tradition comes to mind another author who is Mauritian in the strong sense of the term: Abhimanyu Unnuth. Writing in Hindi, he too lives the problems that he addresses in his work; he lives them even more intensely than Cabon with regard to the Indians, given his origin.... Both these writers ... carried and still carry the flame *of a true Mauritianism*, incarnating at the same time the struggles and aspirations of the labouring classes].

Once again, the authenticity of the Indian experience within the national sphere surreptitiously becomes the point of departure. The suggestion is, then, the adequacy of Indianness to account for Mauritianness *tout court* in a sort of synecdochy not at all uncommon in prominent nationalist discourse. In Callikan-Proag's presentation, Cabon and Unnuth reach a true Mauritianism by way of Indianness—the former by the "Indian" inspiration and content of his work and the latter by virtue of his "Indian" origin and the experience it implies. For Thomas H. Eriksen, the anthropologist who has studied Mauritian society in detail, "[t]he culturally homogenizing tendencies of nationalism and globalization should be counteracted through institutional arrangements which secure some form of ethnic autonomy and encourage cultural pluralism" (*Communicating* 49). In the history of Mauritian politics, this cultural pluralism has played out in the electoral strategies with the rhetoric being that of ethnic autonomy and cultural pluralism.[8] As a result, there has been a greater tendency toward coalitions around ossified notions of ethnicity and a cultural pluralism that continues to be conceived in the terms inherited from the institution of colonialism in Mauritius.

Language, as follows from the earlier discussion of this question, becomes a political tool that can manipulate questions of identity for groups vying for greater power. Mauritius, as a postcolonial nation, is certainly not unique with regard to the volatility around the issue of language. Still the formation of group identities around language mascots in a cultural affiliation that was not necessarily linked to any competence in the language is peculiar to this situation. Indians and Chinese from Mauritius have been quick to establish links with the peninsula and China, respectively, via language. Mauritius was, for example, notably represented at the World Hindi Convention held in Nagpur, India in the early seventies; Mauritius itself was the site for its second convention. Teachers of Hindi, Tamil, Telegu, Urdu, Marathi, and Chinese were appointed, several coming from India and China, while English and French remained the main languages of education. Even if Creole is the undisputed lingua franca, it enjoys no official status. In fact, as recently as in 1982, when the radical MMM (mouvement militant mauricien) wanted to introduce Creole as the national language, the unified protest came from almost all segments of the population.

Some discourses around this protest were linked to ethnicity. Claims were made that since Creole "belonged to" the Creole (i.e., mixed) population, that section of the population would be privileged in the nation. The fact that everyone spoke and speaks this language, regardless of claimed ethnicity, could not defeat this symbolic relation between ethnicity and language. Creoles themselves objected, preferring the more international and prestigious French. In fact, many working-class Creoles and Indians were against rendering official the only language they themselves knew well. Lionnet explains that:

> Mauritians of Indian origin [. . .] are a numerical majority in Mauritius. Among them, the urban educated elite speak both French and English as well as Hindi or Tamil, whereas the rural Indians are generally bilingual in Bhojpuri and Creole. The white or mixed Mauritian minorities [to be read "mulâtres"], on the other hand, speak Creole, French, and English, and take pride in the fact that it is this very diversity of linguistic ability that makes Mauritius both unique and a truly nonhegemonic nation." (Créolité 105)

Yet these minorities can indeed be seen as constituting a hegemonic group within the nation, because of their legitimacy in speaking the language of prestige, French, and the advantage ("diversity of linguistic ability") they have, given the specific language choices available to most of them. Once again, while the "Indian" space and the space of the "white or mixed minorities" are clearly demarcated, no space is envisioned for the "less mixed" (more obviously African) minority. Indeed, getting out of this overworked racial identification could augur a Creole-speaking majority group of Mauritians, which would not, in fact, be marked by ethnic categories.

Returning once more to Ramgoolam's political discourse, Africanness enters it precariously and is treated delicately by him. The prime minister, on the occasion of the inauguration of the School of Mauritian, African and Asian Studies noted:

> Our people are a mixture of the people of Africa and Asia. Our inheritance is evident in our whole personality. Because the immigration from India was more recent than the arrival of the people from Africa we have preserved much more of our traditional ways, in our dress, in our speech, in our music and literature. Our African inheritance was too long neglected and a conscious effort must now be made to rediscover it and bring it to the light of day. There are African words in our Creole speech; there are African traditions, half-buried in our folk-tales, and there are African rhythms in our dance, the *Sega* (119).

Despite these gestures to "Africanness," Ramgoolam's speech glosses over slavery and does not "bring it to the light of day"! The fact of having preserved "Indianness" is attributed to the more recent arrival of Indians. The conditions under which Africans lost their ways under slavery is once again left out. The government, after independence, followed (British) colonial practice, and recognized four distinct ethnic groups: Hindus (55 percent), Muslims (16 percent), Chinese (3 percent), General Population (26 percent). This last category has been described by Boisson and Louit in their work on Mauritian politics, as the most diverse. It includes "pure" Europeans (read whites), the least "racially" mixed people of African or Malagasy descent (called Creoles), and different "métis" or "mixed-bloods." "General Population" actually implies all sections of the population excluding Asians, and the motley group has historically rallied around issues that became articulated through the cause of the French language illustrated so well by Boisson and Louit. The Creole population has not found a niche in the collective memory, as the prime minister's Independence Day speech testifies. There is no space to resurrect the African or Malagasy slave. The reticence shown in the Independence Day speech examined earlier is protracted here in a celebration of Africanness that can be no more than a token gesture without its being granted a historicity as are other "inheritence[s]" of the Mauritian "personality."

When viewed historically, much of the General Population (excluding the so-called whites) includes descendants of the illegitimate offspring of the colonialists with slaves. Their current existence is rarely addressed historically and materially. That is to say, illegitimate children (mostly of white masters and black slave women) were generally not allowed to inherit land, titles, or property. Indians, on the contrary, did manage to inherit land from their indentured ancestors, as they were able, with much hardship, to purchase plots of the land on which they toiled. The illegitimate offspring of whites and slaves, most often received no land or wealth but sometimes did receive, as was the case in various other colonies, a European education. They also participated, to some degree, in that culture, acquiring, at that time, greater skills in

French in general than the Indians had the opportunity to do. This population gradually moved into the administration where some "passed" for white. As a result, assimilation had greater expediency, in their case, and permitted them entry into some areas formerly restricted to whites. Those who did not gain such access into the "white" areas, however, continued to ally with those who could and with the whites themselves. There was no alternative space, no real Creole space that might articulate the in-betweenness of this part of the population, while their entry into the vast (and equally varied) "Indian" spaces was neither desired nor desirable from both the (not!) Creole and Indian perspectives.

Returning to the prime minister's speech (cited above), what he fails to address—and there is a silence on the part of all sections on this subject—is the conditions in the case of early African immigrants to Mauritius under slavery. Such conditions did not permit a preservation of speech, clothes, etc. The mythical ties with the African continent are hardly accessed, most Creoles and "métis" still preferring to be more French or "Frenchified." Those who are "less creolized" racially and, ironically (as well as euphemistically considering the color spectrum as set up in Mauritius), called Creoles are perceived as having darker skin. There is no monumental "Gandhian" figure that links Mauritius with Africa in the way it is linked to India in Ramgoolam's speech, for example. A notable counter discourse is, of course, produced by Edouard Maunick, the Mauritian poet and, as his poem goes, "nègre de préférence" [negro by choice].

Nation, as Homi Bhabha points out, becomes "a space that is *internally* marked by cultural difference and the heterogenous histories of contending peoples, antagonistic authorities, and tense cultural locations" (*Nation and Narration* 299). I have discussed how, in Mauritius, language functions as a marker of difference within the nation and examined the way African heritage is elided in the negotiation of cultural difference in Mauritius. This latter elision creates a constant tension that is registered in discourses of/about the nation. It is furthermore cooperative with the impossibility for this heritage to be linked symbolically to a language, as are other heritages in political discourse on the Mauritian national scene. It also projects an impossible space—the space of the Creole—whose "aridity," I propose, is both a consequence of a lack of an ethnic language marker and also the cause that prevents the claiming of an ethnic language marker. The difficulty of claiming Creole as an ethnic marker arises, first because virtually all Mauritians speak Creole. It therefore loses any power of exclusivity to demarcate an ethnicity. Second, there is a negative value ascribed to Creole almost univocally by all sections as seen in the response to officially recognize this language. By the same token, although a large portion of Indo-Mauritians might speak French, I offer that their use of French is not regarded as sufficiently *legitimate* and therefore forecloses their identification with those who are seen as legitimate speakers of French.

Given this position of Creole, and, simultaneously, the position of "ethnifying" Indian languages and Chinese and even French, it is quite evident that the lack of any kind of functioning for an African language in Mauritius supports the elision of things African. The impossibility of this connection in the case of "Africans" (who cannot even be named in this way) therefore renders untenable the formation of such a group. In its contingency, Africanness is "outside the sentence" in Bhabha's terms. If Bhabha writes that it is outside the sentence that he wants to explore "the question of agency, as it emerges in relation to the indeterminate and the contingent[,]" (*Location* 182) it is in the inarticulated (and even invisible) that he locates agency. How this agency is actualized remains less evident. How does the unnamed and unnameable, and therefore entirely contingent, "African" become a subject of his/her history?

The fate of the Mauritian nation (and perhaps all nations) is doomed if Ernest Renan was correct when he pronounced that:

> [a] nation is a soul, a spiritual principle. Two things, which in truth are but one, constitute this soul or spiritual principle. One lies in the past, one in the present. [. . .] *To have common glories in the past and to have a common will in the present; to have performed great deeds together, to wish to perform still more—these are the essential conditions for being a people.* [my emphases] (19)

What today constitutes the Mauritian nation consists of a population including groups that have historically had vastly different interests. The great deeds of one group prove to be the damnation of another; the glories of one being the shame of the other. On this point, Lionnet reminds us that "[i]ts multiracial society was faced with the burdens of two centuries of colonization first by the French, then by the English, whereas its survival has been ensured by the labour of Indian and black populations who were not natives either" ("Créolité" 213). On one hand, the Creole population denies its own historicity and connection to slave labor, thus rendering impossible any group identity based on this. On the other hand, the lack of Africanness that arises from an impracticable "ethnification" toward Frenchness through language by Creoles and such a disavowal of its historicity that I have shown can be productively viewed. Such a productive view would regard this African space, in all its impossibility within Mauritian society, as nevertheless generating a site from which the rather rigid lines of identity patterns—that one tends to replicate even in analyses—can be disrupted. This lack and disavowal bear within them the possibility of thinking "less [of] a question of mixed identity *d'identité métissée* [sic] than of the *mestizaje* of identity itself, of any identity" (Nancy 123).

It is evident from the above remarks that the difficulty of articulating Africanness in Mauritius is a very specific problematic that has to do with the particular history of Africans in Mauritius and especially with their relations with other groups. Therefore, it would follow that the possibility to generalize these analyses to other situations of postcoloniality is limited. In the Mauritian context, because the troubled idea of Africanness can be traced to the lack of a language "mascot," it can reopen the issue of the different emblematic languages in their narrow functioning with the corresponding ethnic group. An engagement with this problem also consistently reveals the universality of Creole (language) and shows up various other language-ethnic affiliations to be imaginative and important links to the country of origin from a situation of diaspora. Such affiliations are, however, not usually conducive to relationality or creolization in the new land. The lack of Africanness can thus weaken the "racist" thinking of identity Balibar criticizes in the context of politics and alliances. It can make room for a more realistic deliberation of the interests of groups and individuals in their current functioning within Mauritian society and their aspirations for themselves. What I mean is that in rethinking Africanness, groupings within Mauritian society exercise a greater engagement with creolization or relationality in the new land in lieu of the rather obsessive diasporic fantasy (toward India, China, or even France, and its lack in the case of an African diaspora) that has pervaded nationalist discourse.

Contemporary Mauritian Politics: Who Speaks for African Pasts?

The Indian prime minister's visit to Mauritius in April 2005 and the question of monetary retribution to descendants of slaves, which had received international attention in the form of the United Nation's 2002 statement on this issue, are two events that position Mauritius as part of the Indian and African diaspora respectively. For Paul Gilroy, diaspora "[. . .] is a concept that problematizes the cultural and historical mechanics of belonging. It disrupts the fundamental power of territory to determine identity by breaking the simple sequence of explanatory links between place, location, and consciousness. It destroys the naïve invocation of common memory as the basis of particularity in a similar fashion by drawing attention to the contingent political dynamics of commemoration" (Gilroy *Between Camps* 123). These words from Gilroy invoke hybridity as creolization rather than diaspora (although the latter is Gilroy's preferred term) in the sense given to these two terms in chapter 1. By examining some of the ways in which these two events explicitly call forth a hybrid definition of the Mauritian people, I show that the conception of this "plural" nation is refashioned by activating both the question of common memory and the politics of identification. Gilroy's conception of the Black Atlantic seeks "to transcend both the structures of the nation state and the constraints of ethnicity and national particularity" (*Black Atlantic* 19). Here I explore how such a Black Atlantic double consciousness of diaspora and creolization plays out in Mauritius. The different groups that comprise the plurality of Mauritius are implicated in the analyses that follow, although we will be most specifically concerned with this nation's "African" and "Indian" past and present.

Paul Bérenger, the first prime minister of non-Indian origin to be elected since Mauritian independence in 1968, was chastized for intending to manipulate the imminent arrival of Manmohan Singh, his Indian counterpart, in order to garner support for himself among the Indo-Mauritians, who form more than 60 percent of the Mauritian electorate. An Indian journalist in Calcutta (India) reported: "Singh [. . .] finds himself unwittingly caught in the vortex of the island's politics" (Ramaseshan 1). Even though it is obvious that the relatively large size of the Indian population makes the latter visible and allows "Indianness" to play a dominant role in public discourse,[9] other historical factors explain Bérenger's complex position vis-à-vis his electorate and underscore a more general aspect of public discourse in Mauritius, namely, the uneasy position of "Africanness."

The official emancipation of slavery (1835 for Mauritius) spurred massive Indian immigration to replace slave labor in the fields while Chinese immigrants hailed primarily from the merchant class. Indo-Mauritians are primarily Hindus and Muslims, but also include groups that cohere around language and ethnicity, such as Tamils, Telugus, or Gujaratis. Such linkages between categories of immigrants based on their region of origin and their role in the new colony are not completely stable, as noted. Still, at the time of Mauritian independence in 1968 and in the discussions regarding representation that preceded it, whites were historically linked to the colonizers, and accounted for most plantation owners. Those of mixed-blood (usually black and white) were seen as descendants of the offspring of slaves and their white masters and refered to as *métis* or *mulâtres*, while those of African ancestry, identified by dark skin and "African appearance," were called Creoles and linked to the mixed-blood or métis group and to the white population through a cultural alliance, often characterized by the use of and attachment to the French language.[10] Since independence, this "plural" nation has experienced a major recession following a slump in sugar prices and then made a comeback with a diversified economy relying on an educated workforce, tax-free havens, and a boom in textile and technology-related industries.

For electoral purposes, as we have seen, whites, métis, and Creoles make up what is called the "General population," while other categories including Indians and Chinese are registered separately. These categories become significant, and almost unavoidable, as representation of the electorate is understood in these terms.[11]

The road leading up to the September 2005 Mauritian elections was not smooth for the incumbent. Through a complex mechanism, ethnic groups are identified as requiring protection in the electoral process, and then accorded seats. This "best-losers" system was put in place to ensure equal representation to all visible "ethnic" groups of the island as the electoral process was being worked out, even prior to independence. The coalition currently in power in Mauritius has proposed to have this "best-loser" system additionally extended to women and allotted them seven of its "best-loser" seats. Women of different convictions expressed their dissatisfaction with this hasty effort to include them in active Mauritian politics. As Pauline Etienne reports, not only do women aspire to increase their visibility from the current 4 percent (or the proposed 8 percent in this proposal), but they refuse to be considered "second-class citizens," as the system of "best-losers" might imply (2). This adds greatly to the complexity in the process of public representation in Mauritius, with a gender group now becoming increasingly vocal alongside the existing ethnic groups.

Paul Bérenger, a visibly white Franco-Mauritian, belongs to the small elite 3 percent minority of the total population. His political success has depended on, among other things, massive support from a majority of the electorate that is identified as Indo-Mauritian. It is this appeal that was highlighted in the questions raised by the Mauritian press regarding the Indian prime minister's visit. According to K. Venugopal of the *Hindu* (an Indian newspaper), Manmohan Singh's visit has a strictly economic objective, namely to increase commercial exchange through a treaty between the two nations. Mr. Singh inaugurated various sites during the course of his visit, including a cybertower, financed in large part by Indian companies. This inauguration was to be suggestive of the closer ties with regard to information technology that the two nations are seeking. Bérenger's position as the incumbent seeking reelection forces him into a web of relations with his potential voters and is reminiscent of the fact that "India" for Mauritians cannot simply function as the "basis for particularity" through common memory for a single group, but is also part of the "contingent political dynamics of commemoration" (Gilroy

Between Camps 123 cited earlier). The Indian premier's visit, then, implicated the Indianness of Mauritius, the Frenchness of its prime minister, and in this manner, called up other ethnic, racial, and cultural "aspects" of Mauritian society. But the visit also simultaneously established a more dialectical position between this nation's past and its present, situating it as diasporic rather than simply pluralistic.

The increased recognition of "oriental" languages and the use of language as an ethnic marker further point to the ease with which Indianness has entered public discourse in Mauritius. We have seen how the institutionalization of surveys regarding language affiliation and use from the 1930s onward as well as the subsequent inclusion of "oriental" languages in the curriculum have given the language/ethnic marker greater "reality." As we noted, no African language has ever been taught in the public curriculum. Likewise, though virtually all Mauritians speak and understand Mauritian Creole and the fact that Bérenger's party, the mouvement militant mauricien (MMM), supported its official recognition in the 1970s and 1980s, most of the population has been opposed to giving it any official credence.[12] Mauritian Creole is seen as not sufficiently international or prestigious to be a national language but it is also subliminally attached to the "Creoles" as a demographic group. If whites are perceived in Mauritian culture as the legitimate speakers of French, the tendency of most Mauritians is to aspire to speak this language with ease and authority. English functions as a language of prestige and international use, although more recently it has become intertwined with independent India's adoption of English as its official language. Although we cannot discuss here all the ramifications of the language situation in Mauritius and its connections to ethnicity, it is to be noted that while language became an official way of "ethnification" for Mauritians of Asian descent, there has been no comparable mechanism for ethnification in the case of "Africans," an appellation that is almost never heard in Mauritian public discourse. Today's prime minister, as any other public figure, engages this issue in his interactions with his electorate.

Paul Bérenger is no newcomer to Mauritian politics. One of the founding members of the radical MMM, Bérenger is also remembered for leading the General Workers' Federation to a general strike that practically crippled the economy in 1979. This was a period of economic crisis for Mauritius, with the country having to approach the International Monetary Fund (IMF), and the rupee being heavily devalued. During the 1982 elections, the Labour Party, represented by the first prime minister of Mauritius, Sir Seewoosagar Ramgoolam who is also known as the Father of the Nation, accused the MMM of Libyan connections through the Muslim faction of the party. The MMM swept the polls, winning 64 percent of the vote with its alliance with the self-proclaimed Hindu Parti Socialiste Mauricien.[13] Paul Bérenger served as finance minister following this election. In 1995 he became deputy prime minister to Navin Ramgoolam's Prime Ministership while Jugnauth led the opposition.

Despite these rapidly changing alliances, which might legitimately make a voter cynical, Bérenger's support by a fairly large section of the Indian majority is now indisputable. Following the historic defeat of the Indian dominated Labour Party in 1982, the new coalition government was soon beset by its own problems, which came to a head in a rift between Aneerood Jugnauth, the prime minister and comember of the MMM, and Bérenger. New elections were held in 1983, with Jugnauth garnering the support of a huge coalition of various parties under the banner of the Alliance. Bérenger disregarded traditional Mauritian concerns with ethnicity, which would have entailed a more proactive approach to ensure overt connections to all ethnic groups, and continued to lead the self-proclaimed nonsectarian MMM against this coalition. Though defeated, he entered Parliament as the leader of the opposition through the "best-loser" system mentioned before. In a reversal of fortunes (for Bérenger's future), the timely arrest of four members of Jugnauth's Alliance for drug trafficking in Amsterdam provided sufficient scandal to help fuel the future 1991 win of the coalition formed by the MMM with Jugnauth's mouvement socialiste mauricien (MSM)!

Bérenger's election, in some ways, reclaims authorship of the MMM's slogan "Ene sel lepep, ène sel nasyon" [One people, one nation]. A white Franco-Mauritian who can secure sufficient voters' support in a small "plural" country with a large Indian majority, Paul Bérenger can be seen as exemplifying the spirit of the "nasyon" and its future. A more cynical view might see his shifting loyalties, attributable to the different alliances he has made, as mere opportunism. Nevertheless, any understanding of his victory has to contend with the over-determined, communally understood Mauritian electorate.

Indian Representation: Historical Perspective

The question of Indian representation entered public discourse in Mauritius well before independence. The misery of the Indian indentured laborer in Mauritius and his lack of representation were documented as early as 1832 by the lawyer Plevitz in the *Petition of the Old Immigrants*, which he addressed to the King of England. The long list of petitions regarding beatings or dupery led to the appointment of a Protector. The collusion of the overseers and the proprietors to the detriment of the Indian laborers is also recorded in this same document:

> For each day in hospital [the Indian laborer] forfeits the pay of that day, but for each day that he is absent from his work he forfeits two days's [sic] pay. The overseers are in the interest of the proprietor, and are unfortunately but too often valued in proportion to the sum which they can enable the proprietor to deduct from the wages of the Indian labourers. Accordingly the labourers are frequently marked as absent when not absent and stoppages are made from their wages for the noncompletion of tasks almost impossible to accomplish or for other reasons invented by the ingenuity or caprice of the overseers, who must adopt this means to retain the favour of their employers and their situations. (22)

If not intentionally pernicious, the Protectors have also been noted to be just unsuitable, as recorded in the *Memorial* presented by the Inhabitants of Mauritius. Here, it is noted that the Protectors are often "strangers to the Colony and unknown to its inhabitants, enjoy no public confidence, [...] are regarded as enemies; and are consequently distrusted, shunned and hated" (15). A note informs that "[o]ne of the Protectors discovered only after his landing in the Mauritius, that he had forgot [sic] to learn French!" (15).

Historically, representation in island politics has been a charged issue for all sections of the population. From 1810, when the British took over Mauritius from the French, until 1831, the governor, who received direct orders from the colonial administration in Britain, held complete power over all aspects of the governance of this colony. Until 1881, the only input received in decision making was from the officials named by the Governor himself. Gradually, with much agitation from powerful sections of the French population, concessions were made for greater representation of the French planters and sugar barons.

When universal suffrage was being debated in the Legislative Council on 25 July 1950, most Indo-Mauritians were in favor of it. Their desire to be represented became incarnated in Seewoosagar Ramgoolam, who was to take over as first prime minister of Mauritius.[14] The linking of representation to ethnic groups, however, caused some acrimonious exchanges on the issue of communalism during the 1950s debates on universal suffrage. Mr. Kœnig, a non-Indian representative, remarked sarcastically in reaction to the ways in which Indians began to anticipate their full-fledged entry into Mauritian politics on the eve of independence: "When we are asking for posts in the Judicial Department, we are Indo-Mauritians, but when we are asking for universal suffrage, we are all Mauritians" (Mauritius Legislative Council 21). Although he believes that "all representatives of all the communities living in this country should have a share in the administration of the colony" (Mauritius Legislative Council 20–21), he puts forth his views on universal suffrage in this manner:

My friends have found it extraordinary, and I agree with them, that in the past with the old constitution, in spite of the fact that the white community represented some 1.5% of the whole population, the general elections returned a great majority of white members in this house. Well, if we are not careful, what will happen? What will happen in the future? If we resort to universal suffrage, when we know the real results of the last elections, with this suffrage which is not totally universal, it goes without saying that the members of that community who were elected in the past will be replaced by members of another single community in the future. What about the past? Is it because in the past the overwhelming majority represented only one community. That is the point. The point is, being given the communalistic feelings of the mass of the population, we are bound to be careful and see not only that the white community should not be trempled down [sic] but that the other communities should not be trampled down. (Mauritius Legislative Council 21)

Mr. Bissoondoyal, representing the "Indian" and quite specifically "Hindu" side, retorts to this that "[w]e claim that it will not be reasonable to say that if universal suffrage is granted, all the Hindus of Mauritius, because they are the bulk of the population will vote for Hindu candidates, and that only Hindu candidates will sit in this house, that they will entirely forget that there are other communities living in this country [. . .]" (Mauritius Legislative Council 22). Bissoondoyal further cites various examples of how Hindus can think outside of their community and defend other constituents. He concludes that:

> Now, if we were to go and look into the texts of the newspapers of Mauritius, we would see that people are not communally driven. Thousands of people of the Hindu community are not the subscribers of the Hindu paper. They are the subscribers of the "Cernéen" and the "Mauricien" and there are thousands of non Hindus who are not subscribers of the "Mauricien" or the "Cernéen." They are the subscribers of the "Advance" and they buy the Hindu paper. These are the proofs and the evidence to show us that the people of Mauritius are reasoning in a far different way from that in which some members of this House are trying to show us. It is because people are still believing in communalism that they see the shadow of it everywhere around them. (Mauritius Legislative Council 24)

It is against this backdrop of over-determined communal vocabulary and thinking that Bérenger's election under the auspices of the MMM becomes interesting and, indeed, remarkable. Koenig, a white Franco-Mauritian representative, neglected an important aspect of Mauritian reality in his statement that the one community that previously dominated the assembly in numbers (i.e., the whites) would now be replaced by "members of another single community" (i.e., the Indians). This reality is that the latter group comprised, even at that time, a formidable majority of the Mauritian population. A white majority in the assembly indicated the domination of politics by a minority group whereas the anticipated Indian majority would indicate acknowledgment of such domination in the make-up of the Mauritian population itself. The long fight waged by indentured Indians, whose offspring would form the future majority of the Mauritian electorate, continues to fuel Mauritian Indians' emotional investment in the electoral process. This idea of representation remains central to the Indo-Mauritian psyche and Paul Bérenger does not overlook this fact in contemporary Mauritian politics.

The Difficulty of Articulating Africanness

Representation was also central to the colonial planters, who constantly opposed British control of the colony in various contexts, the most contentious being that of slavery. From the 1810 takeover of the island by the British, French planters enjoyed great freedom in terms of language and many other administrative issues. Yet the question of slavery became a sore point in their dealings with the British administration, which was keen to do away with the practice, perhaps in an effort to maintain international credibility. Somehow, slavery is less visible in all forms of public discourse in Mauritius. Although it is true that slavery predates indenture, and that those who actually feel an emotional connection to the period and question of slavery through ancestry is far smaller, this issue remains startlingly invisible, as we have already seen. The question of representation, even as a bone of contention, may have long remained inconceivable to this section of the population historically—precisely because of the lack of power that characterized the position of slaves. As it is noted in the official document of the Colonial Archives as early as 1887, the infamous Code Noir deprived the slave of the experience of his civil rights: he was stricken by an absolute inability to receive any donation or inheritance; he could not appeal to the judicial system, be a witness, play any public role, or participate in a private institution. Marriage between slaves had to be by permission of the master, and children belonged to the master of the mother. Marriage between blacks and whites was not permitted and severely punished; priests were not allowed to preside over them (Archives coloniales 14). This history, although cited in an official document, is never officially summoned in any significant manner for today's Mauritian population.

The most notable discourse on slavery in Mauritius comes from the French writer, Bernadin de Saint-Pierre, who published his *Voyages à l'Ile de*

France in 1773. In 1805, Thomi Pitot refuted Saint-Pierre's published collection of observations. He was in his turn refuted by l'abbé Ducrocq who denounced slavery and its heritage in the early twentieth century.[15] Although these texts are interesting in and of themselves, they are evoked here because their very presence brings back the reality of slavery in a way that no other available official discourse really does. In Pitot's attack against Saint-Pierre, he writes:

> M. de Saint-Pierre s'indigne de la rigueur des châtiments infligés aux esclaves: mais, a-t-il dit la vérité en donnant comme fréquents ces 50, 100, 200 coups de fouets? Non. La calomnie seule écrivit sous sa dictée ces mensonges odieux . . . J'ai habité sept années la colonie; j'ai visité beaucoup d'habitations et j'ai trouvé souvent plusieurs centaines de noirs réunis, et jamais, je l'atteste, je n'ai vu infliger à un noir plus de 25 coups de fouets. (154)

> Mr. Saint-Pierre complains of the harshness of the punishments inflicted upon slaves: but has he been truthful in citing as frequent these 50, 100, 200 lashes of the whip? No. It is only malicious gossip that gave rise to these odious untruths written under his pen . . . I lived in the colony for seven years; I visited many of the habitations and I often found several hundreds of blacks together, and never, I swear, I never saw a black subjected to more than 25 lashes of the whip.

This refutation of 50, 100, 200 whiplashes by confirming a maximum of 25 only serves to verify rather than deny the terrible treatment of slaves. Also speaking of the Code Noir, Ducrocq cites the following article:

> Voulons que les esclaves qui auront encouru les peines du fouet, de la fleur de lys et des oreilles coupées soient jugés en dernier ressort par les juges ordinaires et exécutés sans qu'il soit nécessaire que tel jugement soit confirmé par le Conseil supérieur, nonobstant le contenu de l'article 25 des présentes qui n'aura lieu que pour les jugements portant condamnation à mort ou de jarret coupé. (qtd in Saint-Pierre, Pitot, Ducroq 194)

> It is necessary that slaves who will have undergone punishment by whiplash, by branding and by severing their ears be judged as a last resort by ordinary judges and that they be executed without it being necessary that such a judgment be confirmed by the Superior Council, notwithstanding the content of article 25 of this document which will not occur except for judgments of death penalty or of cutting of the hamstrings.

Ducrocq points out that these ordinary judges were most often friends and acquaintances of the owners. "Le misérable, condamné sans recours, n'avait donc aucune aide à attendre en ce monde. Il était absolument à la merci de son maître" (Saint-Pierre, Pitot, Ducroq 194) [The wretched one, condemned without recourse, therefore had no help in waiting in this world. He was completely at the mercy of his master]. A return to these historical texts does not serve here to provide a more accurate account of slavery in Mauritius—a task opened by Karl Noël's 1991 publication[16]—but rather to draw attention to the manner in which Africans, and slaves in particular, entered public discourse in mediated, indeed mitigated ways, as this occurs in the quotation from Pitot. There is some continuity between the Protector's inadequacy as a defender of Indians' interests and the efforts of Indians to gain credible and satisfactory representation. However, there is no such continuity from the supposed intent of the Code Noir to "protect" slaves to any mechanism of representation of descendants of slaves. Instead, they are grouped with (and ally with) the white population. This could be seen as a very positive development in the postcolony insofar as former masters and slaves would require no further mediation. In reality, the wide disparities in income, status, and representation between white Mauritians and "Creoles" (or their perceivably black counterparts) give the lie to such an interpretation. It is implausible, then, to consider as productive this lack of "ethnification" in the case of "Africans" in Mauritius.

The presence, today, of various languages (French, English, Hindi, Mandarin, Bhojpuri, Gujarati, Telugu, Tamil, for example) in Mauritius provides a forum for representation within Mauritian culture of a history and a link to something greater than, and outside of, the colonial structure. No African language is inscribed in the Mauritian educational system in the way these other languages have been promoted, to different degrees, of course. Yet it is not always the case that the Indian languages in question were widely spoken in the island before their introduction into the system. This move was one that acknowledged a particular history and provided a vehicle for the development of an "ethnic" identity, which, by virtue of appearing in the idiom of the "cultural" escaped being a racial nomination derived so directly through colonial purpose. In the recent electoral history of Mauritius, those of African descent have tended to ally themselves with the small French minority. The term "Creole" to denote this population can also be seen positively because it previously referred to whites born in the colony: such interchangeability of the term could suggest that the previous difference in situation and signification between whites and blacks no longer counts. At the same time, the lack of any "African" referents as symbolic landmarks for this group, which for electoral purposes is considered no different from whites (within the category of "general population" beginning from the period prior to independence), seems artificially construed. In other terms, it is surprising that a common history of labor in the plantations, albeit under different circumstances, between Africans and Indians who came to Mauritius should not link their descendants more closely. What the rubric of "general population" encompasses suggests that former slaves and former white masters have more in common with each other than what could be expected between former slaves and former indentured laborers.

Since virtually all Mauritians speak Creole (or "morisyen") with facility, there is no argument to be made that actual language becomes a barrier between those of African descent and those of Indian descent. The impossibility to really enunciate the term "African" in contemporary public discourse in Mauritius simultaneously trips up any legitimate reference to slavery. "French" culture or Mauritian French culture proved easier to reclaim by métis and Creoles. It follows that, in general, alliances between Africans and Indians would be forestalled due to the very different strategies these groups deploy for group identification in modern Mauritius.

As we saw earlier, Seewoosagar Ramgoolam's elision of this very question in his speech, in the capacity of first prime minister of Mauritius, on Independence Day only continues a tendency that was already entrenched. Still, several more recent cultural ventures have provided a forum for exploring African pasts. Gilroy has shown the significance of music in the transatlantic dialogues of diaspora (*Black Atlantic*). The Mauritian-born "séga," which derives from the music and dance of the slaves, and which grew to encompass within it European dances such as the polka, could well be seen as capturing an African past as well as reaching out beyond the nation or the region in a dialogue with jazz, reggae, or hip-hop as well as other kinds of music of fusion. The artist, Ti Frère's renown as a séga musician was acknowledged on a night of music shortly before Mauritius's independence. Since then, new séga artists and groups such as the Windblows, which have enjoyed great popularity that reaches beyond Mauritian shores, have replaced or augmented the traditional instruments of the "maravane" and "ravanne" with various newer instruments and even electronic synthesizers.[17] Even at the academic level, discussion of the origins of Mauritian Creole has led to a consideration of the impact of slavery on Mauritian culture. Linguists Baker and Corne have argued that there is a far greater connection of African languages to Creole from the period of slavery than acknowledged. Notwithstanding these cultural and academic ventures, it remains a fact that since the period preceding independence, official Mauritian discourse on the nation elides, formulaically, the question of slavery.

In the animated debate in the Legislative Council evoked earlier, Mr. Bedaysee, an Indian representative, made a passionate plea for universal suffrage. During the course of his debate, he evoked the need for education in Mauritius to catch up for all sections of the society in order to render such suffrage legitimate, rather than looking at it the other way around by saying the masses were not sufficiently educated for universal suffrage. He makes a very interesting elision of slavery in the course of this discussion: "Intelligent men were caught in Africa and sold to the Americans as slaves. In India thousands of poor and intelligent people were led to the sugar cane planters and sold for sixty million rupees and they were denied education . . ." (Mauritius Legislative Council 27). Locating slavery in distant America and using rupees as the currency paid by planters, the member simultaneously shifts indenture as being the sole issue at stake in Mauritius. This blatant neglect of the Africans brought as slaves to Mauritius appears to be the naturalized impulse in official Mauritian discourse concerning the nation.

It is evident that Bérenger has been focusing his electoral preoccupations upon the Indo-Mauritian electorate, and that he must now pay attention to a newer discourse of difference, namely gender.[18] To suggest, as I have done here, that an acknowledgement of "African" identity is lacking in Mauritian public discourse is not necessarily to also suggest that establishing this cultural or geographical or racial identity is the only political choice to be exercised. Nevertheless, during Bérenger's term, the issue of slavery has finally come back, boomeranging into official Mauritian national discourse.

This question was raised in Mauritian parliament as recently as 15 February 2005, following the African Union Commission's statement regarding compensation of descendants of slaves. Since the United Nations' 2002 statement by the general assembly that slavery and the slave trade were a crime against humanity, this question had to be addressed in this former French and then British colony. The prime minister was asked to state his position on this issue and whether it would inform the Mauritian government's initiatives:

1. Sir, With your permission, Sir, I will reply to PQ B/59 and PQ B/74 together.
2. Mr Speaker Sir, I wish to remind the House of the commitment of Government on this issue. At page 70 of the MSM-MMM Electoral manifesto for General Election 2000, it is mentioned that, I quote, "Le gouvernement MSM-MMM s'engage à souscrire à toute action internationale visant au paiement d'une compensation aux descendants des esclaves. Vu la spécificité de Maurice, nous envisageons qu'une telle démarche puisse également inclure le paiement d'une compensation aux descendants des travailleurs engagés."[The MSM-MMM government

undertakes to respect all international action that attempts to pay compensation to decendants of slaves. Given the specificity of Mauritius, we envisage such a process would also include payment of compensation to descendants of indentured workers]
3. I am informed that Mr Adam Thiam, spokesperson of the African Union Commission, made a statement on 4 February 2005 to the effect that, I quote, "la Commission de l'Union Africaine va relancer le Comité panafricain sur les réparations des dommages causés par l'esclavage" [the Comission of the African Union is going to once more put to work the panafrican committee on the reparations of damages caused by slavery]. The "Comité panafricain" was set-up in 1991 but has been dormant since the late 1990s. The Government completely associates itself with this proposal of the African Union Commission.
4. I am also advised that the Chairperson of the African Union Commission has called on the Parliaments of African countries to adopt legislation along the lines of the French 10 May 2001 law which described the slave trade and slavery as "crimes contre l'humanité." [crimes against humanity]
5. We are gathering information from the African Union to see how Mauritius can participate fully in this initiative of the African Union and are examining how this issue should be brought to Parliament. (1)

The simultaneous consideration of indentured servants in the debate on compensation for the descendants of slaves is a double-edged sword. On the one hand, it may be seen as depriving slavery of its specificity and exercising a grouping in which once again descendants of slaves lose their specificity as has been the case in the grouping of "Creoles" with whites and métis as "general population" in the election process. Still, perhaps such a move would finally enable a connection between "Africans" and "Indians" in Mauritius within a particular and well-defined collaborative project, no matter what its aims turn out to be, that could open the door to greater dialogue as well as more consequential sharing of a history of struggle and hardship.

The way representation will play out with regard to this issue, both in Parliament and in the society at large, and the influence that the creation of some identity, which assumes an "African" and postslavery character will exert on identifications based on gender remain open for future analysis. The issue of slavery and Africanness has remained beyond the vocabulary of contemporary official discourse in Mauritius but the question of slavery, arising from outside the nation, makes imperative some mechanism for representation within the nation of this "section" of the society. It is premature to speculate on how representation in this case will develop, but it is evident that the issue reintroduces a vocabulary and history that will require some practice in Mauritian public life before they are pronounced and remembered, respectively, with ease.

These mechanisms within Mauritian public discourse to call up particular, ethnically defined groups are short-circuited by ongoing processes in less official spheres. Additionally, the question of gender provides a concrete instance of new types of potential affiliations that could function in defiance of the groupings that have continued to operate largely by adhering to the colonial conception (in the sense of birthing as well as thinking) of this island. The recent visit of the Indian prime minister and renewed international attention to slavery, both emerging quite literally from without the nation, require a notable response in the public sphere. The controversy surrounding Bérenger's handling of the first with regard to manipulating Indian sensibility shows how invested in Indianness his electorate still remains. In the second case, Bérenger is not able to state his "position" on the issue. The very word slavery remains somewhat foreign to the Mauritian psyche. His response above, which is very measured and careful, indicates he has been "informed" and "advised" about the issue and that his government is still "gathering information" and "examining how this issue could be brought to parliament" (Berenger 1).

If the question of diaspora, as Gilroy explains, records the "desire to transcend both the structures of the nation state and the constraints of ethnicity" (*Black Atlantic* 19), simply positioning Mauritian society as diasporic already puts pressure on the more secure idea of a "plural" society. Plural, in this sense, privileges the existence of difference *within*. However, this "doubleness," when exercised, acts like a centripetal force that stretches to tautness Mauritians' identifications. To privilege it is to require this diasporic society to acknowledge, within the *same* act of identification, various connections with the "original" lands of its immigrant population *and* those with similar and dissimilar others within the nation. The Indian prime minister's official visit and the entry of the issue of slavery in Parliament both function to position Mauritian society in this way. In the case of slavery, the question of who are the descendants of slaves as well as of what is the idea of Africa for them (and by extension for the society in which they live) are yet to be convincingly posed. In this context, Gilroy acknowledges that these desires to transcend narrow definitions (in what he has observed in America, the Caribbean, and Europe) "have always sat uneasily alongside the strategic choices forced on black movements and individuals embedded in national political cultures and national states [. . .]" (Gilroy *Black Atlantic* 19).

However, one might suggest, in viewing the African past of Mauritius in light of the remarks above, that "[t]o articulate the past historically does not mean to recognize it 'the way it really was.' It means to seize hold of a meaning as it flashes up in a moment of danger" (Walter Benjamin qtd. in Gilroy *Black Atlantic* 191). If this moment of the entry of Africanness into Mauritian public discourse can be seen as one of "danger," in the sense of exigency, it is indeed a moment to creatively seize hold of a hitherto unarticulated "meaning" of Africanness. It is conceivable, then, that Mauritians might invent a new way of thinking, in which Africanness need not be restrictively connected to slavery, and where slavery need not lead back only to an identifiable *African* part of the population, but rather be owned as the history of the totality of the Mauritian nation. In this way despite Benjamin's reminder of the claim the past has on our ability to envision the future—a "claim that cannot be settled cheaply" (Benjamin 254)—the notion of the "diasporic" itself might be transformed.

These analyses suggest that the idea of Africa remains largely untapped in the model of creolization envisaged in Mauritian society, and particularly in the way in which such creolization has been conceived from within official discourse of this nation. Anticipating the directions creolization in Mauritius might take in the twenty-first century signals an exciting moment for the conception of this African diaspora and, due to the rather unique situation of Africans on this island as outlined, for the notion of diaspora itself.

CHAPTER FIVE

Ethnicity and the Fate of the Nation

Reading Mauritius

> The truth is that there is no pure race and that to make politics depend upon ethnographic analysis is to surrender it to a chimera.
> —Ernest Renan ("What is a Nation" 14)

As we have seen briefly, Marie-Thérèse Humbert's novel, *A l'autre bout de moi*, dramatizes the ethnicity-class relationship in pre-independence Mauritius through the experiences of a family of mixed-blood Creoles.[1] The twin girls Nadège and Anne have very different strategies with regard to their self-image and the one that they project outward. Anne is the narrator of the novel and in this sense creates herself and her twin through the narrative. Anne does all she can to assimilate in order to pass as white and, in this way, exemplifies the classic case of the non-("pure") white in the "general population" of Mauritius that we discussed in chapter 4. Her twin Nadège embraces all that is nonwhite and ends up dying from aborting the child she shares with her Indian boyfriend.

Hierarchy and Structure

When Nadège's uncle André is at the police station after Nadège's death, he is in a rage that his attempt to bribe the policeman has been rebuffed. In the passage below, narration occurs from the perspective (in free indirect style as well as direct quotation) of uncle André. This tense situation highlights an almost frantic effort to distance himself and the group with which he allies from the Indians:

> *Ce policier indien* qui a recueilli des dépositions—un travailliste fanatique, et crypto-communiste de toute évidence [. . .]. Pensez donc! il a refusé de se taire en échange de la somme rondelette que l'avocat [André] mettait à sa disposition! Pis encore il a osé porter plainte: 'tentative de corruption d'un fonctionnaire de police!' Laissez-moi rire! 'Ten-ta-tive de corruption!' Je vais t'en foutre, moi, de la corruption! Comme si ça ne se faisait pas couramment, [. . .] Oui mais voilà: *ces gens-là* ne pensent qu'à une chose, nous couvrir de merde. Et quel merdier, bon Dieu, quel merdier! [my emphases] (445)[2]
>
> *That Indian policeman* who took the depositions—a fanatic "travailliste," and a crypto communist by all evidence [. . .]. Imagine! He refused to be silent in exchange for the nice round sum that the lawyer [André] was offering him! And worse still, he dared to complain: "Attempt to corrupt a police employee!" You have to laugh! "At-tempt to corrupt!" Screw corruption! As if it wasn't routinely done, [. . .]. Yes, but that's it: *those* people only think of one thing, and that is to cover us in shit. And what shit, my God, what shit!

The demonstratives "that" and "those" reinforce the distance between the group of Indians to which the policeman belongs and André, who sees himself as a respectable middle-class person whose position renders him almost white. What irks André is not just the rebuff, but the place of its origin: from that Indian policeman, especially when he knows that *those* people, and in fact the same policeman in question, surely accept "de petits bakchichs de ce genre" [small *bakshish* of this kind] (445). The term "*bakchichs*," from Hindi, means gift given to a paid employee in appreciation of a service rendered. The choice of this Creole word of Indian origin (from Turkish) reinforces the truth or truth-value of the statement—after all, the word used to describe their underhand practices is from *their* language!

Simultaneously, and still at the police station, Yolande, his wife, who is considered "pure" white, anticipates the remarks resulting from this "scandal" of her husband's niece having died hemorrhaging, trying to get rid of an Indian baby. The frequent visitors to their palatial home at Cassis (at the seaside) were:

> déjà moins aimables, déjà devenus si blancs soudain en face de *ces* moricauds [. . .]. Que voulez-vous ma chère, on veut bien avoir l'esprit ouvert, consentir chrétiennement à fréquenter les gens convenables qui vous font

des avances ... [...] Moi je me demande comment Yolande a pu épouser *cet* André Morin. Après tout, *ces* Morin, on ne sait pas trop *d'où ça vient.* [my emphases] (444)[3]

already less amiable, had already become so white suddenly when faced with *these* dark-skinned people. [...] What do you expect my dear, we'd like to have an open mind, to agree in a Christian manner to socialize with suitable people who approach you... [...] As for me, I wonder how Yolande could have married *that* André Morin. After all, *those* Morins, one doesn't quite know *where they come from.*

So, for André Morin, unlike his impoverished brother (Nadège and Anne's father), success and material advancement as well as a "white" wife, enable him to penetrate the sanctuary of the whites, even though he is a mulatto. His "doubtful" (i.e., not pure white) origins were overlooked until the scandal brought on by his niece forces the reconsideration of his position amongst them. Behavior is always justified by "who" or "what" people are; that is, where they came from, their history. Note the demonstratives emphasized in the quotation, indicating *position* within the structure that the speaker conceives.

The impediments posed by historical notions of cultural difference to the forging of a "mass of people," are underscored in *A l'autre bout de moi.* Sassita, the maid in the Morin household is constantly presented as a Hindu by focusing on her behavior, her docility, the way she rationalizes her fate. The other female character who knows a harsh reality due to position in structure is Mme Lydie. She "helps" Nadège with her abortion and brings about her death. Mme Lydie is also constantly described as Creole. Putting aside the obvious differences between these two characters, there is nothing in the novel that brings them together as women operating under patriarchal forces: Sassita, discarded by a man twice her age because the sheets were not stained with her blood on the night of her wedding; Lydie, raising her children alone on the outskirts of society, operating outside the official domains of Medicine and Law. Sassita remains in Quatre Bornes with the twins' father while they are sent off to the coastal Cassis to get over the scandal caused by Nadège's association with the Indian politician, Aunauth Gopaul. This distance is also inscribed in the body of the printed text, with most of Sassita's story being told at the beginning whereas the character of Mme Lydie only figures at the end of the story after Nadège is pregnant.[4] This serves to separate their paths, their fate, and their comparable position in the general structure much as all else occurs in Mauritian society to separate Indians from Creoles as chapter 4 demonstrated. Gaston Daronville from *La Maison qui marchait vers le large* also acts from such an understanding.

Carl de Souza's Gaston Daronville is a mulatto whose ancestors must have had some "standing" in Mauritian society. This character understands how historical privilege functions in people's minds: as a child, he resented the "gens de maison qui, [. . .] par leur servilité de tous les instants, les avaient ancrés dans cette supériorité factice" (182–83) [the servants who, [. . .] by their servility at all times, anchored them in this artificial superiority]. Daronville's anger and resentment stem less from the superiority he is granted, but rather from its falseness. Daronville describes a scene from his childhood when he and his classmate Emile Laqueyre climb a tamarind tree and look out to sea and then back at the island and their neighborhood. He sees his family's house and gets into a rage when he glimpses the dilapidated condition of the roof, which was not visible from inside:

> Hé oui, il l'avait bien vu, le toit désigné par Emile, émergeant au-dessus des bouquets de manguiers. Son aspect lui avait fait l'effet d'une trahison. D'en bas, quand il jouait dans la petite pelouse devant la varangue, il s'était rendu compte, bien entendu, des quelques rides que la maison avait prises mais, aux yeux du gosse qu'il était, elle conserverait son allure de vieille douairière, éternellement. Indestructible. Ils avaient grandi avec l'idée que rien ne pouvait être plus beau, mieux que leur maison. "Ton père est plus fort que mon père, ta voiture va plus vite que la mienne, d'accord, mais ma maison est plus belle que la tienne." A cela, aucun des cousins n'avait jamais rien trouvé à redire. (181)

> Oh yes, he had seen it, the roof that Emile pointed out, emerging over the bouquets of mango trees. Its appearance had seemed like a betrayal to him. From down below when he played on the little lawn in front of the veranda, he had noticed, of course, a few cracks that the house had developed, but to the eyes of the boy that he was, the house kept its allure of an old dowager, eternally. Indestructible. They had grown up with the idea that nothing could be more beautiful or better than their house. "Your father is stronger than my father, your car goes faster than mine, okay, but my house is more beautiful than yours." None of the cousins had ever found anything to say in response to that.

It is this same house that Daronville refuses to sell as an old man even though his daughter tries to convince him to do so due to his failing health and inability to manage the large dilapidated building. In a twist of fate, the house, along with the rest of the slope on which it rests, will begin its slow descent toward the sea: "la maison qui marchait vers le large" as the title of the novel characterizes it. The house is but a symbol of old privileges held in place by the colonial system and then preserved "symbolically," we might say. Daronville's reaction is that of one who is unable to accept this change in situation and status:

"... il s"était refusé à reconnaître ce faîtage indigne, cette espèce de vieux crâne frappé ... L'enduit spécial dont on avait badigeonné le bois, [. . .], avait troqué sa noble couleur de jais contre un gris délavé par la trop longue succession de pluies et vagues de chaleur" (182) [. . . he had refused to recognize this lowly construction, a kind of old beaten up head. . . . The coating with which they had whitened the wood [. . .] had bartered its noble color of jade for a gray that had been washed by a lengthy succession of rain and heat waves].

The final and decisive death of these class privileges in the movement of the entire slope and the Daronville mansion toward the sea is hard for him to accept since, as his grandfather told him, it was built with "quinze peids de fondations dans le roc" (45) [a foundation fifteen feet deep in the rock]. Yet, the truth of the crumbling French Empire elsewhere during Daronville's childhood had to be faced. Refusal to accept this descent characterizes Daronville and his class in their inability to see themselves as they *are*, or even what they could be, rather than what they were.

Historical Considerations

Early writing from Île de France, as Mauritius was then known, tended to reflect the concerns and dilemmas of the newly established colony.[5] Even though attachment to the "mother country" remained strongly articulated, there was also a trend, which established the superiority of the Creoles (at that time indicating whites born in the colony), given the hardships under which they were to function. In the nineteenth century, Thomi Pitot writes in praise of these Creoles (to which group he belongs) regarding their "conduite régulière" [proper behavior] and the fact that they remained "les dépositaires fidèles des vertus de leurs aïeux au milieu de la corruption que l'Europe a tenté, sans relâche d'y introduire . . ." (cited in Prosper *Histoire* 28) [the devoted holders of their ancestors' virtue in the middle of the corruption that Europe has continually tried to introduce here . . .]. Preserving the noble character and superiority of the colony's whites accounts for the basic preoccupation of the "colonial novel" discussed in chapter 3.

Slavery was an issue around which much of identity was "worked out" by the white population, often in defense of slavery and against metropolitan abolitionist positions. This was a clear point at which a certain nationalism can be said to form: nationalism, in a consciousness of the geographical space that was conquered and settled as well as the collective will that enabled these acts. To the white settler, abolition was a threat to this space and its functioning. Abolition as an injustice to the white Creoles (colonists) was bemoaned and reactions against the British government, under whom it took place, formed a movement in which one can identify such a nationalism. Such were the efforts toward defining and consolidating French identity, which necessarily opposed itself to the British administrators who really did not have a vested interest in Mauritius as a colony. The space of the nation was prominently seen as legitimately belonging to those who formed it (i.e., the white French who believed they had built it). The shift was thus from organization against metropolitan France to that against imperial Britain.[6]

With the importation of massive Indian labor in 1865, one can see how the nationalist sentiment of the French population coalesced through the various battles they had to wage against British protectors of indentured laborers sent from India. The protectors were seen as troublesome to the colonists when they insisted on certain conditions ordered by the British colonial administration in India with whose authorization the immigrants arrived in the new colony. In addition, French plantation owners would send their own "recruiters" who used various means to entice Indian coolies to board the immigration ships (including lying and kidnapping). Early revolts by African slaves were sparse and no notable movement was launched, for obvious reasons, the most significant of which was the coopting of the *commandeurs* by the colonists.

Despite some movements against planters and sugar barons, no consolidated movement can be said to challenge this strand of nationalism on the island until the organization of peasants and workers in the early part of the twentieth century (1920s–40s). This is the first time a movement of some magnitude against what we can term the nationalism of the elite occurs. Even if there is not enough information on maroons and their opposition to the colonial system, and slavery in particular, such workers movements also record prenationalist activity from a different source.[7] It is to be noted that the majority participating in the movement given an impetus by the revolt of the workers were "Indians." However, many from other "races" participated as well. At this point, however, the significance of being, within the Indian community, Bihari versus Tamil still has not acquired the significance it will in the period preceding the independence movement. The categorization of "race" does not yet really become inadequate by the claiming of ethnicity.

Considering ethnicity as a communication of cultural difference in an anthropological model, though valuable in other ways, cannot properly account for the functioning of ethnicity in the national context of Mauritius. Chapter 4 underscored the process of ethnification of the Indian groups (and this is the case with the Chinese as well) through language. We have noted also the formation of a new intermediary class made up of different figures. This included the Indian bourgeoisie and the Creole bourgeoisie formed by education, professionalization, and through the administration. Claims to Mauritian Indianness, as seen in chapter 4, are nowhere matched by similar claims to Africanness. There is a devaluation of things African because, in the politics of difference, alliances with the French (Franco-Mauritian, especially through language and its politics) have seemed more attractive and advancing to the Creole (especially mulatto) population—in the later sense of mixed-blood. The anthropologist, Thomas H. Eriksen notes this fact when he writes that "[n]ot sensing belonging to a continent [sic], *Mauritians of non-African origin* [thus excluding Creoles] tend to turn to their real or postulated ancestral homelands for a self-identification of loftier scope than the options locally available" [my emphases] (*Communication of Cultural Difference* 13), confirming the ambiguous position of the Creole in Mauritian society.

Given the importance of the diasporic aspect of hybridity in connecting with the homeland, privileging trauma, and valorizing the past, the figure of the Creole could be an ideal expression for nationalist sentiment by bringing together the variously positioned nationalisms at least symbolically. The body of the Creole carries the history of the slave and that of the master—of oppression and of subordination as well as resistance and survival. If the idea of "the" Mauritian nation is so hard to imagine due to the different histories and positions, as I have indicated, the figure of the Creole, could take on the role of healing and integration, even if this is not through solidarity and good will: the explosion of the Creole as a proper actor is the point at which the racial (as innate, given, immutable) gave way to a new category, even before the systematic communication of cultural difference would become part of the propelling force of Mauritian nationalism.[8] The role of the Creoles, who constituted a new intermediary group functioning during the colonial period between the group of laborers and former slaves, and the white colonialists, thus allows a consideration of class. The complete exclusion of Indians from this group even at that time is conceptually implausible, although this idea tends to be repeated in public discourse in Mauritian society.

Simultaneously, though, if this new bourgeois section takes on its "revolutionary" role, recognition by Creoles and Indians who are in a similar position would necessarily follow in order to facilitate their cohesion as a group. In this intermediary bourgeois class (made up primarily of Creoles and Indians), the essentially defined African slave or the Indian laborer can be transcended in a creolizing move through the common vehicle and experience of professionalization that recognizes a past history of trauma. Such an understanding becomes all the more pertinent given the opening up of the Mauritian economy of the 1980s to various sources other than sugar to make up the gross national product.

Still, foreseeing for this new bourgeoisie a revolutionary role is not (necessarily) a restriction to its economic role of entrepreneurship and risk.[9] It includes rather an imaginative and creative role (entrepreneur-like in that sense) to think its destiny. This is not to proscribe a selfless or unrealistic "good" role of putting the nation or people before self-interest, even if Fanon can want that "[i]n an underdeveloped country an authentic national middle class ought to consider as its bounden duty to betray the calling fate has marked out for it, and put itself to school with the people: in other words to put at the people's disposal the intellectual and technical capital that it has snatched when going through the colonial universities" (*Wretched of the Earth* 150). As I see it, the most nationalistic act that this new bourgeoisie can conceive of is to write itself into the national context, to narrate its own reality as a group that exploits (in every sense of the word) its situation, instead of remaining a weak appendage to the traditional bourgeoisie, or the white (and other new) capitalists. As Fanon remarks (unhappily), "[t]he national middle class discovers its historic mission: that of intermediary" (*Wretched of the Earth* 152).[10] In my conception, a revolutionary role, as seen in earlier chapters, will inevitably reveal the impossibility of an alliance for identity/politics based on the ones inherited from colonialism. These revolutionary moments can be significant acts of creolization, turning the stagnation of identity politics upside down.[11]

Revolution and the Image of the Creole

Lionnet notes that *A l'autre bout de moi* is the story of "Mauritian métis, these 'apatrides de la race [racially homeless people]'[12] [...], the coloreds or mixed-bloods, whose marginality is partly the result of their own inability to assume their non white heritage because they have internalized the ideals of the racist colonial society" (*Autobiographical Voices* 208). In the context of the Mauritian nationalisms that I have described, perhaps one might say that they are nonqualified (or homeless) "ethnically" through a lack of parallel connections to ancestral claims.[13] Nadège and Anne can be seen to represent two "types" of Creoles (*mulâtres*), or two possibilities for Creoles: revolutionary and (false) assimilatory, respectively.

Anne's entire struggle is against her sister, not only in claiming her own identity against her stronger twin, but also in rejecting the "lower" ranked part of her "mixture." Her attempts to penetrate "white" society are similar to her uncle André's. She frequents the Church and pays visits to the old dowagers she meets there; she believes herself to be in love with the white neighbor, Pierre Augier, because he is white, even though she despises the way he treats her. He keeps the relationship clandestine at all costs. Anne dresses as simply and "elegantly" as possible to avoid association with Nadège's "wild" style and all things Oriental.[14]

Nadège, on the contrary, does not hide her scorn for the whites (ce sont tous des cons [they are all stupid]) and her embracing of anything nonwhite is reflected in her vocabulary, her actions, her dress. She loves to recite songs learned from Sassita, and will not hesitate to be seen in the Hindu quarter, nor adorn her arms with all sorts of bracelets and wear clothes that are loud to the Western (i.e., cultivated) eye. Anne's struggle against Nadège is revealed to be a struggle against parts of herself: "Etre en dehors d'elle, être à tout prix, voilà ce que je désirais, je ne savais pas encore que ce que j'étais ainsi amenée à renier, parce que trop semblable à elle, constituait souvent la partie la plus authentique de moi-même" (419) [To be outside of her, to be at all costs, that is what I desired, I did not yet know that what I came to deny, because it was too similar to her, often constituted the most authentic part of myself]. Yet, this separation turned out to be an impossible task: "[. . .] dans les rêves je parle souvent comme Nadège, je me gargarise des mots de Nadège) [. . .] il y a moi qui parle et moi qui vis le rêve . . ." (Humbert *A l'autre bout* 74) [(. . .) in my dreams I often speak like Nadège, I gargle Nadège's words (. . .) there is me who speaks and me who sees the dream . . .]. But further, Anne's inability to truly be part of either Nadège's world or the white one her mother would like to inhabit is brought out. The dream continues:

> [. . .] [I]l y a moi qui parle et moi qui marche . . . Tranquille avec ça, tranquille l'idiote, alors que l'autre moi crie arrête, hurle, bat du cœur, des pieds, des bras. Rien à faire. La chose est là devant nous, dans l'eau . . . une masse blanchâtre et visqueuse, une masse de poissons agonisants. Quelques-uns frétillent, encore, la tête couverte de sang [. . .]. Je me cabre tout entière, emplie d'une seule certitude: cet entassement ensanglanté vient d'un charme irréversible, destiné à nous fixer là pour le reste de notre vie. (74)

> [. . .] [T]here is I who speak and I who walk . . . Calmly, too, calmly, the idiot, while the other I cries stop, screams, fights with her heart, feet, arms. Nothing doing. The thing is there before us, in the water . . . a whitish and viscous mass, a mass of fish in agony. Some of them are still tossing about, their heads covered with blood. [. . .] I stumble backward, filled with one certainty: this bloody mess comes from an irreversible magic source that was destined to pin [fix] us there for the rest of our lives.

The doubling of herself where she *is* the twin in her dream marks the certitude of being other than what she projects. In confronting the frightening bloody mess of dead and dying fish, the "I," that is already split assumes a "we" [us]. The sorcery is aimed at fixing them there for the rest of their lives. The I who walks and talks seems to do so in a stupor—it is the Anne of assimilation. The other I is involved in a struggle for, we might say, a more authentic identity in its relationship to otherness, beginning with the identification with Nadège. But the struggle between the two possibilities in Anne's case results in paralysis. In an allegorical reading, Anne's inaction shares in that of the class of Creoles (mixed-bloods) who, instead of determining their own course of action to match their interests, continue to constantly evaluate themselves unfavorably with regard to the small group of whites from whose company they are nevertheless banished. Anne continues that she is unable to decipher the dream, and although there is no answer to the question, she does point out that "[c]ela m'oblige à revenir si loin en arrière. A cette epoque de l'enfance dont nul d'entre nous n'a jamais reparlé" (75) ([t]his obliged me to go so far back in time to a period of our childhood about which none of us ever spoke again). For Mauritian society, this initial sin, as it were, is the sin of slavery (and its daughter indenture), which, as we have seen in chapter 4 is silenced in the collective memory. Within the novel, the sin is that of being born dark-skinned and it haunts Anne for the anguish it brought their mother.

Anne's quest for a singular identity can be read as the effort of the Creole population for an unambiguous white identity. When the twins discover their mother's diary after her death, Anne cannot bear the disappointment (her mother's and her own) of not being white: "[. . .] je crie je voudrais renaître, Nadège, avec des joues roses, des cheveux blonds, je voudrais renaître blanche pour ne pas la decevoir" (130) [And I cry out that I want to be reborn, Nadège, with pink cheeks, blond hair, I want to be reborn white so as not to disappoint her].

When Mme Morin leaves her husband, she goes to the decrepit seaside house because she cannot tolerate his infidelities and the way he wastes their resources on alcohol. The children are left to fend for themselves in the hot sun. The bloody mess in the sea (in Anne's dream), which has power over them, is related to two aspects of Anne's life, both entering the narrative in this same chapter of the novel. The first is her impossibility to separate herself from Nadège: "S'il m'arrive d'être seule, on est choqué, on s'inquiète, on m'accuse. "Où est ta sœur?' demande Père impératif. 'Où est ta sœur?' gémit Mère. 'Où est ta sœur?' me reprochent doucement les religieuses . . ." (75–76) [If I happen to be alone, people are shocked, they are worried, they accuse me: "Where is your sister?" asks Father urgently. "Where is your sister?" cries out Mother. "Where is your sister?" the nuns gently scold . . .].[15] Any effort to disjoin from Nadège would thus be violent and bloody. The second is her impossibility to enter white society, as she will find out from Pierre's reticence and hesitation to fully embrace her socially. Pierre's behavior is in fact a violent rejection of her personhood. Anne's paralysis results in an in-authenticity that is recorded as a marionette's actions (the I who walks and talks) as seen earlier. This dramatizes in a different way Fanon's massive struggle recorded in the narrative of *Black Skin, White Masks*, and which we shall examine later in this book. The idea of authenticity, then, that is considered dubious and thus summarily dismissed in many contemporary contexts, and particularly in postcolonial theory, is not excluded from the experiences and desires of those who occupy hybrid social locations.

Anne's isolation is underscored in the same chapter when she recalls the drive by taxi from their home in Quatre Bornes to the beach house: "C'est ce jour-là que j'ai fait pour la première fois *l'expérience de la solitude*: entre cette femme aux yeux bouffis et ma sœur endormie" [my emphases] (85) [That was the day that I knew for the first time *the experience of solitude*: between that woman with the swollen eyes and my sleeping sister.] This can be read as the solitude of the nonethnified Creole, who struggles to produce at both the individual and collective level, an authentic idiom of selfhood. Nadège is rejected by "les gens bien," [decent folk] and welcomes this, while her mother tries at all costs, in almost Jansenite fashion, to continue to behave with what she sees as the greatest virtue, knowing/living her rejection all the time. Between these two attitudes of mournful striving to conform by her mother ("yeux bouffis") and happy acceptance of her rejection by her sister ("sœur endormie") Anne remains with no society of her own, while sitting between them. What is presented as "solitude" for Anne can be read as "nonengagement" with reality for the intermediary group outlined earlier.

The single moment of triumph for Anne with regard to this white identity that she seeks is, inevitably, a moment of extreme emotional and physical violence. Nadège takes her to the beach as she wants a beautiful expansive place to announce her happy news. She announces there that she is pregnant with Aunauth Gopaul's child. Anne's reaction is one of violence and hatred. Nadège's choice is not just a foil for the "bourgeois marriage" that she aspires to with Pierre. It provides her with a moment to savor an instance of singularity—through the *act* of dissociation. Singularity in identity against her sister, her twin who haunts her life becomes a moment of comparison that can render her pure. Her reaction to Nadège's news is revealed (in the narrative) at the moment when she is being questioned in court before a judge: "Je l'ai giflée" (426) [I slapped her]. Then the narrative continues after the courtroom scene is described. She is given a pause and led out of the room to recover emotionally. Yet the veritable violence and triumph of the moment is in Anne's continuing narrative to herself, to the reader:

> Et il n'y eut plus en face de moi qu'un bizarre visage convulsé, une sorte de défroque. Non. Je n'éprouvai pas de pitié, mais de nouveau cette affreuse jouissance dans son acuité plus proche de la douleur que de la joie: devant ce masque sans expression, enfin, moi, j'avais un visage." (427)

> And before me there was just this strange convulsive face, a sort of empty shell. No. I did not feel any pity, but again this terrible ecstasy [jouissance] that was, in its intensity, closer to pain than joy: before this mask devoid of expression, at last, me, I had a face.

It is only at this moment that Anne steps out of her marionette-like self and claims her being through action. It is the point where one is called on to make an ethical decision, a moment that is of great significance to Edouard Glissant's conception of hybridity, as we shall see. In keeping with the fact that there can be no prior determination of the type of action, its morality, or outcome, Anne's shocking behavior is the only one that was authentic for her, perhaps even ethical, at that moment. In this way, such authenticity and ethics can only be understood and theorized at the individual level and cannot be given in advance. Anne finds Nadège "grotesque," she has a feeling of "répulsion" (422) [repulsion] and "répugnance" (425) [repugnance] toward her. But she continues inexorably in her violence to reach that point at the very brink of her self, of her own subjectivity: "[Q]u'il crève ton sale bâtard, qu'il crève dans l'œuf! Je criais comme d'autres frappent, assourdie [...] mais enragée à frapper, à frapper encore, à frapper toujours..." (428) [(M)ay he die your dirty bastard, may he die in the egg! I screamed as others might strike, loud [...] but obsessed with striking, with striking again, striking forever...]. When she finally cries: "Fœtus! Horrible Fœtus! Crève[!]" [Foetus! Horrible Foetus! Die(!)] she is referring less to the child in Nadège than the Nadège in her. Nadège is at this moment on the ground, curled up "la tête caché dans ses bras repliés, les jambes ramenées sous elle" (see 428) [her head hidden in her folded arms, her legs curled in under her]. It is clear that Anne's outrage is directed toward herself and that the violence she does to Nadège is the best way to be violent to herself:

> Mais en la regardant, je sus que j'étais arrivée là où je l'avais voulu: à l'extrémité de la souffrance et à l'autre bout de moi, le seul horizon où je pourrais jamais la rencontrer. Car celle que je contemplais à mes pieds, dans une atroce et saignante satisfaction. C'était moi-même; à cause de cela, je ne pouvais rien pour elle." (430)

> But looking at her, I knew that I had arrived at the point where I had wanted to go: at the limit of suffering and at the other end of myself, the only horizon where I could ever have met her. Because the one that I considered at my feet, in an atrocious and bloody satisfaction. It was myself; because of that, I couldn't do anything for her.

This is an example of the movement of "aggression," which is pertinent to Fanon's examination of the choices available to individuals that we will examine in chapter 7. In the encounter with otherness, it signals at least the beginning of a decision to "be." It is from this point that any future *Relation* (which is the focus of chapter 6 on Glissant) can even be envisaged. In heeding the end of the story, we would need to resist here the temptation to stretch an act of interpretation to claim that this is Anne's moment of whiteness by annihilating the Creole.[16] The story ends with Anne walking alone, after her father's death, to Aunauth Gopaul's house and taking Nadège's place there. I prefer to see in this moment the long-deferred action by which Anne chooses to step out of her twin's shadow and which was initiated in the violent moment of authentic selfhood, which (individually and even for Anne) implied a close alliance with the Indian part of her island's society. That it has to be a cruel and violent act only signals the necessity for it, just as the moment of realization in *Métisse*, examined in chapter 3, came at the violent moment in which the narrator's mother calls her father a nigger. Such a moment of violent epistemological shock that highlights contradiction is required to spur action to be counted as agency. For the Creole, whom we have allegorically linked with Anne, this entails any kind of self-conscious, even self-interested, action through a breaking out of the syndrome of "bad faith" that we shall examine in chapter 6 in the context of the Antillean that Fanon describes. Anne's bad faith consists in casting her self-image in the reflection of the small white population who, in reality, are so far removed from her social sphere and the material conditions of her existence that her identity politics border on the absurd.

By her own admission, Anne can never *be* Nadège, that is, all that is sensual and whole and beautiful, or life itself: "Nadège, douce, violente, et perverse sirène, le regard scintillant, la lèvre sensuelle, respirant autant que j'étouffais, avec une liberté de mouvement qui m'apeurait" (120) [Nadège, sweet, violent, and a perverse siren, with a scintillating look, sensual lips, breathing while I suffocated, with an ease of movement that scared me]. Afraid of movement, of giving up the possibility of the fixed inherited position of privilege through lighter skin in Mauritian society that she so covets:

> l'image que j'essaie de saisir de moi me trahit, m'échappe; c'est toi qui es là dans la glace, il y a seulement dans le regard une autre expression et le

> reflet que je vois, ma propre image, me semble une mauvaise photo: oui, c'est l'expression qui manque, l'expression des yeux de Nadège. (122)
>
> the image that I try to glimpse of myself betrays me, escapes me; it is you who are there in the mirror, only, in your look there is another expression and the reflection that I see, my own image, seems like a bad photo to me; yes, it is the expression that is missing, the expression of Nadège's eyes.

Anne cannot see herself the way she wants to (i.e., white) because of interference from the image of Nadège within hers. Still she ends up being only a poor copy of her sensuous twin, lacking the life of the latter. Throughout the story, Anne is fearful of action, of seizing a new space, claiming a new path, until she is capable of coming into being as an individual, which for her occurs in a violent moment of assertion. Reflective of the ambiguous space of the Creole, of the lack of insertion into the national framework Anne asks: "Où est l'espace où je dois vivre?" (122) [Where is the space where I should live?]. Nadège, on the contrary, does not use a mirror (12), but sees herself, constitutes herself, through the gaze of others (419). There is a tension between such a restrictive (for Anne) as well as liberating (for Nadège) power invested in the other's gaze. Fanon will also theorize this question, as we shall see. Anne allows it to determine what she can be while Nadège uses it to construct a counter-image in which she becomes heroic.

Returning to the pitfalls of consistently reading the allegory of the Creole in Anne, brings me to the oft-discussed idea that "all Third World texts are necessarily [...] allegorical" (Jameson "Third World Literature" 69). Debates around this question have shown that to qualify them *all* as allegorical is reductive and cannot account for the creativity of individual authors; that it implies a high-handed and essentially Western notion of understanding History in privileging the "national" allegory; that it settles for the adequacy of categorizing texts as being of the "Third World."[17] I am mostly in agreement with the general criticism of the thesis as it has been taken up in the critical views of this essay. Still the more interesting aspects of the essay such as the suggestion of the national allegory as a legitimate framework for reading Third World texts in a particular context and Jameson's wider stake in the critique of capitalism from a Third World context become obscured in many of the indignant responses. What makes the allegory so tempting in the national context of postcolonial regions? My own reading of Anne was self-proclaimedly "allegorical," and the narrator of *Métisse*, as we also saw overtly invites such an allegorical consideration.

Réda Bensmaïa's central criticism of Jameson on this point is that in reading postcolonial writing, the split between the "pedagogical" and the "performative" (this is from Bhabha's *Nation and Narration*) in the narrative disallows such a recuperation under allegory. Invoking Paul de Mann's *Allegories of Reading*, he explains the impossibility of distinguishing between the "literal" and "figural" meaning (Bensmaïa 155), quite essential to Jameson's allegorical reading. However, what if we were to consider Jameson's article, as not being *about* nationalist literature, but rather as part of the narrative *of* the nation, stemming from his (intellectual) desire to preserve it as an analytical and legitimate political category? That is, can one not read in Jameson a very clear nationalist *sentiment* described by Gellner? It is not for his *own* nation, but rather for (particularly) Third World—here postcolonial for our purposes—nation(s). My point is that mirroring the impossibility of distinguishing between the literal and figurative, and the interference of the performative on the pedagogical, the functioning of discourses *about* the nation also become discourses *of* the nation through their own performance, and especially in this instance through the performance of their reading. It is for this reason that the anthropological study of cultural difference in Mauritius (about the nation) that we shall consider joins up with a certain model of Mauritianness in which history and totality can be elided as was pointed out with regard to the Mauritian prime minister's public speeches (of the nation) from chapter 4. These speeches betrayed insufficient engagement with certain aspects of Mauritian history, primarily slavery and its consequences, generating an incomplete vision of both the history of the nation and the current unit or totality that it incarnates.

Without over-emphasizing the point here, I think that texts of the nation come in unexpected forms. The power of the national, especially for/in nations of more recent construction, must be recognized as having multiple sources and texts. In the context of nationalism and ethnicity, the construction of ethnicity is far more complex within the national sphere of Mauritius than the account provided from an anthropological understanding of the plurality of Mauritius. If, as Trinh T. Minh Ha has pointed out, "writing as a system by itself has its own rules and structuring process" (21), so too do discourses of the nation. Any analytical gesture must, then, pay attention to these rules and structuring processes, which can only be understood with a proper accounting of both the specific histories involved and the totality that it calls up.

Ethnicity as the Communication of Cultural Difference

Eriksen presents Mauritian nationalism as on the one hand, "ostensibly nonethnic" in character due to the depiction of the "mosaic of cultures." He points to the cultural shows on Independence Day where the different ethnic groups are represented (for example, Sino-Mauritians with a dragon, Hindus singing Indian film songs, Creoles with a séga).[18] Along with this, he notes, on the other hand, a "trend" in nationalism that "encompasses or transcends ethnicity rather than endorsing it." This happy coexistence of the universal in the particular and vice-versa is echoed as a goal by the first prime minister of Mauritius, Sir Seewoosagar Ramgoolam, on Independence Day in 1974:

> We are now well set on the path of success and the country knows that in a multiracial society like ours we must forge unity out of diversity. This must always be an essential part of our *national policy*. [. . .] Independence has ceased to be an issue dividing one Mauritian from another.[19] We have come to treasure it as the greatest achievement of the country and to honour and venerate the flag which was born out of the sacrifices of our people. (131–32)

Yet even in these lines we can adduce the tension around the term diversity, which has to be reflected in "national policy." One must conclude that when Eriksen writes that Mauritius is "ostensibly non-ethnic," this means not single-ethnic. He adds that the Mauritian situation is more complex than this outline and that "[t]here is some ethnic tension, and there are conflicts between nationalism and ethnicity" (*Ethnicity and Nationalism* 117), as Ramgoolam's lines also suggest. The acknowledgment on Independence Day by the prime minister that Independence and the nation-state were not *common* goals and dreams for "the Mauritian people" is not insignificant. On this occasion of the sixth anniversary of independence, Ramgoolam speaks against a "narrow nationalism," which is "against the mass of the people from which we derive our strength" (132).

Eriksen evokes several intellectuals who have been concerned with race and ethnicity as categories.[20] If, for the purposes of analysis, ethnicity is a subcategory of race, all ethnic categories then carry in them their superordinate racial category. For Eriksen, "[i]deas of 'race' may or may not form part of ethnic ideologies, and their presence or absence *does not seem to be a decisive factor in inter ethnic relations*" [my emphases] (*Ethnicity and Nationalism* 5). When interethnic relations are studied in the context of a *national* structure in Mauritius, however, one cannot fail to see the significance of the superordinate in their "ethnic" or subcategorical level, especially in light of the "ethnification" of racially understood groups through the symbolic use of language, as we have seen in chapter 4. A proper accounting of the totality in which particular Mauritian ethnicities are coherent would reveal the specific relationship to race. Nationalism—at least in Mauritius—inevitably invokes (some form of) the term or concept of ethnicity: ethnic diversity; ethnic relations; ethnic categories; ethnic conflict/harmony; "communalism;" ethnic-language correspondence, etc. And such ethnically articulated relations clearly relate to historical groups that were constructed and understood racially.

In Mauritius, it is impossible to distinguish between race and ethnicity by claiming that the former is a categorization from the outside and that the latter is claimed by the group (Banton paraphrased in Eriksen *Ethnicity and Nationalism* 5). Indian immigration documents in Mauritius reveal how every new immigrant was listed according to his/her port of origin, and the "ethnic" category, which often coincided with the language spoken. African immigrants did not have the opportunity to posit ethnic differences due to massive and rapid homogenization under French planters, given the disparate nature of the demographic make-up of slaves and the urgent need to learn Creole. In their case, then, ethnification through language was blocked and therefore they have remained racially read. Even though the "pure" whites and Creoles share common language identification (French), the whites also remain racially read, thus preserving the distinction between themselves and mixed-bloods. As noted in chapter 4, there is hardly a noticeable population with British ancestry, most administrators having served for specific time periods in Mauritius and then moved on. In the case of indentured laborers arriving under British administration, the categorization on paper, which was part of the immigrants' documents in the new land, surely served to inscribe this ethnic category in his/her psyche and worldview. The importance of being Bihari or Tamil [sic] became far more pertinent once the immigrant was issued papers confirming it upon arrival in the new colony. Birth certificates, for example, in "British" India contain information about "caste" and "religion," but not about language or ethnicity.

The more recent rhetoric of being Indian in Mauritius discussed in chapter 4 must be viewed in light of this fact. Moreover, all statistical information groups Indians into, at least, Hindus and Muslims—often Tamils and Telugus [sic] as well. Among the Tamils, many were converted Christians. Also, the Bhojpuri speakers make up the largest part of the Hindu population. Gujarati "speakers" are often Muslims as well. Recent surveys on language can be read as claiming (the use of) language in a symbolic gesture, related to those papers issued by the government to the ancestral immigrants. So, ethnicity is seen to function most actively in the Indian community. Perhaps one should also remember that many Muslim Indians were later arrivals—they were merchants and are historically concentrated in the Port-Louis region—as the majority of the Chinese population (also traditionally merchants). The Bhojpuri speakers—here the actual language use is higher than with other groups given the large immigrant population from this part of British India—make up an important part of the rural, or at least traditionally rural, population, that is, indentured laborers who over generations acquired parts of the land that they toiled.

Quite obviously, the historical reality of these diverse ethnic groups has had a material impact on their role and functioning. Although there is a common reality shared by the group not only through language, but also common memory, the "imagined," shared "origin" is made explicit or "real" through colonial documents. The relative histories of these groups also placed individuals belonging to them in similar positions within the new colony owing to the fact that they performed similar functions. Indentured laborers from Bihar arrived in large numbers at the same time, worked on fields, gradually saved money, bought small patches of land to which they added over generations; sent their children to schools, and then, more recently, to university, often abroad, creating a first generation of the "Bihari bourgeoisie." The entry of these inheritors of the indentured laborers into the middle class can be seen in light of the idea of a new middle class replacing an older one. "By new middle class was meant the growing stratum of largely salaried professionals who occupied managerial or quasi managerial positions in corporate structures by virtue of the skills in which they had been trained at universities—originally, primarily the engineers then later the legal and health professionals, the specialists in marketing, the computer analysts and so on" (Wallerstein 140).[21] These aspects or actions seem more significant in generating a common "culture" than any other primordial or essential idea of the "ethnic." "Tamil" immigrants in smaller numbers, from Pondichéry and Madras, came earlier, during slavery and certainly during the governorship of Mahé Labourdonnais, whose tenure ran from 1735 to 1747 (Hazareesingh 2). They were skilled workers and clustered in the urban areas, especially Port-Louis, after which many converted. The language did not survive and their affiliations with Hindus, as Indians, as well as the Creole population, as Christians (but also as closer to administration than labor), should be figured with the more recently arrived Tamils who also did not keep their language to any great extent. In addition, some of the early Indian arrivals are grouped with the Creole population, some even intermarrying.[22]

The use of symbols in the service of nationalism, chiefly those that have to do with kinship are noted by Eriksen. The reality of the nation-state is proclaimed by postulating that "political boundaries" are "coterminous with cultural boundaries" (*Ethnicity and Nationalism* 109). Further, in describing the nation-state more generally as a political system, Eriksen mentions the use of legitimate violence and taxation, the use of a bureaucratic administration and a written legislation encompassing all citizens, uniform (or ideally uniform) educational system, a shared labor market, and often a national language that might preclude the use of vernaculars in certain situations (see Eriksen *Ethnicity and Nationalism* 109). As opposed to ethnic nationalism, where "a successful nationalism implies the linking of an ethnic ideology with a state apparatus" (*Ethnicity and Nationalism* 108), Mauritius is proffered as providing an example of nonethnic nationalism (see *Ethnicity and Nationalism* 116–18), with two approaches: multiculturalism and the nation as a nonethnic (ethnically neutral) entity. As I have shown in chapter 4, it is precisely within such a positioning (examined through the prime minister's speeches) that the historical reality of Africans could be elided.

We have noted the revival of Indian languages as well as of Chinese in the educational system with no such move having been made with regard to any African languages, real or imagined.[23] The idea of introducing Swahili was proposed around independence, but this never gained any currency.[24] The most visible valorization of Africa comes in a connection with négritude by the Mauritian poet Edouard Maunick.[25] More recently, as suggested in chapter 4, connections especially through music and other newer means for the younger generation to connect with international currents are already changing the identity politics of Mauritius. The lack of adequate and easily accessed symbols for the Creole population calls attention to the division in this section between the *mulâtres* (of whiter skin and therefore with the possibility of "passing") and the *créoles* (with a definite "trace" of African blood), supposedly by skin color, but also historically to mark the difference between the "ordinary" next-generation of former slaves, and those who could "credibly" claim white blood. The introduction of the latter group into the higher echelons of society through access to education and placement in the administration in fairly large numbers indicates a creation of the new, intermediary class. This is what Wallerstein describes in post–World War II Africa as the "administrative bourgeoisie" (141). He is referring here to the educated "cadres" who are relatively well paid and employed by the government.[26] In the context of Mauritius, we could consider the entry of Creoles, especially the *mulâtres* into the administration, from as early as the mid-nineteenth century in the formation of a certain part of the bourgeoisie. As the reverend Patrick Beaton, who spent five years in Mauritius at this time noted, numerous whites were

> content (to use a local phrase) to live and to die *comme ça même* [just like that], and after death they bequeath their property and their name to their coloured offspring. It is in this way, principally, that the gradual transference of property has been effected and so general and widely

spread are the connexions [sic] to which we allude, that it is probable that in the course of a century or two, the white population will be absorbed by the coloured, or that the few remaining descendants of the former lords of the soil will become the servants of a class whom they detest. (17)

Although the white population did not get completely "absorbed" they certainly did not become the "servants" of the mixed-bloods either, as Beaton suggested. They have, however, become a very small, if still powerful, minority, currently at about 2 percent of the entire population.

Useful from Eriksen is his conception of "nationalism and ethnicity as ideologies which stress the cultural similarity of their adherents" (*Us and Them* 51). Still, one must ask if an investment in cultural similarity within perceived ethnic groups can hinder recognition of structural similarities in relation to the national unit—similarities, which, I believe, can be equally read as "cultural" if not "ethnic." Would a serious acknowledgment of structural position necessarily result in a mitigation of "ethnic" differences? Let us accept that nationalism, based on the preceding discussion on the subject, is an investment in the nation-state as a politically sovereign and legitimate entity; and that ethnicity is the communication or notation of a specific difference within the national sphere, presented in cultural terms. Do structural differences not generate their own cultures, which exist with and in combination with these "ethnic" differences; do they not inform the communication of these ethnic differences? I have suggested that the nation-state in fact requires such structural hierarchies for its very constitution.

The implicit suggestion of the anthropological model is that somehow culture can be extricated from its knotty entanglements with the political history of the groups in question and from its specific articulation within a provisional, structural totality. As Mbembe has noted, in recent scholarly work (on Africa), "[o]nly rarely is there recourse to the effects of the *longue durée* to explain the paths taken by different societies and to account for the contradictory contemporary phenomena" (6). The extrication of culture from deep structural and long historical realities is not incompatible, however, with the new theories of postcolonial hybridity. In both cases, a hybrid quality is what somehow proves to be the result of creativity and agency that escapes historical binding, while the extent to which history and structure themselves produce hybridity is less evident. It is of central concern in this book that radical agency in "hybrid" locations risks being obscured if the particular paths taken by different societies are not accounted for within notions of creolization.

CHAPTER SIX

INTERROGATING HYBRIDITY

SUBALTERN AGENCY AND TOTALITY THROUGH
EDOUARD GLISSANT'S *POÉTIQUE DE LA RELATION*

Edouard Glissant's vast writings have entered postcolonial theory in rather tentative ways.[1] Throughout his work, he develops a poetics of *Relation* that is presented more specifically in the work of the same title. Much of the difficulty that is now commonly associated with Glissant's œuvre lies in what I read to be a Marxian attempt to both inscribe a functional-instrumental version of culture as well as fulfill its more utopian ideals. In privileging this double aspect, I will be formulating a reading, against the grain, of Glissant's *Poétique de la Relation*. My central interest is to follow how it seeks to satisfy the deepest Marxist impulses while fleeing a Marxist idiom. In tracing the large theoretical sweeps it shares with Marxism, I see many fruitful connections between Glissant's thought and Western Marxism, which was heavily influenced by a resuscitation of the Hegelian sub-text of Marx and Engels' writing.[2]

Glissant's poetics of *Relation* is primarily concerned with the ways in which different cultures encountering one another in contingent historical circumstances transform themselves and each other into new and unforeseeable entities. Such a concern is central to other theories that abound in postcolonial studies as expressed in terms such as creolization, métissage, hybridity, and even diaspora.[3] In my view, Glissant's departure from the strategy identifiable in many of these theories arises, essentially, from the attention he pays to the notion of totality. This reorientation has consequences for the way in which specific encounters in history can be theorized from Glissant's hybridity.

In his novels Glissant consistently seeks to dethrone the authoritative narrator. But I am less inclined to see this aesthetic move to be indicative of the author's more modest approach to narrative. Michael Dash suggests such an interpretation for Glissant's avoidance of an authoritative narrator, attributing it to the author's belief that "poetic discoveries" are after all likely to suffer the same fate as "historical discoveries" (53). The idea that knowledge is provisional and often revised by subsequent discoveries is not objectionable in the framework of Glissant's work. However, his coining of the terms *Relation* with a capital "R" that informs much else he produces, and Tout-monde, which becomes the title of a novel, suggests something more ambitious. The narrative tactics contain fairly large aspirations that can be better understood alongside Glissant's theoretical stance toward language and subjectivity that we shall examine in this paper. For me, there is no doubt that Glissant is interested in a type of grand-scale theorizing that seeks to transform/realize the large reality/utopia his thought posits and envisions. Glissant's thought, in this reading, has tremendous significance for privileging the notion of agency while understanding hybridity in the contemporary world.

Dialectics of *Relation*

Glissant provides three terms that work together within his theory of hybridy: métissage, creolization, and *Relation*.[4] If métissage is the initial shock ("choc") or encounter ("rencontre") that anticipates a synthesis ("synthèse"), creolization is the more active (altering, differentiating) process that diffracts ("diffracte") (see *Poetics* 34 / *Poétique* 46). Métissage refers to an encounter that is recorded as a cognitive shock, which can then allow us to track difference; it is also identifiable as a moment in reality that opens up the possibility of the process of creolization. While métissage could lead toward a process that privileges synthesis by the erasure, or at least the recuperation, of difference, in it also resides the possibility for the complex process of creolization that Glissant describes and admires. Creolization entails a dynamic process in which difference continues to function and proliferate as a constitutive reality and as a basis for thought and action (see Prabhu and Quayson 226–27). So the significance of métissage is always to be understood retroactively, tracking back to a moment when radically defined difference is identifiable as preceding the encounter. The greater the success of the ensuing process as synthesis accompanied by the erasure of differences, the more the moment of métissage "fades" ["s'en efface"] (*Poétics* 91 / *Poétique* 106).

Marxist thinkers have, likewise, differentially privileged the relationship between action and understanding or practice and theory according to the exigencies at hand. Métissage in Glissant speaks directly to this issue in that it is a retroactive understanding, which can privilege the revolutionary potential of a moment. Glissant's desire to bring together action and thought can be seen as continuing the efforts of a long history of Marxist-informed thought regarding the relationship of theory and practice. Such a move is enabled by his umbrella concept, *Relation*.

According to Glissant's description:

> Relation is not to be confused with the cultures we are discussing nor with the economy of their internal relationships nor even the intangible results of the intricate involvement of all internal relationships with all possible external relationships. Nor is it to be confused with some marvelous accident that might suddenly occur apart from any relationship, the known unknown, in which chance would be the magnet. Relation is all these things at once. (*Poetics* 170–71)

This description is a performance of the idea of *Relation* itself. The reader is put under pressure to hold the ideas of what it is *not* before being instructed that it is all those things at the same time. In this manner Glissant approaches what Fredric Jameson calls dialectical writing, where it is "as though you could not say any one thing until you had first said everything; as though with each new idea you were bound to recapitulate the entire system" (*Marxism and Form* 306). There is no space for a passive consumer of Glissant's writing given the way the reader is drawn into the text. *Relation* requires an explicit engagement of the intellect and, as we will see, Glissant demands of each individual an ethical engagement in encountering otherness. Still, it is clear that Glissant grounds his work in the Caribbean culture he discusses, engages the specificities within it (drawing also from his earlier discussion in *Caribbean Discourse*), and envisages relationships that exceed those within the Caribbean. At the same time, he makes room for unforeseeable contacts, which preclude a completely rational predictability.

A fuller appreciation of the complexity that Glissant wants to preserve emerges upon close examination of his elaboration of *Relation* itself: "[W]hen we speak of a poetics of Relation, we no longer need to add: relation between what and what? This is why the French word Relation, which functions somewhat like an intransitive verb, could not correspond, for example, to the English term relation*ship*" (*Poetics* 27). Here, a Hegelian-Marxist idiom is suggested through a similarity with Hegel's rejection of pre-Kantian thought, which relied on understanding and functioned by attributing predicates that could keep categories separate and mutually exclusive. Glissant's reticence to allow a one-to-one relationship and his preference for the more complex notion of *Relation* can be seen as the espousal of dialectical thought privileged by Hegel and taken up as a central feature of analyses by Marx and Engels. *Relation* requires a constant figuring of the entire totality within which specific concepts and interactions become coherent. While discrete moments are privileged as in postcolonial theories of hybridity, which focus on the contact of otherness, such moments cannot be left as discrete and isolated in the act of understanding.[5] Likewise, for a Marxist critic: "There is no content for dialectical thought, but total content" (Jameson *Marxism and Form* 306).

Specifically in unearthing the Hegelian subtext of Glissant's theory of *Relation*, we could see the progression in Glissant from métissage to creolization and then *Relation* as carrying the flavor of Hegel's three "moments" of understanding, dialectical thought, and positive or speculative reason. It is of course to be understood here that for Hegel, reality implies that which we can speak about in the sense of a totality: it is the unity of the subject that can know the object and the object that can be known by the subject. Métissage and Hegel's understanding rest upon the heterogeneity of real objects, which are given in their specific difference. Creolization and dialectical thought involve an acknowledgment of the fact that every characteristic is self-contradictory. For Hegel, everything contains its negation and in being linked with its opposite must, in a sense, become what it is not. The tendency in creolization to seek out opposition and privilege a process in which each element does not remain the same but approaches its opposite, with which it is confronted in the moment of métissage, contains the spirit of Hegelian dialectics. In its final stage of Reason, for Hegel, thought transcends "the 'either-or' mode of thinking and [. . .] recognize[s] the unity, the difference, and the identity of opposites which, according to the Understanding are incompatible with each other" (Jordan 102). In *Relation*, likewise, this idea of opposites is not collapsed, but rather embraced just as it is "recognized" in Reason. Hegel characterizes this final stage of speculative reason by "the grasping of opposites in their unity or of the positive in the negative" (Hegel 56).

Glissant preserves this sense of opposition in processes of relationality with his idea that every people has the right to opacity. But he also, like Hegel, links this sense of contradiction not simply to the objective world but also to subjective cognition. The suggestion of some kind of resistance in opacity has deep resonance, in this comparison, with Marx's explanation of the seemingly consensual relationship between the capitalist and the worker: "[. . .] [T]hat relationship only constitutes itself *within* the process of production, and the capitalist, who exists only as a potential purchaser of labour, becomes a real capitalist only when the worker, who can be turned into a *wage-labourer* only through the sale of his capacity for labour, *really* does submit to the commands of capital" [all italics in original] (Marx *Capital* 989). The suggestion right through this passage is that breaking out of this process of production and delinking from this relationship with the capitalist are truly in the hands of the worker, who makes the entire system "real." Such a relationship is only conceivable within the established system of capitalism. In *Poetics* opacity protects the sanctity and inaccessibility of "poetic intention" throughout the successful process of writing and reading themselves (see 115). In *Relation*, opacity functions as a corrective to essentializing or reducing the entity behind action without canceling the value of subjectivity because, as we shall see, its ethical engagement will be called upon to face contradiction. In this sense, for Glissant refusal to fully expose poetic intention through the notion of difference is the authorial refusal to be recuperated by the system of Europeanization, recolonization, canonization, or perhaps even capitalization. But opacity as a concept only functions in this relationship with a/the dominant other(s). The aesthetic task before the writer seeking *Relation* can be seen within the same project as that of the class-conscious proletariat (seeking revolution). In each case, what we find is a theoretical acknowledgment of the power of the worker and the writer, respectively, to short circuit an entire system.

Glissant suggests the impossibility of grasping *Relation* in terms of anything but itself. "We must [. . .] abandon this apposition of Being and beings: renounce the fruitful maxim whereby Being is relation, to consider that Relation alone is relation" (*Poetics* 170). For Hegel

> [. . .] *there is not* an infinite which is first of all infinite and only subsequently has need to become finite, to go forth into finitude; on the contrary, it is on its own account just as much finite as infinite. [It is therefore erroneous to assume] that the infinite, on the one side, exists by itself, and that the finite which has gone forth from it into a separate existence—or from whatever source it might have come—is in its separation from the infinite truly real; but it should rather be said that this separation is *incomprehensible*. [italics in original] (153)

Clearly, then, particular instances of being do not somehow all together simply become Being; likewise, in order to understand *Relation*, it is not enough to figure various instances of particular relations. Therefore, while examining *Relation* always implies the relation of all possible things and their interrelations, it is impossible to name that totality, capture it or delimit, once and for all, its boundaries. Here, Glissant activates the Hegelian dialectic of the universal and particular, and ends up "siding," like Hegel in Adorno's words, with the universal (326). But this should in no way be seen as sacrificing the particular for the universal. What Adorno noted for Hegel can be seen as a strong tendency in Glissant, for whom "not only particularity but the particular itself is unthinkable without the moment of the universal which differentiates the particular, puts its imprint on it, and in a sense is needed to make a particular of it" (328). Hegel's statement is that although Being is indeterminate, it does not become the "opposite of determinate being" (Hegel 153). Neither métissage nor creolization can be understood without the all-encompassing notion of *Relation*, within whose logic they come to function as the conflictual, productive processes Glissant describes. In this way, we can see that Glissant's ultimate interest in Caribbean creolization is anchored in a larger totality of processual *Relation*.

Glissant's writing—both theoretical and fictional or poetic—has the effect of circularity, with characters who reappear, ideas that come back and are repeated, changed, and revised.[6] While a spiraling repetition that occurs at a higher level is a typically Marxian metaphor the idea of thought as an integral process of reality itself in Glissant will allow for further development of this parallelism.

Contradiction and Alienation in Glissant

The importance of the moment of métissage in Glissantian thinking is clear. Métissage as a stage in the apprehension of reality has been shown in the comparison with Hegel's stages of thought. Here, however, I want to show how this idea additionally activates a clearly Marxian concept of contradiction in its strongest terms: contradiction as the essential catalyst of change. In a rather more traditional Marxian formulation, contradiction is registered at various levels in society. But the most salient and pertinent type of contradiction is that between the interests of groups that then, in this formulation, must coalesce into classes in the conscious identification of these contradictory interests. It is most strongly articulated, of course, in the concept of alienation. In the process of production, the relationship between the laborer and product as subject and object becomes reversed when the former loses control over what is produced, resulting in an alienation of the laborer from the product. Further, when what counts is objectified labor itself, the laborer is alienated from both the product of the labor and his/her humanness.

The root of the problem for Marx, as explained in *Capital* is the distancing or alienation in the sense of divestiture [Verräusserung] that accompanies the process of commodification, when these products "strip off every trace of their natural and original use-value, and of the particular kind of useful labour to which they owe their creation" (204). The process in which the laborer alienates [entfremdet] his labor-power by treating it as a commodity as s/he enters into its sale to the "buyer," is vividly described in these terms: "He who was previously the money-owner now strides out in front as a capitalist; the possessor of labour-power follows as his worker. The one smirks self-importantly and is intent on business; the other is timid and holds back, like someone who has brought his own hide to market and now has nothing else to expect but—a tanning" (Marx *Capital* 280). The alienation of the product of labor from labor, between the objective conditions of labor and subjective labor power is the basis of capitalist production and indeed draws in and creates the capitalist and the worker as such. The worker's power is transformed not only into commodities but also into capital, an alien power that dominates the worker (see Marx *Economic and Philosophical Manuscripts* 71). The capitalist produces labor-power abstracted from the laborer. In this way the worker as a wage-laborer is reproduced or perpetuated and becomes the necessary condition for capitalist production (see *Capital* 716). The awakening of the laborer's consciousness and his realization of the scope of his own agency in the process are crucial to Marx's conception of revolutionary change, as we have already noted.

For Glissant, on the other hand, métissage is a moment of a brutal shock, or an encounter of radical and irreconcilable difference. As we saw, it is in tracking backward from a diffracting process of creolization that métissage is restored in all its fullness. The idea of class-consciousness involves awareness of a particular relationship of an exploited group to a larger reality and also has to be anchored in an historical consciousness. We may recall Glissant's call on the ethical subjectivity to bring together the theoretical and the social through his notion of opacity. Such a desire is recognizable in Fredric Jameson's writing, which shares many of the same impulses as Glissant's work. In fact the frequent inscription of the problematic of the distance between thought and reality becomes the very fertile ground for much of Jameson's investigative energy.[7] From Lucien Goldmann to Raymond Williams to Fredric Jameson, Marxists in different guises have struggled to bring together the aesthetic and the social in the context of their projects. The processes ensuing from métissage construct it as a cognitive shock in Glissant's theory, and participate in progressive consciousness of reality, as we have seen.[8] For Glissant, differences and their encounter do not work toward homogenizing difference upon the resolution of contradiction. Still, when difference is historicized, the challenge is to preserve it while simultaneously maintaining equality across differences that have, most often, been predicated upon inequality.

If a Marxian idea of contradiction is understood as the precondition for a productive antagonism that creates social upheaval, Glissant's refusal to abandon radical difference provides a revised view of this idea. It indicates that even in a utopian mode, it is now impossible to envisage a classless or at least a nonhierarchical society. Furthermore, it is also unproductive to do so, for this would be to endorse a static configuration, which can today be made to suggest a negative hegemony. Such a view is not incompatible with contemporary post-Marxist theories. For Laclau and Mouffe, "there cannot be a radical politics without the definition of an adversary. That is to say, it requires the acceptance of the ineradicability of antagonism" (xvii). Similarly, for Jameson, it is essential to conceive of a "perpetual cultural revolution, [which] can be apprehended and read as the deeper and more permanent constitutive structure in which the empirical textual objects know intelligibility" (*Political Unconscious* 97). Glissant's thought, then, in this respect, makes similar moves to those of more recognizable, even if diverse, contemporary Marxists and post-Marxists.

Glissant tackles contradiction in his study of the dissociation between language and subjectivity in the Martinican psyche. French was imposed on vast, different, non-French, and then Creole speaking classes. At the same time, Glissant incisively argues that Creole is not tied to any form of real production and hence has become a sort of folklore. Language for Glissant is the privileged site for *Relation*, but his treatment of language is intricately linked to the actual language situation in Martinique. With Martinique's departmental status, there is no authentic self-generated production in the island. Creole language has not been allowed to develop with and through the creative production of a people and this is the case particularly after departmentalization.[9] Therefore, Glissant's opposition to an accelerated and institutional development of Creole was informed by his belief that until we can claim a language develops from within a process of productivity, to promote it in any artificial manner is to encourage a folkloric space of inauthenticity. Still, French has functioned, like much else in Martinican culture, as an import. It does not carry the inflection of a sustained history, remains spoken with unease, and cannot, therefore, be the site of forging effective *Relation* until it is appropriated through a process of production in which it participates and is embedded. The arising alienation from language in Martinique separates the individual from society and from a process of production (or a lack of it).[10]

I believe Glissant's concept of alienation is a development of and from the Marxian account of it. What is innovative here is the fact that it is not only "work" but also a distance and isolation from it and from the production of what is simply *consumed* (French culture, language, education, images), that can bring about alienation. Glissant's critique of the lack of consciousness of this alienation from language in the adoption of French and an inability to see the need for the centrality of Martinicans' engagement with their production, culture, and language calls up the way in which Marx explains the distortion operated by the capitalist mode of production. In this context, "it is not only things—the products of labour, both use-values and exchange-values—that rise up on their hind legs and face the worker and confront him as '*Capital*.' But even the social form of labour appears as a form of development of capital, and hence the productive forces of social labour so developed appear as the productive forces of capitalism" (Marx *Capital* 1054). Conversely, Martinicans' adoption of French and their command of it give them a self-satisfied appearance of success or progress whereas, as Glissant explains, their inability to participate in the process of creating and shaping the language (an inability that has far reaching significance for its perpetuation in every aspect of their existence within a French Overseas Department) is neglected. In capitalist production "the development of the *social* productive forces of labour and the conditions of that development come to appear as the *achievement of capital*, an achievement which the individual worker endures passively, and which progresses at his expense" (Marx *Capital* 1055). In a reversed situation, Martinicans believe they are fully participating in French culture when in fact they are only passive consumers of it. On the other hand, the achievements of the worker in capitalist production are presented as the achievement of capital. This not only obscures his contribution but also does not materially recompense it, thus stripping the laborer of the means to participate in the fruits of such achievements.

I have suggested earlier a more ambitious project in the narrative of Glissant's novels than might be evident. His narrative structure delivers the type of dissociation he envisages between authoritative speakers and language. Many other postcolonial authors experiment with the narrative authority of a singular, speaking subject as part of a strategy to posit collective, disjunctive voices in their fiction. Here, this historically marked split between language and subjectivity ensues from the alienation of Martinicans from their labor in a particular way. In understanding Martinicans' relationship with French Glissant activates the senses of alienation (especially as Entäusserung) Marx uses in describing the ways in which the laborer is alienated: the idea of alienation in the sense of selling something and renouncing that which is intrinsically yours (for Martinicans we might say their identity or more poetically, their "soul") such as your own relationship with a culture and history you create; as well as alienation in the sense of making external to oneself: here by adopting and living in a language in which the self that is created cannot be annexed to the creator, much as labor gets separated from the one who labors. As Karin Barber has shown, such an engagement with "real" "indigenous languages is woefully lacking in postcolonial studies of all persuasions. Postcolonial theories of hybridity in their most sophisticated (generalized) guise are unable to embrace and explicate concrete language politics as elements of the hybrid. Instead they opt to strategically engage with language in a metaphorical sense.

Glissant Historicized

Glissant's innovative accomplishments can be seen against at least two contexts. The first being the properly Martinican context where Glissant's two compatriots automatically become interlocutors of his thought. Frantz Fanon, proclaimed Marxist in his early association with François Tosquelles as well as with his revolutionary work in Algeria; the other, Aimé Césaire, representative in the French Constituent Assembly on the Communist Party ticket. Both figures with mythical status within Martinique as well as in the postcolonial world. Césaire only resigned from the French Communist Party in 1956 to form the Parti Progressiste Martiniquais. It was around this time that Edouard Glissant would be expulsed from Martinique for his work with the Algerians. If Glissant, in his public persona, resisted the type of huge monumental "arrival" that the revolutionary figures of both Fanon and Césaire evoke, this gesture can also be read as an attempt to differentiate his career and image from those of these figures.[11] Glissant's own style is adapted to one who will linger and stay and whose career would be more easily characterized by the rhythms of a long relationship between himself and a reading public rather than by the sort of love at first sight of a brilliant, but short, affair.

The second context I wish to evoke includes two significant moments in French intellectual history, the first being Alexandre Kojève's Hegel seminars between 1933 and 1939 at the Ecole Pratique des Hautes Etudes. These seminars were, as is well known, a clearly Marxist rendering of Hegel in which the master-slave dialectic was privileged to propel the image of the proletariat as the emancipator of mankind.[12] While the seminar itself was attended by such figures as Maurice Merleau-Ponty and Jacques Lacan, the full impact of these lectures can be said to have hit the intellectual scene in 1947, when Raymond Queneau published the students' notebooks and other articles by Kojève. The second moment is the seminars by Jean Hyppolite at the Sorbonne and the Ecole Normale Supérieure from 1949. He translated the *Phenomenology of the Spirit* into French between 1939 and 1941, and his lectures were attended by the likes of Michel Foucault, Gilles Deleuze, Louis Althusser, and of course, Jacques Derrida. He privileged, for his part, the unhappy consciousness as man's recognition of the absolute and his awareness, at the same time, that this absolute is beyond humanity. Hyppolite's lectures were very much concerned with the individual as a subject of history as well as a product of it. The self-other relationship became pertinent in conjunction with the importance accorded to dialectical thinking, in which life could not be separated from thought. These ideas were making their indelible mark on French intellectual thought in the 1960s when Glissant was forced out of Martinique for subversive activities. By this time,

Fanon was already a notorious figure with his untimely death in 1961 adding to the mythic status of his revolutionary life. Glissant's investment in thought as revolutionary suggests his own preparation of a revolutionary moment for and from his writing.[16]

I believe that Glissant's work is further illuminated when seen in the long view of his career of some six decades of theoretical and artistic production. While Glissant might not "invok[e] [. . .] Marx, Breton, Sartre, nor Césaire" (Dash 2), there is no doubt that the thought of these and other recognizable figures is deeply entwined with his own—our task here is restricted to the Marxian subtext. From my reading, Glissant submits a transformed Marxism, in which there is a less restrictive vocabulary that can account for the contradictions arising with and beyond class or colonialism. He works away from a simplistic instrumental vision that rests upon one-to-one correspondence between theory and society. He also demonstrates an original and radical way of linking the individual and society, the enunciative and the historical, the cognitive and social. These moves are suggestive of a creative, forward-looking thinker whose very elusiveness works resolutely toward productive meaningfulness. Dash writes: "The political thrust of earlier ideologies such as cultural universality, negritude, indigenism, Marxism was clear. It would however be impossible to derive a systematic politics from Glissant's poetic and generously open-ended ideal of irreducible plurality and diversity for the Caribbean" (24). While Dash is quite right that Glissant's work resists neat categorization, the substructure of his entire thought rests on what we can identify as the Marxian dialectic. Contra Dash, then (and polemically here), Marxism is not an "ideology" in the sense that a particular (or even distorted) way of thinking gains hegemony by influencing how people view important aspects of reality as natural: Martinicans from Frantz Fanon to Raphaël Confiant describe a deep-seated feeling of inferiority in their culture's relationship with France, a situation that does not accord with a real dominance of Marxian thought. The euphoria associated with Césaire's early politics, even if self-proclaimedly Marxist, was, in the general consensus, unsuccessful in forging the type of collectivity any version of Marxism would envisage and culminated in departmentalization for Martinique. In fact, the way in which Glissant frames the most urgent problems faced by Martinique is based in clearly Marxian terms: alienation and a lack of productivity. Also, while the word "systematic" might intuitively be counter to Glissant's impulses, plurality and diversity do not preclude a notion of totality, as we have seen. Glissant's utopian vision is fiercely committed to a political agenda for *Relation*, which aims at changing the world.[14]

Agency

That the language, structure, and processes of Marxian (inseparable from Hegelian) thought are an essential part of Glissant's, whether they are in opposition, disguised, or overtly present, is what I have indicated and shall further argue. In the process described by Glissant, it is essential to first identify the significant moment of (most often violent) contact: this is métissage, although it cannot be recognized as such in the present of its appearance. As we have seen, the moment of métissage has to be retroactively constructed. When métissage is followed by a diffracting process rather than one of synthesis it is possible to track back to this moment and call it up as métissage: this difference occurs in the moment of enunciation. We might bring together Bhabha's notion of difference (as opposed to diversity) and the kind of alterity within creolization that Glissant advocates as a move toward *Relation*.[15] A process of synthesis would have rendered such a move impossible because the moment of métissage is then (retroactively) figured as "weak," as we have seen earlier. Here, contingency in both its spatial and temporal dimensions becomes clear. Bhabha's rather abstract idea that "the contingent is contiguity, metonymy, the touching of spatial boundaries at a tangent, and, at the same time, the contingent is the temporality of the indeterminate and the undecidable" (186) is explicitly figured in Glissant's description of the process of creolization. The contingency of the moment is seen in time because one cannot tell if a moment is métissage until the diffraction has been witnessed; it is also recorded in space in that the moment of shock functions to identify a border between differences. More interestingly, Bhabha's notion of active difference versus a more passive diversity goes further in Glissant who describes the "other of thought" and "thought of the other" in much the same way. The most basic thrust of Glissant's thought and his theorizing impulse come from the *encounter* (and not the parallel and incommensurable existence) of radical difference. For Glissant, a reality, when under analytical consideration, becomes a theoretical process, which transforms the thinker into an agent.

> Thought of the Other is the moral generosity disposing me to accept the principle of alterity, to conceive of the world as not simple and straightforward, with only one truth—mine. But thought of the Other can dwell within me without making me alter course, without 'prizing me open,' without changing me within myself. As an ethical principle, it is enough that I not violate it.
>
> The other of Thought is precisely this altering. Then I have to act. That is the moment I change my thought, without renouncing its contribution. I change, and I exchange. This is an aesthetics of turbulence whose corresponding ethics is not provided in advance. (Glissant, *Poetics* 154–55)

The act of "thinking" (with the specifications made for it) propels action in Glissant's bid for collective reflection. Glissant's métissage and creolization startlingly privilege a conception of *qualitative* difference being articulated in an encounter in the *first* place, rather than the classic Marxian notion (also present in Hegel) of quantity being cumulatively transformed into qualitative difference. It is perhaps in pushing this point further that the central task (of privileging subaltern agency) identified by postcolonial theories of hybridity could be better clarified. Rejecting, at the same time, an unrealistic idea of happily coexisting otherness, Glissant's notion of radical otherness requires change through the cognitive process.[16] While such a requirement of "deep" transformation proceeding from antagonism forms the basis of a Marxian view of historical change, for Glissant, the encounter of otherness itself transforms people into agents by their experience of this otherness. He pays greater attention, in this way, to agents in the process than does the Marxian rendering of "the people," as central in the revolution. If the energies of Marxism are in many ways directed toward prediction, Glissant rejects this predictability for the unforeseeable, but only within his total concept of *Relation*. This vision disallows any kind of essentializing or even reduction of an acting individual or agent or group (in terms of class, but also gender, race, or any other such category) without restricting, as in Bhabha's enunciative moment, any and all possibility of coherence to that immediately available in the moment.

The other of Thought for Glissant and difference (as opposed to diversity) for Bhabha are both prerequisites for pressing agency. In both cases they lead to an active role of differentiation, which, for Bhabha, questions the limits of sameness while for Glissant it explodes the cognitive into a social act. In Bhabha's proposal, agency becomes visible after the fact in particular enunciative moments, and, in this way, it ends up privileging a linearly defined textuality. This results from the necessary though implicit theoretical distinction of the hybrid from the nonhybrid, which privileges interpretation as the realm in which that past action enters the present. In Glissant, the moment of contact leads to action in the present, which is accomplished by registering contradiction as being uncontainable within textuality (within the particular mode of its inscription). In the sense of the "Other of thought" signification cannot continue without *change* that necessarily breaks out of this modality (representation). Introducing, in this manner, a definitive break in progression for any kind of signifying chain, such a moment is worked into Glissant's conception of an aesthetics of turbulence in which is produced the ethical acting subject through the encounter of difference. Seen as an ongoing process, métissage at different points (*from* different points) makes of *Relation* a "chaos-world" that cannot be understood within a linear inscription. Glissant clearly indicates the extent to which relativizing difference is insufficient just as predictability allows an easy morality that this poet wants to surpass: his insistence therefore that there can be no pre-given ethics but rather one that has to be constantly re-invented through the act of changing/exchanging/relating.

Otherness in Bhabha's version of hybridity first challenges the coherence of hegemonic (unitary) discourses. The notion of Nachträglichkeit draws heavily from psychoanalysis and the telling process the latter involves. The fact that social realities and their processes are closely connected with processes of cognition in Glissant's view of hybridity places the latter close to psychoanalytic anamnesis. Regarding the latter, Lacan writes that "it is not a question of reality, but of truth, because the effect of full speech is to reorder past contingencies by conferring on them the sense of necessities to come, such as they are constituted by the little freedom through which the subject makes them present" (Lacan *Ecrits* 48). If the limits of *Relation* are not so easy to describe or represent in the Tout-monde of absolute *Relation*, the same difficulty is evident in the psychoanalytic process with which Lacan is concerned. In a more idealistic (early) moment, Lacan comes close to the utopian element in *Relation*, when he anticipates the "omnipresence of human discourse will perhaps one day be embraced under the open sky of an omnicommunication of its text" (*Ecrits* 56). The chaos (not disorder) that Glissant identifies in this totality is also instinctively suggested by Lacan: "This is not to say that human discourse will be any more harmonious than now" (Lacan 56), but no less meaningful. But most significantly for us in Lacan, the inadequacy of the intersubjective is indicated even if it is the soil for anchoring agency: "But this is the field that our experience polarizes in a relation that is only apparently two-way, for any positing of its structure in merely dual terms is as inadequate to it in theory as it is ruinous for its technique" (Lacan 56). Glissant's interest begins with social realities and their processes only to move inward to the most basic processes of individual recognition and construction. While his theory begins with the wide historical sweeps of his earlier work, *Relation* itself often returns to the language of the self. In the end, it shares much with the more primeval knowing of the self through otherness with which psychoanalysis is concerned. In Lacan, the direction is reversed in the sense that the truth of the subject in the analysis lies beyond it: in the structuring realities of the self that necessarily expand outward. This truth, following Freud, is to be found in monuments (the body), archival documents (memories), semantic evolution (the individual vocabulary), traditions (legends of the past), and the distortions arising from the links of the traumatic moment to others around it (see Lacan *Ecrits* 50). Although each of these pertains to the individual in question, it is easy to see how they all implicate without fail, in their very vocabulary, a larger societal reference. It is quite remarkable how this eminently subject-driven theory meticulously connects to notions of collectivity. In Glissant the question of who I am is insignificant when compared to the question who we are (*Caribbean Discourse* 86). In these ways, the insistent pull of the process of knowing beyond a self-other dialectic is suggestive of an implicit totality in both Lacan and Glissant. On the other hand, while Bhahba strongly identifies with Lacanian psychoanalysis, he rejects any discussion of totality because "[t]he postcolonial perspective resists the attempt at holistic forms of social explanation" (*Location* 173).

Disjunctive experience forms the very basis of the Caribbean worldview for Glissant, whereas for Bhabha, it is the hybrid that, when sought out, can disrupt what is otherwise known and knowable in a linear modality. The Caribbean experience of resistance and agency has necessarily led its creative agents to resort to a type of disjuncture from narrative and language by lengthening the terms of its "moment" and thus altering the "time" of judgment (or representation). One might say that in Glissant's conception the labor of the maroon (runaway slave) and storyteller to "disjoin," is an activation of alienation that cuts across the entire production and its social actants.[17] The creative production involved in breaking away from the plantation economy by the maroon and from the bequeathed narrative of History by the storyteller respectively, while recording a form of alienation, is insufficient until action proceeding from it is turned into social upheaval that can lead to *Relation*. *Relation* in its dialectical movement between thought and reality, the particular and totality, cognition and action, aspires to nothing short of perpetual revolution. In the moment of métissage, like in Jameson's epistemological shock in dialectical thinking, lies the utopian possibility for change that is both objective and subjective, but necessarily beyond the realm of interpretation.

To be sure, the full possibility of the sign is not accounted for if we do not acknowledge that it "itself faces simultaneously in two directions: it faces toward the object in a 'passive' relation of being determined, and it faces toward the interpretant in an 'active' relation of determining" (Peirce qtd. In Parmentier 29). Most postcolonial theories of hybridity, in their eagerness to privilege agency, seem quick to validate the active relation and prove less enthusiastic about acknowledging the other direction. It is in this sense that critics such as Benita Parry have questioned the disengagement of much postcolonial theory from material reality (see *Postcolonial Studies*). Glissant's work readily embraces both and transforms the signifying process in pursuing contradiction and engaging an ethics in its resolution, which necessarily exceeds the particular interaction. One might see in it: "the simultaneous recognition and transcendence of immediate appearances [which] is precisely the dialectical nexus" (Lukács 8).

We can state following Glissant, that no social explanation is adequate that does not itself seek (to be) change within a conception of totality. Glissant's hybridity in its meticulous movement from one stage to the next in *Relation*, and in its bid for an ethical engagement called upon by contradiction, accomplishes precisely this. His theory of *Relation* establishes a dialectical relation between heterogeneous entities and of these entities with themselves. It engages the relationship between them by also enlarging it to encompass all other possible relationships. Glissant's use of the umbrella term *Relation* places his theory quite close to the more explicitly Marxian account of inequalities that would be resolved only through total revolution.

Hybridity and Totality

With the many changes in the Twentieth Century, the Lukácsian idea of an expressive totality and its essentializing of class became less possible to maintain in Marxian analyses alongside too many constituencies, which were competing for a central and nameable collective agent. Althusser's interpretation of totality as a structure of structures made of it a theoretical form for understanding with less concern for a corresponding referent in reality. For Jameson, if totality is mode of production, in his work, capitalism forms the ultimate structuring force within which actions and events of all kinds occur and are understood. Now, in a postmodernist vocabulary, to refuse totality also questions the very representability of reality. While the question is interesting in and of itself, some locations, and here I wish to specify the postcolonial, have a vested interest in the ways in which oppression is carried out and expressed in reality. In Bhabha's theory, the immediacy of the enunciative does not allow the kind of abstraction and distance that is required to think a totality. It is in this way that differentiation in the immediate is anomalous with respect to the concept (or ideology, if one wishes) of totality. The crux of the differences between much postcolonial theory on hybridity and more robustly Marxist thought comes to rest in the position within each of them of the concept of totality.

We might say that, in such a Marxian framing, Glissant's version of hybridity, through the idea of *Relation*—necessarily and always with a capital 'R'—implicates both "the world space of multinational capital" while at the same time "it achieves a breakthrough to some as yet unimaginable new mode of representing this last, in which we may again begin to grasp our positioning as individual and collective subjects and regain a capacity to act and struggle which is at present neutralized by our spatial as well as our social confusion" (Jameson "The Cultural Logic" 54). In this sense of "cognitive mapping" any individual or collective act of political will necessarily engages with its situation and struggles to project its imprint outward to this vast but interconnected space. As we have seen, Glissant is equally concerned with what has remained a central Marxian problematic of the particular and the general (what in Jameson's formulation above contains the echo of class-consciousness). This process of anchoring the enunciative moment in something other than itself is what is explicitly neglected (or rejected) by Bhabha who stubbornly fixes the idea of totality as static, foreclosing any discussion of an enlargement or expansion out from the particular: "The epistemological is locked into the hermeneutic circle, in the description of cultural elements as they tend towards a totality" (*Location* 177).

For the enunciative, Bhabha figures a more fluid space: "The enunciative is a more dialogic process that attempts to track displacements and realignments that are the effects of cultural antagonisms and articulations—subverting the rationale of the hegemonic moment and relocating alternative, hybrid sites of cultural negotiation" (*Location* 178). It is less clear how subverting the rationale of the hegemonic moment translates into action for the subaltern from alternative locations. Subalternity is experienced, even in the enunciative moment, in the relationship of the subaltern with the hegemonic. While the rationale of such hegemony might be shown to be "irrational," or at least contingent, any theoretical project purporting to empower subalterns should somehow address the question of undoing this hegemony—a project that necessarily exceeds the (immediate) textual at some point. The point at which the hybrid moment enables the move between a particular representative mode and the "outside" of such a provisionally sutured whole, which is presumed and whose dominant logic maintains the subalternity of the subaltern would be crucial. The method ends for Bhabha where, for us, it must begin.[18] Endless relocation to alternative sites of negotiation which would once again reveal the irrationality of hegemony at that point, only to revert to relocation once more can be, somewhat reductively, named as the postmodernist idea of endless textuality as process. It allows no way to connect discrete "illogics" of hegemony.

The association of *Relation* to "chaos-monde" and "tout-monde" in Glissant is a reckoning with totality. Creolization is, for him, the earthly approximation of his idea of total *Relation* (of everything to everything else, simultaneously and equally): "What took place in the Caribbean, which could be summed up in the word creolization, approximates the idea of Relation for us as nearly as possible" (*Poetics* 34). In evoking the comparison made with Hegel earlier in this piece, the confusion here of moving one stage of thought to the next reflects a more consequential tendency in Glissant to blur totality and utopia. If *Relation* is a totality that is required for métissage and creolization to gain coherence, without the complex process of creolization as a model (which depends on the encounter in métissage), *Relation* would be unthinkable. But *Relation* contains within it the utopian element of Glissant's thought as a world in which there is total on-going creolization without exception. We can theorize further from Glissant *Relation* as totality and *Relation* as utopia. However, in *Relation*, we find a complex linking of analytical totality to an original theorization of agency, guided by an impulse to move that totality toward utopia. The lack of a proper intervention of any idea of totality to accompany the privileged agency of the subaltern, noted in Bhabha's enunciative present and characteristic of most postcolonial understandings of hybridity, is what marks the incommensurability between these theories and Glissant's more particularly Marxian rendering of the same. In this, we might say with Neil Lazarus, at least with specific reference to hybridity in postcolonial studies, that "the conceptual reach of Marxism is superior to that of the problematics prevalent in the field" (*Nationalism* 15). Glissant's *Relation* is predicated upon a more immediate connection between thought and reality than even a Marxian derived formulation of dialectics while it simultaneously addresses the idea of the subject mediating between them.

Glissant's poetics of *Relation* has begun a most provocative reframing of Marxism for a world where the idea of "difference" could simply collapse into incoherence, or worse, lead to complacency. The challenge that difference poses for a conception of revolution is seen in the maneuvers of postcolonial hybridity. Such maneuvers include a general resistance to accord a more consequential place to true contradiction and its potential for restructuring as well as to conceive of an analytical category of totality within which this might be theorized. Utopian longings for revolutionary agency without these concepts become meaningless. Glissant's writing, under the aegis of *Relation*, rethinks precisely the notion of revolution and responds to inexhaustible claims or branding of "difference." My suggestion is that all those interested in theorizing difference in the contemporary world (and Marxist-minded thinkers in particular) would find reason to pause and consider his thought.

CHAPTER SEVEN

Narration in Frantz Fanon's *Peau noire masques blancs*

Some Reconsiderations for Hybridity

Frantz Fanon's writings remain one of the most influential œuvres from which postcolonial criticism draws. His work is referred to in discussions on, among other things, violence, nationalism, inequality, racism, capitalism, elitism, sexuality, and ethnicity in both the postcolonial nation state and various metropolitan contexts. Given that the essays in *Black Skin, White Masks* (hereafter *BSWM*) are all about the unremitting opposition of black and white as ontologically incompatible spaces, the keen interest in Fanon by theorists of hybridity requires further thought. One of the pitfalls of Homi K. Bhabha's appropriation of Fanon has been to read hybridity in Fanon in ways that are untenable, undoing or at least playing down the oppositionality on which much of Fanon's thinking is predicated even in this earlier text.[1] As Neil Lazarus has noted, the appropriation of *BSWM* by this influential theorist of hybridity has been from "back to front" "thereby falsifying the testimony of Fanon's own evolution as a theorist" ("Disavowing Decolonization" 87). Nevertheless, for Paul Gilroy Fanon is less helpful in the current world because "his thinking remains bound to a dualistic logic we must now abjure" even to ask how cultural analyses and politics "might contribute to the new humanism he called for thirty years ago" (*Small Acts* 253). I will show the continuing relevance of Fanon's thought owing, precisely, to the multiplicity of strategies he employs, which could potentially tie it to a notion of hybridity. Critics have also demonstrated that, in general, Fanon has been read out of context by theorists and isolated from the body of his entire work.[2] Here, I provide a close reading of parts of *BSWM* to show the ways in which Fanon's text (a) could give a different profile and understanding to the notion of hybridity and (b) requires keen attention to its narrative processes. In doing so, I will also draw attention to the manner in which the affect of this text becomes central to its theoretical moves.

Some Specifications for the Following Reading

My interest in this text is to first note how a certain conception of agency is programmatically laid out. This idea is of central importance to contemporary notions of hybridity, for which agency is a central preoccupation. Stuart Hall and Homi Bhabha, to take the most prominent readers of Fanon in such a context, pay little attention to Fanon himself *as* providing a coherent theorizing on the in-between. Rather, the metaphors, language, and tone of *BSWM* are extended and even adopted in a rereading in which, particularly with reference to Bhabha, it is hard to see where Fanon's discourse ends and the later critics' begins.

As the title of his book indicates, Fanon's writing is about two radically different spaces: the space of the white colonizer and that of the black (often specifically Antillean) native. Fanon writes from his experience of being a black man in France in *BSWM*. The poignancy of these inspiring, poetic, personal essays comes, in effect, from such a separation between black and white. The fact that the black skin and white mask are configured from the *same* subject position—simultaneously or alternately—generates the need for negotiation that theorists such as Bhabha or Stuart Hall have rightly seized in their readings of Fanon.[3] The idea of delaying the definitive interpretive moment, suggested early in this text by the "perpetual question" (*BSWM* 29), is a seductive invitation to acknowledge in Fanonian thought the precursor of postmodernist deferral and holds great possibility to read Fanon through Bhabha's notion of hybridity. However, I will further explore Fanon's text in an attempt to elucidate the wider implications for, and critique of, this dominant conception of hybridity in relation to Fanon.

Hybridity, in its colonial version was predicated on the superiority of the white race. Hybrid examples of humans were seized to either reiterate that humans formed one species (by the monogenists) or to contest this conception by suggesting these different groups were incompatible and therefore to be considered naturally distinct (by the polygenists). Hybrids were of interest and presented a challenge to the colonial administration in its categorization of the different groups to be administered in the colonies (Dubois 99). Still, whether monogenist or polygenist, whether the argument was used for or against slavery, race subordination remained a constant. Robert Young defends hybridity (or hybridizing readings) as theorized by Bhabha, against the bulk of criticism of the latter's work. Such criticism focused on aspects of Bhabha's work in general (along with that of Said and Spivak in postcolonial criticism) that privilege textuality without paying sufficient attention to a politics of action. According to Young's defense, Bhabha's work is not incompatible with, and does not preclude, a more politically engaged form of analyses or indeed opposition, providing instead a "significant framework for that other work" (163). What becomes evident in my reading of Fanon's narrative, however, is that at a more basic textual level, Bhabha's hybridity, despite the latter's ceaseless return to Fanon, is indeed incompatible with Fanon's central ideas about the encounter with otherness. Relying on what he calls the "language metaphor," which he identifies in the work of Cornel West and Stuart Hall in contemporary cultural studies, Bhabha shifts the emphasis from a more bland idea of cultural diversity to cultural difference. Even though this reorientation is indeed powerful, his development of the notion of agency "outside the sentence," (*Location* 180) remains unconvincing. This is because it is unclear how the specification of the "enunciative present [. . .] provide[s] a process by which objectified others may be turned into subjects of their history and experience" (*Location* 178). Without engaging in a full discussion of this issue, we may note with others the conflation of the realm of interpretation with the realm of other forms of action that occurs consistently in Bhabha's book. Fanon's disagreement with Sartre, which we will examine, clearly indicates the inadequacy to him of a notion of agency that could be "deprived of subjectivity" (*Location* 191). Agency, for Fanon, is deeply intertwined with, and can only proceed from, a feeling of "authentic" subjectivity. As we saw in chapter six, Bhabha's picture of totality, which is constraining and nondialectic in the association he makes between this concept and the epistemological (*Location* 177) as opposed to a more processual description of the enunciative is also incompatible with another basic requirement of Fanon's analyses. This lack of any notion of totality in Bhabha as well as his unwillingness to name the subject cannot be reconciled with the fundamental impulses of Fanon's work.[4] For Fanon, on the other hand, the black man's subjecthood within the totality of colonial domination becomes the substructure of *BSWM*.

In what follows, I will examine two key passages that, to my mind, present Fanon's writing (*BSWM* in particular), as not just an inviting text on which hybridity can be projected, but one where there occurs a specific dramatizing of the moves essential to a theory of hybridity. My close reading of parts of Fanon's text will show that neglect of the specific chronology and tactics in the narration, particularly of "The Fact of Blackness," makes for rather inaccurate assertions regarding statements that are attributed to Fanon's authorial "I."

Theorizing from Fanon: Consequences for Hybridity

Fanon lays out how a reading of interactivity must proceed from the level of the individual consciousness. Such a conception cannot be overlooked by those allying Fanon's thought with hybridity because the latter concept in postcolonial studies is concerned with theorizing and enabling the agency of subaltern subjects, which can be seen as the main impetus of intellectual and political activity in this field. In this framework, Fanon gives a very clear articulation of a notion of totality. This is the first of two key passages I wish to signal in relation to a theoretical discussion of hybridity via Fanon:

> L'homme est mouvement vers le monde et vers son semblable. Mouvement d'agressivité, qui engendre l'asservissement ou la conquête; mouvement d'amour, don de soi, terme final de ce qu'il est convenu d'appeler *l'orientation éthique*. Toute conscience semble pouvoir manifester, simultanément ou alternativement, ces deux composantes. Energétiquement, l'être aimé m'épaulera dans l'assomption de ma virilité, tandis que le souci de mériter l'admiration ou l'amour d'autrui tissera tout le long de ma vision du monde une superstructure valorisante" (*Peau noire* 33).

> Man is motion toward the world and toward his like. A movement of aggression, which leads to enslavement or to conquest; a movement of love, a gift of self, the ultimate stage of what by common accord is called *ethical orientation*. Every consciousness seems to have the capacity to demonstrate these two components, simultaneously or alternatively. The person I love will strengthen me by endorsing my assumption of my manhood, while the need to earn the admiration or the love of others will weave, consistently along my vision of the world, a validating superstructure. [translation modified] [my emphases] (*BSWM* 41)[5]

As mentioned at the beginning of this chapter, the possibility to assume both the black skin and the white mask simultaneously or alternately is what has been identified in dramatizing hybridity for the very existence of the évolué under colonialism as described by Fanon. Here, Fanon describes aggression, which leads to enslavement and conquest, and love, which is the final stage in one's ethical orientation. Both these basic impulses of every consciousness for Fanon play out, first, in the inter-subjective space. Manliness, or the more neutral idea of strength, is produced at the level of the individual in assuming such a characteristic in one's identification with the other. Still, the desire to be worthy of the other's love or admiration—in other words in one's identification as a consciousness—presupposes an overarching totality of coherence for the self's perspective. While still quite definitively in the context of the black man, these remarks suggest a wider notion of struggle for an ethical orientation in interacting with otherness both within oneself and between individuals or groups.

Fanon's conception of the healthy encounter between the black man and the world implies the same kind of ethical engagement. After showing to what extent the black Antillean has absorbed white perspective even in relation to negative stereotypes of blacks, he remarks that the black "vit une ambiguïté qui est extraordinairement névrotique. [...] [L]'Antillais s'est connu comme nègre, mais, par un glissement éthique, il s'est aperçu (inconscient collectif), qu'on était nègre dans la mesure où l'on était mauvais, veule, méchant, instinctif" (*Peau noire* 155) "lives an ambiguity that is extraordinarily neurotic. [...] [T]he Antillean has recognized himself as a Negro, but, by virtue of an ethical transit [slip], he also feels (collective unconscious) that one is a negro to the degree to which one is wicked, sloppy, malicious, instinctual" (*BSWM* 192). This is an interesting idea drawing from Sartre's notion of responsibility in that the black man can be a "nigger" only through such a lapse in his *own* ethical mode. It is for this reason that such cultural hegemony can occur in Martinique: "L'imposition culturelle s'exerce facilement en Martinique. Le glissement éthique ne rencontre pas d'obstacle"(*Peau noire* 156). "Cultural imposition is easily accomplished in Martinique. The ethical transit [slip] encounters no obstacle" (*BSWM* 193). I have modified the English translation to better express this idea of an ethical slip (in the sense of a mistake or a lapse in concentration in the process of reasoning, as well as the idea of "glisser sur" or to "skim over" something without properly entering into the detail). The black man's compromise or lapse in ethics, which then allows him to ratify and hold up the white man's lie, is not compensated in the end by any privileges gained by him.

In fact, his ethical slip is facilitated by the relationship between blacks and whites in colonial culture, whereby his negative image of himself as a nigger is validated all around him. Instead of being compensated the Antillean is rudely reminded of the falsity of his white mask by the white man who chides him that "it is not enough to try to be white, but that a white totality must be achieved. It is only then that I shall recognize the betrayal" (*BSWM* 193). The latter is the betrayal of the French promise of assimilation in the colonial relationship. In the end, black skin comes back to haunt the Antillean and crudely marks his exclusion from white culture. It is to an already constituted totality that he was first invited and then denied a proper space within it because he has no agency in its construction. The monumental ethical and material engagement to undo such a situation will be theorized as revolution in Fanon's later work.

In the passage cited at the beginning of this section, Fanon draws attention to a notion of totality within which the individual engages with another.

Here, this totality is sustained by a certain logic by which the individual seeks to be loved and admired; such love from a partner sustains and strengthens the position of the self. A complex web of interdependency thus holds the entire conception of the world together. Already in this early work, even (or especially) at the level of the individual, Fanon is keen to establish how liberation involves a strong comprehension of totality. Interdependency with the other who "endorses" his "assumption of his manhood" and the need for acceptance and "love" become the bases for the self's understanding of both its place in the world and the limits and contours of that world. Fanon's close attention to the necessity of radical difference (distance) between the self and other in this, and to their mutual dependency in this process of identification were also evident in the two movements he describes of aggression and love.[6] Although "The Fact of Blackness" is an inexact rendering of the French title, "l'expérience vécue du noir" [The lived experience of the black man] it captures quite accurately the facticity against which the black man poetically forges a mode of thinking.[7]

The chapter begins with a dramatic presentation of this fact (of blackness) as it is lived in the person of a black man. The narrative opens with the oft cited confrontation of the "I" of the black man by the eye (gaze) of the white world which fixed him in the form of an object. This draws much from Jean-Paul Sartre's theorizing of the formation of selfhood in its relation to otherness and the struggle for claiming subjecthood. The interesting part about this introduction is that the other is the source of both anguish and liberation; of both objectification and the basis for subjecthood. This twin function of the other's gaze is noted by Fanon below. This is the second quotation I find pertinent to a theory of hybridity available from Fanon.

> "Sale nègre!" ou tout simplement: "Tiens un nègre!"
>
> J'arrivais dans le monde, soucieux de faire lever un sens aux choses, mon âme pleine du désir d'être à l'origine du monde, et voici que je me découvrais objet au milieu d'autres objets.
>
> Enfermé dans cette objectivité écrasante, j'implorai autrui. Son regard libérateur, glissant sur mon corps devenu soudain nul d'aspérités, me rend une légèreté que je croyais perdue, et, m'absentant du monde, me rend au monde. Mais là-bas, juste à contre-pente, je bute, et l'autre, par gestes, attitudes, regards, me fixe, dans le sens où l'on fixe une préparation par un colorant. Je m'importai, exigeai une explication ... Rien n'y fit. J'explosai. Voici les menus morceaux par un autre moi réunis. (*Peau noire* 88)

Dirty nigger! Or simply, "look, a Negro!"

I came into the world imbued with the will to find a meaning in things. My spirit filled with the desire to attain to the source of the world, and then I found that I was an object in the midst of other objects.

> Sealed into that crushing objecthood, I turned beseechingly to others. Their attention was a liberation, running over my body suddenly abraded into nonbeing [transformed into smoothness] endowing me once more with an agility [a lightness] that I had thought lost, and by taking me out of the world, restoring [restores] me to it. But just as I reached the other side, I stumbled, and the movements, these attitudes, the glances of the other fixed me there, in the sense in which a chemical solution is fixed by a dye. I was indignant; I demanded an explanation. Nothing happened. I burst apart. Now the fragments have been put together again by another self. (*BSWM* 109)

Thus, the black man becomes a nigger under the white gaze. From such a position of objecthood, he implores the other to alter this state. It is the searching gaze of the other that paradoxically discovers and delivers the subject that is formed from within the body of the narrator. This momentary attention to his specificity lifts him out of objecthood, allows the gaze to pass smoothly over him, separating him from the thickness of the world, and endowing him with a lightness that he so craves. But then, the culturally charged look (now buttressed by attitudes and gestures) "fixes" him within a limited sphere of personhood that cannot match his own enthusiasm, his own understanding of the vastness of his soul as a being-in-the-world. Once again, it becomes clear that the metaphysical encounter of these two entities is forced into its "worldliness," by a grounding in the cultural context (here defined by colonialism) in which it occurs. Surprisingly, Fanon uses the term "dye" recalling Mayotte Capécia's attempt to negrify the world by throwing black ink on those who were unkind to her at school. In her case, he dismisses it as an ineffective and ridiculous act. In this dramatic presentation of the encounter with the other, Mayotte's disparaged metaphor avenges its author by appearing in Fanon's text and recalling, despite Fanon's harsh criticism of Mayotte, their common story of being "French" Martinicans. It is, of course, ironic that this metaphor becomes the most adequate form Fanon finds for expressing the pigeonholing that negatively defines the narrator's very existence, given Fanon's refusal to understand affectively Mayotte's use of the very same. In the above quotation, no rebellion is capable of dislodging this pigeonholing except that of explosion.

I wish to restore the significance of the last line quoted above to the narrative of this chapter in following what it means to speak of hybridity through Fanon. Re-assemblage of the body that is split apart enables the black man's subjectivity. All possibility of subjecthood lies in the narrator's willingness and ability to accept that point of explosion, which blasts apart the black male body as it is known within colonial culture: Y'a bon banania;

the grin; the obsequious attitude that structures this body noted elsewhere by Fanon. It is in a conscious and conscientious reconstruction of the idea itself of the body of the black man that any kind of legitimate subjectivity can occur. Since the black man is always to assume responsibility for his body, for his race, for his ancestors (*BSWM* 112), which all come to rest in the singular black man when he is encountered, one of the ways in which hybridity intervenes as a method of resistance to this is in privileging the individual black man in his multiplicity. All attempts by white culture and history to "fix" the black man in his blackness are blasted open by an explosion that comes from the ethical agency of the black man's consciousness. The subsequent construction, in this chapter, of a coherent, but multiple, narrative "I," which we will examine shortly, is a lesson in this hybrid project. Although this multiplicity can easily be compatible with Bhabha's ideas of negotiation and ambiguity, the ethics that guide such a project and their origin seem to sit less comfortably with his theory of hybridity. In Fanon, the urgency of recognizing the black man's subjectivity is tied to an ethics he prescribes, which comes from his own bodily experience. In this way, because of the responsibility placed on the black man for his agency, Bhabha's privileging of unconscious and fortuitous resistance enabled through ambivalence collapses under the greater project of emancipation envisioned by Fanon. Hybridity as a response to reductive stereotyping replays that troubling aspect of the métis, which is to disturb the terms of the hierarchy in place, an aspect of hybridity that is central to Bhabha's analyses. However, simply disturbing them is not an end in Fanon. Fanon's project is tied to a more explicit project of liberation from specifically colonial subjugation, which begins at the level of subjecthood. Young's defense of Bhabha cited earlier picks up on the fact that a more clearly political activism would be the "other work" that Bhabha's theory does not purport to fulfill. In considering Fanon's narrative here, it is evident that hybridity is called up in the necessity of a double response to stereotyping. This double response is accomplished here through the strength of the collective in the assumption of what I have called the historical-universal narrator and through simultaneously reclaiming the affect of the individual, idiosyncratic narrator. Bhabha's vision of hybridity prompts him to chide Fanon for his belief in a human essence: "Fanon is not principally posing the question of political oppression as the violation of a human essence, although he lapses into such a lament in his more existential moments" (*Location* 42). This is to misunderstand that for Fanon it is impossible even to pose the question of political oppression unless it employs the idiom of existential impossibility arising from the black man's experience of de-subjectification.

Re-reading BSWM

Here, I reconsider several important passages that illustrate the historical-universal position of the narrator and privilege the overall affect of this chapter. With such a focus, I suggest some reconsiderations for its interpretation via Markman's translation. What Fanon demonstrates so clearly here is that Sartre's notion of existentialism is rendered impossible from the subject position of the black man. While Sartre writes, for example, in defense of his version of existentialism that existence precedes essence, or you have to begin with subjectivity [il faut partir de la subjectivité] (*L'Existence est un humanisme* 17), Fanon provides us the terms within which this is impossible with regard to the black man's subjectivity:

> J'arrive lentement dans le monde, habitué à ne plus prétendre au surgissement. Je m'achemine par reptation. Déjà des regards blancs, les seuls vrais, me dissèquent. Je suis fixé. Ayant accommodé leur microtome ils réalisent objectivement des coupes de ma réalité. Je suis trahi. Je sens, je vois dans ces regards blancs que ce n'est pas un nouvel homme qui entre, mais un nouveau type d'homme, un nouveau genre. Un nègre, quoi! (*Peau noire* 93)
>
> I move slowly in the world, accustomed now to seek no longer for upheaval. I progress by crawling. And already I am being dissected under white eyes, the only real eyes. I am fixed. Having adjusted their microtomes, they objectively cut away slices of [structure the contours of] my reality. I am laid bare [betrayed]. I feel, I see in those white faces that it is not a new man who has come in, but a new kind of man, a new genus. Why, it's a Negro [nigger]! (*BSWM* 116)

In the passage above, with no illusions of erupting into the world, the black man enters unobtrusively, crawling slowly. Still he is captured, fixed and dissected by the white gaze, under which he is not at liberty to construct his own reality. I have modified the translation in square brackets (while leaving the original English intact), suggesting here that it is not that his reality is "cut away" but that it is structured—a point we have examined previously. Thus, I evoke the verb "réaliser" in the sense of making something real or concrete. I suggest the tem "betrayal" to connect this passage to a lack of acknowledgement of the individuality and emotional reality of this black man (see the word "objectivement" and note the metallic coldness of the microtome) who has been dissected. It also connects to betrayal through the broken promise of assimilation, which remains out of reach for the black man in the real encounter with whiteness. The word "betrayal" itself, as we shall see later, is used elsewhere in this chapter to record the narrator's dismay at being ultimately rejected by the white culture that he has systematically interiorized. Although "laid bare" accords very well with the sense of violence from the white gaze and the more general Sartrean idea of the gaze of the "other," I have preferred to evoke the idea of betrayal from the word "trahi," thus connecting it urgently through affect to the following sentence, where such betrayal is tied to stereotype.

Following from this betrayal, the black man remains nothing but a "type,"—a Negro (nigger). It is from this point that we must understand the desire for absolute originality and the numerous assertions of independent personhood, despite, in other places, the clear recognition of the dialogism within which it has to be claimed. The historical lack of recognition in the self-other relationship is at the base of these efforts. The "I" in this chapter is that of the black man trying to be original, full of enthusiasm, and a complete human being in encountering the world, but being deprived of all such possibility by the white gaze. This gaze has been held up by dominant structures historically and has fixed and limited him: "I came into the world imbued with the will to find a meaning in things, my spirit filled with the desire to attain to the source of the world, and then I found that I was an object in the midst of other objects" (*BSWM* 109). This is followed by the passage quoted earlier when the "I" explodes by seizing its agency in response to the fixing accomplished by the culturally loaded white gaze. Next follow a series of observations and statements about the Black (man) [le Noir]. Before resorting back to the generic black "I" there is a slip into a "we" that could easily be missed, but which clearly points to a purposeful forging of a collective consciousness based on this experience of blackness that can be known through the bodily experience of the white gaze:

> Et puis, il *nous* fut donnee d'affronter le regard blanc. Une lourdeur inaccoutumée *nous* oppressa. Le véritable monde *nous* disputait *notre* part. Dans le monde blanc *l'homme de couleur* rencontre des difficultés dans l'élaboration de *son* schéma corporel. La connaissance du corps est une activité uniquement négatrice. C'est une connaissance en troisième personne. Tout autour du corps règne une atmosphère d'incertitude certaine. *Je* sais que si *je* veux fumer, il faudra que *je* me recule. . . . (*Peau noire* 89)

> And then the occasion arose when *I* [*we*] had to meet the white man's eyes. An unfamiliar weight burdened *me* [*us*]. The real world challenged *my* [*our*] claims. In the white world the *man of color* encounters difficulties in the development of *his* bodily schema. Consciousness of the body is solely a negating activity. It is a third-person consciousness. The body is surrounded by an atmosphere of certain uncertainty. *I* know that if *I* want to smoke *I* shall have to reach out. . . . [my emphases] (*BSWM* 110–111)

What Fanon underscores is that even though the black man's body is given to him through the harsh gaze of the white man through a cultural lens informed by stereotypes inherited from colonialism, there remains a knowledge of the body in space that is purely physical, which can only be experienced singularly by each individual. It is unfortunate that the English translation does not record the use of "we" in the first three sentences. Although in and of itself, this might be a legitimate translation, I do believe that in this particular instance the movement from "we" to the general "he" and then to "I" is quite significant. Even though, for the black man, consciousness of the body is in the "third person," re-knowing the self as body consists in re-claiming through action as a means of knowing. The full possibility of this re-knowing is suggested in the notion of "certain uncertainty" that each claim to the self as body actualizes differently, but necessarily individually. We have already encountered the passage where a lapse in ethics at this point will lead back to cultural hegemony in which the black man is stereotyped. It is in relation to this consciousness, to this certain uncertainty that a move toward a collectivity has to occur. As we have seen, such a connection between the body and its experience of itself by the black man is central to Fanon's development of an individual ethics that is fundamental to any kind of political action. In the same manner, Fanon is at pains to indicate that marking black collectivity through stereotype has to be properly responded to through the black man's reassertion as a consciousness, full of possibility, recalling Sartre's words: I am a freedom or I am a project:

> Et tous ces gestes, je les fais non par habitude, mais par une connaissance implicite. Lente construction de mon moi en tant que corps au sein d'un monde spatial et temporel, tel semble être le schéma. Il ne s'impose pas à moi, c'est plutôt une structuration définitive du moi et du monde—*définitive*, car il s'installe entre mon corps et le monde une dialectique effective. (*Peau noire* 89)
>
> And all these movements are made not out of habit but out of implicit knowledge. A slow composition of my self as a body in the middle of a spatial and temporal world—such seems to be the schema. It does not impose itself on me; it is, rather, a definitive structuring of the self and of the world—*definitive* because it creates a real dialectic between my body and the world. (111) [*BSWM* my emphases]

Therefore, this passage from "we" to "I" indicated in the previous passage becomes significant. While colonialism stamps the other in such a way that, within the group, one is indistinguishable from the other, the more primeval drama of the self-as-body and the experience of literally being-in-the-world in interacting with space and time are so purely individual that any idea of agency for Fanon has to proceed from this level of subjecthood. The central modality of dismay in this chapter comes from a realization that access to this basic relationship to the self is blocked for the black man; and it is all that blurs the path to this experience of selfhood that dismays him, because it is from this point of selfhood that some agency in participating in the process of structuring a totality can be theorized. Here inheres a reciprocal form of interactivity between self and world in which the body encounters space, and space is reoriented through the agency of this body-subject. This process involves knowledge of the self that the self, alone, can attain through experience. It is here that one can find an effective delivery of the basic Sartrean formulation that existence precedes essence. Much is at stake, then, in this quest for the black man's most basic encounter with himself: his body as structuring his experience, and thus a reestablishment of his selfhood outside the various constraints that have been actualized through the history of colonialism. Access to this, if we follow Fanon, has been blocked for the black man as he is "epidermized" and fixed in a negative generality before he can think of experiencing his positive particularity. Working exclusively from the English translation, as we have seen, we would be unable to track the movement of the narrative subject in its accounting of the most basic construction of the self.

Accosted as a nigger, the narrator is first amused, and then laughs openly at the white child's fear, but is not able to sustain this reaction, because, "assailed at various points, the corporeal schema crumbled, its place taken by a racial epidermal schema" (*BSWM* 112). Referring to, and even assuming, the move made by the poets who would be called the authors of négritude, Fanon writes: "Since the other hesitated to recognize me, there remained only one solution: to make myself known" (115). Fanon clearly had a more ambitious project, which was at odds with such a reductive image producer of the black man as the claims of négritude when articulated simplistically. However, the narrator's dependency on negritude as politics and aesthetics shows how indispensable it remains in the story of black liberation. In fact, in this very chapter the narrator assumes a historical-universal "I" of the black man in tracing out, before the white man's gaze, his many tactics, one of which is, indeed, the "I" of négritude. In what follows I will show that such a reading of the narrative here speaks to Henry Louis Gates Jr.'s early identification of two aspects of Fanon's thought in any possible "Fanonism." The first—drawing from Gayatri Chakravorty Spivak's reversal of Derrida's notion of "writing" to mean "colonial discourse"—being that in this context, "all discourse is colonial discourse" (Gates 466) and the second being the interminable relationship between the individual and the collective in *BSWM* already identified by Stephan Feuchtwang (Gates 46).

Fanon's Historical-Universal Narrator

Our narrator remarks, "Je hélais le monde et le monde m'amputait de mon enthousisame. On me demandait de me confiner, de me rétrécir" (*Peau noire* 92) [I had been shouting a greeting to the world, and the world severed from me all inspiration. I have been instructed repeatedly to confine myself, to contract my infinitude] [my translation] (see *BSWM* 114–15 for the English: "I shouted a greeting to the world and the world slashed away my joy. I was told to stay within bounds, to go back where I belonged"). I have worked substantially with the English translation here. First, the use of the imperfect tense becomes consequential to this historical narrative I have privileged. Here, the theoretical historical-universal narrator and his struggles gain poignancy from the long history of repeated crushing of the spirit. The alienated black man with the inferiority complex is not one who was created from one day to the next. Therefore, I have chosen to emphasize the long period of domination ("had been shouting" and "have been repeatedly instructed"). Second, it is not that white domination simply slashed at his joy; the situation is far worse. It systematically cut off all connections he could make with his joyful self. Thus it is agency at the primordial level of being in touch with oneself that is amputated. The reductive aspect of the words "confiner" and "se rétrécir" are not conveyed properly in the translation by "stay within bounds" and "go back." These words and their meaning (in their connection to dismemberment, severing from wholeness, longing for the accomplishment of the potential for the absolute) resonate throughout the chapter. It has been my aim to follow the affect of this narrative and, here, to give greater amplitude *within* Fanon's text to the metaphor of dismemberment. Over and over in this chapter, Fanon returns to the idea of a shrinking of the black man's spirit by various machinations of colonialism.

Next follows a passage that is characterized by its indignant tone but which is also full of resolve to assume agency against the numbing, reductive, and generalizing white gaze. It ends with: "Since the other hesitated to recognize me, there remained only one solution: to make myself known" (*BSWM* 115). But this aggressive stance is short-lived. In contemplating Nineteenth-Century theories of race that advocated racial separation to avoid "contamination," the historical-universal black narrator decides that the best reaction is to wait. "Quant à moi, je saurais bien comment réagir. Et en un sens, si j'avais à me définir, je dirais que j'attends" (*Peau noire* 96–97) ["For my own part, I would certainly know how to react. And in one sense, if I were asked for a definition of myself, I would say that I am one who waits" (*BSWM* 120)]. This is another well-known characterization of Fanon—as the one "who waits." But in following the narrative thread of this chapter, it should be properly recognized as a specific tactic of the black man in relation to the white man that Fanon is historically recounting.[9] The clue that it is not an aside (quite common in Fanon's writing), and therefore a more general statement of the characterization of the black man, is the use of the conditional (saurais) that can be read as an anticipation (the future in the past). Given these racial theories at the time, the narrator anticipates (in the present of the narrative) what the reaction of the black man was going to be—it would be to wait. My suggestion is that in taking this statement out of context, one is discounting "waiting" as a provisional tactic of the black man at a particular historical juncture. For the next sequence is important: with the end of slavery he feels his "tenacity" (waiting and surviving) pays off as this historical-universal black "I" has gone forward (*BSWM* 121). But then he comes crashing down with the realization that it was: "[t]rop tard. Tout est prévu, trouvé, prouvé, exploité" (*Peau noire* 97) ["[t]oo late. Everything is anticipated, thought out, demonstrated, made the most of" (*BSWM* 121)]. Thus, waiting has now made him "too late." This situation, tracing the continuing impossibility of the position of the black man through a chronological narrative, is completely discounted by Bhabha when he remarks that "it is one of the original and disturbing qualities of *Black Skin, White Masks*, that it rarely historicizes the colonial experience"(*Location* 42).[10] This chapter is all about historicizing the experience of the black man; and of understanding the history into which he must erupt as a subject. Confirming Fanon's recognition of the use of the ideas of négritude as a resistive tactic of survival, the narrator states: "*On comprend que, devant cette ankylose affective du Blanc, j'aie pu décider de pousser mon cri nègre*" (*Peau noire* 98) [In the face of this affective ankylosis of the white man, *it is understandable that I could have* made up my mind to utter my Negro cry" (my emphases) (*BSWM* 122)].

Specifically, Senghor and Césaire's appropriation of blackness and frequent return to pre-colonial richness of black culture, even if seen as an act of "unreason" is ratified by the "necessities of the struggle"; in fact, this move is also subsumed in the narrative of *BSWM* and assumed by the historical narrator: "Since no agreement was possible on the level of reason, I threw myself back toward unreason" (123). Of course one cannot miss the irony of the end of the following quotation: "Out of the necessities of my struggle I had chosen the method of regression, but the fact remained that it was an unfamiliar weapon; here I am at home; I am made of the irrational; I wade in the irrational. Up to the neck in the irrational. And now how my voice vibrates!" (123). Still, the narrator couches his irony in the realization (from hindsight) that this reaction was one of necessity and circumstance. His narration, after all, assumes the folly of such a tactic.

Next the narrator traces, through the voices of Senghor and Césaire, this irrational step: a return to a good primitivism that shows that black culture was independently rich and developed. The quotations are punctuated with an ironic evocation of the excesses of négritude whose aim it is, nevertheless, to "rehabilitate" the image of the black man (see 127). I must stress again that this irony has to be put into the context of the present of the particular narrative in its historical evocation of the different tactics for the survival of black subjecthood within the constraints of colonial domination. In the introduction to Victor Schoelcher's famous text, Césaire rejoices in precisely this rehabilitation of the black man by a white man; a white man who points out various specifics of the richness of the Africa that Europeans would then plunder and destroy. It is in this context that the narrator proclaims: "Get used to me, I am not getting used to anyone" (*BSWM* 131). Again, this quotation is often used to characterize Fanon's general stance toward white culture, when it is actually one he dramatizes in recounting the processes by which blacks have been subjugated in recent history.

Nevertheless, even this step has the black man cornered. It seems that the white man then takes him at his word, and swallows his story about rhythm and the occult, which can be associated with black culture: "Black Magic! Orgies, witches' sabbaths, heathen ceremonies, amulets. Coitus is an occasion to call on the gods of the clan. It is a sacred act, pure, absolute, bringing invisible forces into action" (*BSWM* 126)]. He has to accept, as well, the bond between the earth and the black man: "Between the world and me a relation of coexistence was established" (*BSWM* 128). Césaire's poetry allows the black man to claim, "I made myself the poet of the world" (*BSWM* 129). All this is short-lived. The white man's response is to instruct the black man to study white history, where, he claims, he will find that all this fusion with the earth has already been a stage in the white man's own evolution. For the white man, that is now a thing of the past (see 129). He's been there, done that! Faced with this, our black historical narrator can only weep: "My originality had been torn out of me. I wept a long time, *and then* I began to live again" [my emphases] (*BSWM* 129). This sentence is another convincing moment for the recognition of this chapter as being held together with a specifically historical thread, as I have been arguing here.

What I hope to have shown above in highlighting some of the moves in the narration is that Fanon's text performs what we might call a hybrid reading: on the one hand there is a universalizing "I" that stands in for "the" black man—an implausible concept but one which is reclaimed by the individual black man as a tactic before the stereotypes that precede him as he enters the world. This is the sense of the term being "fixed." It is against this fixing that the agency of the black man has to be engaged. As Fanon writes later, "The object of lumping all Negroes together under the designation of 'Negro people' is to deprive them of any possibility of individual expression. What is thus attempted is to put them under the obligation of matching the idea one has of them" (*Towards* 17). Thus, agency is recognized by Fanon as having to do first with the very basic step of asserting a subjectivity through thought, speech, action—existence. As we have seen, it is asserted that this has to occur at the level of the individual in his [sic] recognition of his self-as-body. Such an assertion of the individual is proved impossible at each turn as the black man is fixed as the stereotypical flesh-eating, white-toothed, grinning, big-footed, earth loving, mother-fucking nigger. His very survival has therefore necessarily depended on privileging a collective, strong, and positive image of blackness; the narrative has necessarily unfolded under the aegis of the historical-universal black narrator. However, Fanon recognizes that there remains a tremendously difficult task of reclaiming the existence of the individual, sensuous, original black man that he heroically (or tragically) wishes to undertake. The tragic role in which the narrator is cast cannot be reconciled with Bhabha's reading of this text: this role implies a conscious understanding and activation of this double role by a specific and specifiable subject, who envisions for itself and for a particular collectivity an escape from precisely the hierarchical situation in which it accomplishes such hybrid moves.

The struggle between the universal, collective, historical "I" and the force of the more subjective personal and still-in-formation "I" makes for a narrative process that can be recognized as hybrid. Hybridity, then, as it emerges from the narrator's project arises not only from simply negotiating between white and black but also from a dramatic struggle with himself and with a construction of his identity. The black narrator locates his selfhood in the process of reconstituting his own body through experience. In this chapter, the tension arising from this dual force is recorded in the irony with which this "I," although assuming the moves of négritude in granting a large part of its narration the first person rather than the third person, still notates the "untruth" of négritude, according to the beliefs of the individual "I." The movement between the "I," the "he," and the "we" examined earlier also produces a more expanded framework to the various statements, requiring greater care in the extraction of the many that might stand in for a "Fanonism."

This theoretical text rests on the authority of the narrating author. Here, the author periodically abandons the authority of his investigative narrative position to recuperate the general self of the experience of the black man under colonialism. This makes it particularly important to follow the moves undertaken in the fluidity of the narrating entity. Still, such a position is not assumed without reservation. These reservations are voiced through the ironical considerations of the narrator that I have emphasized. They point to the necessary solidarity in preserving the collective "I" even with the element of dissent being figured within it. But it also shows the possibility to forge such a discourse of political significance, which does not imply a simple, strategic silencing of difference. Yet, the suggestion is that this collective self must explode at some point in the individual's existence in order to assert a true agency.

The two passages I have pointed to earlier set out the premises and specifications for a methodologically sound reading of interactivity, which is central to the notion of hybridity. They also include a consequential articulation of totality and suggest an ethics that can be tied to the self-as-body before theorizing agency. Further specification included the assertion of the individual's subjecthood as a point from where to re-know itself against colonial stereotyping through its body's interaction with the world. There is no doubt that a certain delineation of colonial culture is taken as the limit that needs to be exploded; but the moves of the narration and the negotiations of the narrating entities occur within the structuring totality of the relationship of the black man to white colonial culture. Fanon's consciousness of totality is underscored by Eileen Julien's examination of the speech he made at the 1956 "First International Conference of Negro Writers and Artists in Paris." Julien notes in this context that "while Fanon on the whole privileges 'national' culture, which is for him a culture born of political struggle, here he seems to admit the vital capacity of 'ethnic' culture, *before* colonialism at least" (159).

Without proper recognition of these narrative moves in Fanon's text, the strong criticism of Sartre's introduction to Senghor's anthology that is frequently commented on loses the sense of poignancy and the deep anguish I wish to restore to it. Fanon expresses dismay that Sartre's text takes away the originality of the black man's struggle in drawing a parallel between the black man and the collective of the proletariat. Following Sartre, just as the struggle of the proletariat is to reach a classless society, so too the authors of negritude wish to render the category of race null and void. The period of negritude, then, becomes a stage in this historical movement rather than an ultimate end. From the reading above, it becomes quite clear that Fanon's thinking does not necessarily clash with such an interpretation. Fanon's hybrid "I" has sufficiently alerted us to the way in which this criticism of Sartre must be read: as a necessary response, for all the veracity and perspicacity of Sartre's analyses, in countering the effect it has on the individual black man. In fact, the narrator must attack Sartre, given the history he has just outlined and the position from which he has outlined it. All this is clear because the irony noted in the assumption of the rhythm-claiming "I" would acquiesce with Sartre's assertion of the transitory nature of this phase. The narrator himself has suggested that this was a phase in the tactics of the strategic survival of the black man under conquest, slavery, colonialism, and the subsequent pigeonholing through stereotypes. It seems, then, following from this, almost an act of bad faith to proclaim that "I needed to lose myself in negritude" (135), when our narrator showed quite clearly that he was skeptical of its truth. This contradiction is not really one, when we are able to validate the multiple functions of the narrating entity, who both mitigated the "I" of negritude with ambiguity through irony, and who now claims before Sartre that negritude needed to be an absolute for the black man.[11]

Sartre's Preface and Fanon's Reaction: Another Look

The anger evident in the narrator's confrontation with Sartre's preface is an emotion that we can pause to consider. As we have seen, at the level of the historical-universal black subject, Sartre's accounting is not altogether implausible. The narrator's rage stems from a much more complex source. It is the rage of the individual black "I" that has strained throughout this narrative to dislodge the universal position, which was the only effective tool against the totalizing discourse of colonialism or at least its totalizing ambition. The poignancy arises from the fact that as readers we have already, if sporadically, encountered the narrator's deep desire to escape the historicity which frames such an assumption of the universal "I," and yet we encounter and follow the moves made in the narration that take it on. This is a remarkable performance of the struggle at the very heart of Fanon's entire project, positioned resolutely between reality and utopia.

Sartre's claim that historical circumstance propelled the black French poet of negritude to assume a position of poetic grace that made it superior to all other poetic attempts of the time (qtd in *BSWM* 134), causes Fanon to protest that: "and so it is not I who make a meaning for myself, but it is the meaning that was already there, pre-existing, waiting for me. It is not out of my bad nigger's misery, my bad nigger's teeth, my bad nigger's hunger that I will shape a torch with which to burn down the world, but it is the torch that was already there, waiting for that turn of history" (*BSWM* 134). He turns on Sartre: "Jean-Paul Sartre has destroyed black zeal. Jean-Paul Sartre had forgotten that the Negro suffers in his body quite differently from the white man" (*BSWM* 138). Here, we must pay attention to the source of the voice that pronounces Sartre's sympathetic, enlightened engagement with the question of the black man to be necessarily inadequate, even inaccurate. Such inadequacy and inaccuracy do not stem from any kind of essentialism but rather from over-determination by external factors.[12] Fanon's narrative voice speaks from a point in history when only a black man (of "epidermalized" blackness) can restore his subjecthood through his own agency. He continues: "I defined myself as an absolute intensity of beginning. So I took up my negritude, and with tears in my eyes I put its machinery back together again" (*BSWM* 138). The repudiation of Sartre has to be accomplished somehow from the point of view of this historical-universal black "I." But within this repudiation also lies the despair of the individual black man who has been cut off from his joyous, individual self and who recognizes that négritude does indeed offer a miraculous weapon.

Given this over-determination, the narrator must turn on this existentialist whom Fanon so greatly admires and whose work provokes a ceaseless dialogue for his own intellectual reasoning. This narrative act underscores the poignancy of the narrator's tears. Sartre's comments become, at the simple level evident from the text, deeply offensive to this narrator. But the tears also signal the other muted "I" whose discourse is as yet (at least in evoking this historical, collective black experience) to be properly articulated. Fanon himself gives us a clue elsewhere: "[w]henever a man of color protests [proteste], there is alienation. Whenever a man of color rebukes [réprouve], there is alienation" (*BSWM* 60). The alienation of the black man from his own psyche, the impossibility to escape the interiorization (specifically for the Martinican) of white cultural values in which he himself is denigrated, and, in the end, the difficulty of assuming an individual subject position, all channel dismay as his required reaction as the historical-universal black man to Sartre's pronunciation. Such an emotional response can be retraced to both the individual and the universal identities of the narrator. This complexity is evident when we recall that Fanon made great efforts to return to Sartre, this time in person, for the preface to the *Wretched of the Earth*. Fanon will later explain why acts of "love" at the individual level must be rejected because of the overarching structure of colonialism in which the black man is denied his individuality.[13]

The gratefulness that we experience toward Fanon, then, despite his oversights indicated by many, is for having somehow given us the experience, through the narrative, of an affective encounter with the reality of the black man's history, but also of all the possibility of an individual "I" within it—a possibility that, nevertheless, this narrative cannot actualize. The reasons for this, of course, as we have already indicated, go well beyond the aesthetic of this text and point to the realities that Fanon will more directly address in his future work and life.

Movement to and fro between a recognition of reality (of the fixing of the black man that is transformed into the historical-universal black "I") and a struggle for utopia (as the assertion of the singular, unique, original, "I" that happens to be black) characterizes the impetus of the narrative in this entire chapter. The narrative positions assumed correspond to historical moments that specifically refer to the subjugation of the black man under colonialism and the as-yet-to-occur full inscription of each individual black man (or at least such a potential) in the societies Fanon describes. The frequent breaking down of the narrative position through the interception of irony as well as references to breaking down by the narrator (weeping), characterize this impossible task of reclaiming black subjectivity that Fanon dramatizes for us in this chapter. Such impossibility within the narrative exceeds the text in its correspondence with the impossibility to express black subjectivity as credible agents in colonial society. Fanon's take on irony in the specific context of the Antillean is an indication of the power of his unremitting analyses of culture. It also confirms our reading of irony in *BSWM*.

In reflecting on the relationship between "West Indians and Africans" in an essay published in *Esprit* in 1955, Fanon writes that while irony in Europe "protects against existential anguish, in Martinique it protects against the awareness of Negritude" (*Towards* 19). The Antillean's cultural anxiety plays out in his relationship with Africa and Africans, with reference to which he constantly needs to reaffirm his difference. Whites, with whom the Antillean (believed he) shared the same culture would, of course, never be mistaken for Africans. "But what a catastrophe if the West Indian should suddenly be taken for an African!" (*Towards* 20). It was Césaire who first articulated that "it was fine and good to be a Negro," which created a "scandal" (see *Towards* 21). But a second event in 1939 would turn the tables on Césaire's fate, which seemed to indicate he would be dismissed for a lunatic. For four years, the French sailors (of the Vichy government) from the ships Béarn and Emile-Bertin flooded Fort-de-France at a time when the economy was already suffering. The sailors, many who were accompanied by their families and brought into contact with the Martinicans who resented their presence due to the particular, added strain of supporting them at this time, inaugurated a "racist" encounter (*Towards* 22–23).

The Martinicans' experience of these sailors' racism allowed them to exercise an interesting intellectual maneuver in order to cling to Frenchness. Before the French racist sailors for whom he was a nigger, the Martinican reasons thus: "Since these men did so consider him, this meant that they were not true Frenchmen. Who knows, perhaps they were Germans?" (*Towards* 23)! If in *BSWM* Fanon showed how it was through his own ethical lapse that the black man could become a nigger, here he shows how he escapes being a nigger by a maneuver that the narrator presents with scathing irony: "[. . .] [T]he

West Indian felt obliged to defend himself. Without Césaire this would have been difficult for him. But Césaire was there, and people joined him in chanting the once-hated song to the effect that it is fine and good to be a Negro! . . ." (*Towards* 23). The Antillean's strategic valorizing or devalorizing of his blackness continues to be a source of Moliéresque irony for Fanon:

> Fifteen years before, [the West Indians] said to the Europeans, "Don't pay attention to my black skin, it's the sun that has burned me, my soul is as white as yours." After 1945 they changed their tune. They said to the Africans, "Don't pay attention to my white skin, my soul is as black as yours, and that is what matters." (*Towards* 24)

It is at the close of this essay that we have a reflection on the irony of the historical-universal black narrator from the specific positioning of the Antillean. "It thus seems that the West Indian, after the great white error is now living in the great black mirage" (*Towards* 27).

The frequent citations made from this much-read chapter of *BSWM* that we have examined here, such as "I am the one who waits," in postcolonial criticism need to better account for the careful positioning of this "I" that pronounces them within the text. The charge (or praise) that Fanon does not historicize should be carefully reconsidered in that the entire chapter is an historical evocation of the possibilities of the black subject dramatized in the narrative position. The poetic evocation of the enthusiasm, individuality, originality, and vastness of the individual black soul who can assume the role of a legitimate interlocutor is constantly cut down by the reality of his existence within the totality of white colonial culture. The black man's entry, through assimilation, into white colonial culture occurs through a disavowal, an ethical slip, or, in properly Sartrean terms, an act of bad faith. It is in this way that Fanon ratifies Sartre's idea of responsibility. As we have seen, although it is evident that it is colonial culture that steroetypes the nigger, Fanon is at pains to reclaim and reassert the agency of the black man within that paradigm: it is his ethical slip that allows himself to become a nigger, because it is the same agency that will have to refuse niggerhood through an explosion—at the level of the individual and also, theorized later, at the level of entire, socially coherent totalities. Fanon's engagement with the problem of the black man's subjectivity is revealed through a hybrid narrative where the terms between which the hybrid appears are clearly stated but, as we have seen, an accounting of both history and totality are properly figured within it. After the somewhat ambiguous critique of the writers of negritude as well as of Sartre's assessment of them, the final lines of this chapter adjust this position by an oblique homage paid to both:

> I feel in myself a soul as immense as the world, truly as souls as deep as the deepest of rivers, my chest has the power to expand without limit. [. . .] I wanted to rise but the disemboweled silence fell back upon me, its wings paralyzed. Without responsibility, straddling Nothingness and Infinity, I began to weep. (*BSWM* 140)

The first sentence is an assumption of the language, rhythm, and spirit of the Cesairean paradigm much as the last is a nod to Sartre's text. The weeping with which the chapter concludes evokes, in the same sentence, the revised title of Sartre's Being and Nothingness. The struggle for transcendence plays out in the first sentence, but it is cut short by the paralysis of silence: speech is Fanon's primary site of analytic operation. Fanon's impossible desire to create a subject without dialogism is related to a need to be without compromise (suggesting a notion of "authenticity") and precisely to escape this hierarchic relationship with the white man. Yet, a fundamental understanding of the dialogism of thought and existence itself is based in his training as a psychiatrist. The primacy of speech for Fanon becomes a point of anguish because it presumes a dialogic quality. The primacy of speech, and its bases in dialogism on one hand, and the need to break out of a dialectical relationship with the white man on the other characterize much of the tautness of the text of *BSWM*. It is also with the negotiation of these two positions that an account of Fanonian hybridity might proceed.

The full import of the end of the quotation above requires further unpacking. We have examined the sense in which the black man is, first and foremost, for Fanon, an ethical being whose responsibility includes a proper recognition of who he is "outside of" or despite white culture. Such recognition would necessarily entail engagement with the structure of white culture within which his lapse turns him into a nigger. Fanon looks back, in his letter of resignation from Blida-Joinville, at the notion of individual enthusiasm that he theorized in *BSWM*: "But what can a man's enthusiasm and devotion achieve if everyday reality is a tissue of lies of cowardice, of contempt for man?" (*Towards* 52). This personal act is one that both ratifies individual agency as well as records its insufficiency. Although Fanon recognizes that an individual's agency is not sufficient to oppose such a structure, he also realizes, as we have shown, that it is essential for the individual to record an ethical stand in his interactions at this level. Such ethical behavior has implications for the totality within which it operates and without which it would have no meaning.[14] It is a lapse in such an ethical duty that allows the black man, and specifically the Antillean, to succumb to an inferiority complex. This entire chapter has been about the tactics of the universal-historical black "I" within an overarching colonial structure. If the black man's being has been under threat in this chapter, the latter ends by showing how he is not grounded in being, but rather uncomfortably placed between Nothingness and Infinity. Because transcendence presupposes immanence, the impossibility of the black man's existence within colonial culture renders absurd any aspirations to transcendence.

Figuring Fanon within the rhetoric of hybridity could be instinctively rejected precisely because we have come to associate with him more revolutionary ideals of anti-colonial struggle. If the many criticisms of the appropriation of a hybrid Fanon in a dominant strain of postcolonial studies with a strong influence of postmodern theory are to be taken seriously, I propose it is time to do so in the name of this hybridizing text. It is my hope that the reading I have provided here can suggest interesting leads into the rest of Fanon's work. I have also suggested, proceeding from an effective engagement with Fanon's text, some concrete theoretical adjustments and limits to the notion of hybridity, specifically with regard to totality and the relationship of the self/body to ethics and agency.

For Fanon, "[t]he characteristic of a culture is to be open, permeated by spontaneous, generous fertile lines of force" (*Towards* 34). Yet, the importance of the notion of "structure" in the identification of a culture is evident: "Exoticism is one of the forms of [. . .] simplification. It allows no cultural confrontation. There is on the one hand a culture in which qualities of dynamism, of growth, of depth can be recognized. As against this, we find characteristics, curiosities, things, never a structure" (*Towards* 35). In this way, Fanon's positive vision of cultural contact privileges the idea of confrontation within historical specificity. Following his thought, viewing dynamism, expansion, and depth in a culture is insufficient and simplistic if individual elements cannot be connected to some kind of overarching logic or totality.

AFTERWORD

Why Hybridity Now?

Given the currency of the notion of hybridity today, it is first necessary to make some basic distinctions and specifications pertaining to its usage in postcolonial analyses. The first is the distinction between what I provisionally termed diaspora and creolization, the former being linked in theoretical discourse to an "older" strategy for the terms in which identifications of groups and individuals occur. The later notion of creolization involves a more dynamic engagement with the question of the past, along with a loss in privilege of the affect of trauma. Still, as we have seen in all instances both diaspora and creolization as strategies are essential to any discourse of hybridity. The characterization of a discourse as hybrid entails the proper recognition of two poles such as diaspora and creolization. These poles are manifested in the oscillation between the past and the present, the collective and the personal, victimhood and heroism, or the national and the ethnic, for example. In each case, the relationship to History as well as an articulation of Totality were shown to be essential for a proper understanding of the generation of such concepts and thus for a restoration of any of their radical possibilities. Following from this, a method of hybrid reading was adduced by carefully following such multiple sources of coherence within particular discourses.

Hybridization has been seen as the watered-down or even apolitical course of action when faced with an encounter. According to this logic, a more revolutionary choice is given as confrontation:

> One of the necessary political tasks today is to rework the difference and the inequality in hybridizations of the global and the local, to discover how the old patrimonies of humanity and the new patrimonies of globalization are at the same time specific modes through which local cultures found themselves and had to decide if they would enter into *war or into*

> *hybridization*. [. . .] Perhaps the patrimonies that are worth keeping formed not only of works in which a self-sufficient history (official or popular) is sedimented or of products well tailored by the market so that everyone is able to digest them, but also with those works in which beats the imminence of uncertain encounter, when a collection of men and women feels challenged by another culture and has to choose *between hybridization and confrontation*. (Néstor García Canclini 50) [my emphases]

I have shown throughout this book how hybridization as a process does not occur without reliance upon the implicit notion of confrontation. Such an understanding culminated in my reconsideration of Edouard Glissant and Frantz Fanon. The method of hybrid reading that Fanon's writing in *Black Skin, White Masks* allows us to describe consisted of seeking out points of confrontation between the personal idiosyncratic narrator and the universal-historical one, between the notion of aggression and love, between self-image and stereotype, or between the dialogism essential to "speech" and the necessity for independent originality that would fall outside the oppressive gaze of the colonizer. Glissant's theory of *Relation*, with the distinctions he makes between creolization and métissage, allows us to configure this notion of confrontation from within a theory of hybridity as a development of the Marxian concept of contradiction.

In my study of language and ethnicity in Mauritius as well as in the notion of métissage in La Réunion, it was evident that within the particular hybrid society in question, a history of precisely such confrontation is implicated. For this reason, History and Totality were found essential to a proper understanding of hybridity. Social manifestations of readable hybridity as well as theoretical methods of hybrid analyses come together, in this way, to provide a more coherent model for hybridized reading, both within a theoretical framework of hybridity and within a societal example of it. It is only what I would call an incomplete notion of hybridity (with the two shortcomings I have consistently elucidated in both theoretical and political/cultural discourse) that can present such a choice of *either* hybridity *or* confrontation.

The idea of "choice" within the hybrid is most productive in a different context. In both Fanon and Glissant, it is connected to the type of dialectic posited between reality and utopia and it is called up at the moment of an ethical decision made by a "free" subject, thus evoking the Sartrean concepts of both freedom and choice. Such estimation calls on individuals to enter into a conscious ethical engagement in their orientation with otherness, in this way disqualifying the activation of simplistic notions of difference without an ethical evaluation of its significance.

Insistence upon the individual might seem somewhat incongruous when speaking of two intellectuals such as Fanon and Glissant, whose work and life are so deeply committed to the idea of the collective. But as we have seen, both consistently return to the individual as the authentic site for working out an ethics of freedom within the larger project of the self-emancipation of groups of people. When hybridity is relocated, as I have done in this book, to its relationship to contradiction and totality, it emerges as fairly robust forms of politics in processes connected to decolonization, diasporization, and globalization. It also becomes the very ethics of forms of cognitive mapping.

Notes

Chapter 1

1. I am not going to engage in discussion of the delineation of this field. For such questions, see Michel, Bahri, Li, Appiah, Dirlik, McClintock, and Shohat and Stam, for example. Suffice it to say, it is not merely to the "periodization" (i.e., after colonialism) that the term "postcolonial" refers; and the centrality of colonialism is also indeed debatable. However, drawing from such discussions, I refer to the complex situation of particular regions in relation to world economics, culture, and politics, as it has been inherited after the vigorous period of official colonialism coinciding with the activation of newer dominating forces, many of which stem directly or indirectly from the colonial venture, from both within and without these regions.

2. See Fludernik and Stewart for a discussion of such terminology.

3. I mean quite seriously that this is provisional even in the context of this book. For this chapter, I am separating the notion of diaspora from that of creolization and assigning them somewhat contradictory meanings. In the chapters that follow, terminology involving hybridity is specified either for the societal context, or for the particular theorist being examined.

4. Still it is important to keep in mind that the idea of diaspora does not immediately imply a homogenization of the diasporic group in question. Consider, for example, Tejumola Olaniyan's sensitivity precisely to the conflicts within notions of diaspora in his *Scars of Conquest / Masks of Resistance*. In fact, the modified use of "diaspora" in the last three decades by Gilroy, for example "is introduced in large part to account for difference among African-derived populations [. . .]." (Edwards 30). In this way, his usage places itself postdiaspora, as described above by the term creolization.

5. Among other revisions to this view, see, for example, the pieces in Yiddel and Kemp's *Arms Akimbo: Africana Women in Contemporary Literature*.

6. With perhaps less success, Jonas Rano, more recently suggests the term "créolitude" in his book of the same title.

7. Gilroy also wants to resuscitate a revised notion of diaspora, placing it with "creolization" as described in this chapter: "With its biblical force somewhat diluted, the idea of diaspora can be useful again here. [. . .] Diaspora allows for a complex conception of sameness and for versions of solidarity that do not need to repress the dif-

ferences within a dispersed group in order to maximize the differences between one 'essential' community and others. [. . .] Identity conceived diasporically resists reification in petrified forms even if they are indubitably authentic" (252).

8. The Gilroy quotation in the previous note also emphasizes this point.

9. Lionnet's second book, for example, in examining a range of postcolonial women writers from Martinique to Egypt shows how they "have been redefining traditional conceptions of history and culture, literature and identity. They create new paradigms that represent, through innovative and self-reflexive literary techniques, both linguistic and geographic exile, displacements from margins to a metropolitan center, and intercultural exchanges" (*Postcolonial Representations* 7). In her earlier work, "renewed connections to the past can emancipate us, provided they are used to elaborate empowering myths for living in the present and for affirming our belief in the future" (*Autobiographical Voices* 7). Similarly, Hall indicates that in the second and more desirable way of thinking of cultural identity, difference is crucial just as is a more strategic relationship to the past rather than the acceptance of an "essentialised past" (see "Cultural Identity and Diaspora" 394).

10. I am considering its impulse as one of creolization in the most elementary way (here postnégritude). Glissant himself will accuse the créolistes of a new essentialism (*Caribbean Discourse* 90). For the emerging idea of métissage in early African Francophone writing, see Lüsebrink. Despite Senghor's ideas of métissage in the sense of a way of being "negro" within a more interactive framework or his conception of négritude as a form of humanism, René Depestre's *Bonjour et adieu à la negritude* shows the way in which such a conception played into the colonial paradigm (see especially 81–82). Abiola Irele rightly points out how a critic of Senghor's negritude such as Soyinka is not as far removed from Senghor as Soyinka would like in his reliance upon some kind of African essence (12). Gilroy himself, as we will see, speaks of such an experience of being black. These points serve to indicate how both impulses described here as diasporic and creolizing characterize many strategies of resistance.

11. This echoes, for example, Deleuze and Guattari's general idea in *Anti-Oedipus* that world-modernity isomorphizes rather than homogenizes.

12. Apart from the discussion here, Bhabha's theory figures further in the following chapters, particularly chapter 3 and later when discussing Glissant and Fanon.

13. The women writers Lionnet examines are characterized by her as *cultural "métis, créoles"* (*Autobiographical Voices* 21).

14. For an excellent critical study of the Latin American context and move from transculturation to hybridity, see Trigo.

15. It is important to bear in mind that Lionnet's views on métissage and indeterminacy are to be understood within the specific framework of her literary project in which she has a "somewhat utopian [] view of writing as an enabling force in the creation of a plural self, one that thrives on ambiguity and multiplicity, on affirmation of differences . . ." (*Autobiographical Voices* 16). Elsewhere Lionnet notes that "writing [to break out from colonizing languages] becomes the only key to the (utopian?) creation of a different, heterogenous, and multicolored future [. . .]" (*Autobiographical Voices* 27).

Endorsing completely the utopian visions of writing, I find, however, that there is a central contradiction in the conception of métissage, which is not resolved theoretically. The idea of métissage as transculturation via Nancy Morejón (where there is reciprocal influence and no single element dominates) (*Autobiographical Voices* 15) is not really compatible with the image of métis who employs an "esthetics of the ruse" (*Autobiographical Voices* 18) because the latter indicates a struggle against domination in a way that the former does not. In *Autobiographical Voices*, the thrust of métissage becomes an "emancipatory metaphor for the inevitably relational and interdependent nature of peoples, nations, and countries [. . .]" (29).

16. See, for example, Hall "Cultural Identity and Diaspora" 394–96 for a very forceful statement of this notion of difference.

17. But this is not to privilege the subaltern as the site of some authenticity. It is rather to understand in what ways hybridity is of interest in subaltern contact, struggle, and negotiation with outright domination or hegemony.

18. This task is admirably accomplished by Nick Nesbitt in his *Voicing Memory*. Nesbitt argues, for example, that Hegel's notion of *Entfremdung* informs not just the dialectical thought of Marx and Kojève but is equally rethought by Glissant, Fanon, and Césaire.

19. I am, of course, referring to the sentence: "*All* third world texts are *necessarily* [. . .] allegorical . . ." [my emphases] ("Third World Literature" 69).

20. This suggestion was previously made in Prabhu and Quayson.

21. My interest is to work out more specifically the ideas of transnational and translational hybridity that Bhabha suggests (see *Location* 172–75 in particular).

Chapter 2

1. Axel Gauvin shows how so-called illiterates, with minimal instruction in a simple script for Creole, can demonstrate reading competence in Creole, though not in French (*Du créole opprimé*). This problem of the relation of a local language to the colonial one, particularly in the context of education, is not unique. See, for example, Rasool and Alexander for a discussion of this issue with regard to the African continent, Rughoonundun ("Les langues") and Chaudenson with regard to Mauritius, and Giraud and Manesse, Bentolila, and Damoiseau with regard to the French Caribbean. As in some of the cases mentioned above, the fact that the writing of Creoles has had to be hastened within such a structural position, of course, has added consequences.

2. For a study on métissage in the literature of La Réunion, see Jean-Claude Carpanin Marimoutou's "Ecrire métis."

3. All translations of Boyer's text are my own.

4. See Nietzsche 102–06.

5. See Nietzsche 96–102.

6. On Chinese immigration to La Réunion see Chane-Kune *Aux origins*.

7. See Nietzsche 106–08.

8. Whites who moved to the highlands and black maroons who escaped to the mountains can be seen in a similar position, structurally, within the economic system of La Réunion. They all farmed their own land and raised cattle, selling the excess in the plains. However, they did not participate in an ongoing way in the larger economic system of the island-colony: i.e., both groups existed outside of plantation slavery, even if slavery gave birth to them in different ways: the ex-slaves through escaping it and the poorer whites because they did not have access to slaves. Monique Agenor's *Be-Maho* explores this historical reality in a fascinating story.

9. Fanon sharply critiques Mayotte Capécia's autobiographical *Je suis martiniquaise* for her constant efforts at what he calls "lactification." He fails to read the position from which this desire is generated as well as what benefits of this "lactification" the character/author seeks (see *Black Skin, White Masks* 41–62).

10. We shall discuss the full meaning of the sense of *Relation* when discussing Glissant in chapter 6.

11. The production of an important study in Creole, entitled *Lanseyeman la Réunion in plan kolonialise*, by a group of five teachers at different levels, including two "*zorèys*" or metropolitans, under the name of "Sarcemate" (the name of a famous maroon or runaway slave) marks a pertinent point. This study or evaluation of the system was done entirely in Creole, using a simple phonological graphic code, thus proving that Creole could be used for serious purposes, as well as providing an analysis of "letoufeman kiltirele" [cultural stifling] that the educational system was accomplishing.

12. While this is beyond the scope of this chapter, ideas about the functioning of the world and herself in it are rendered with some reference or recourse to Creole. For quick example for Creolophone and/or Francophone readers, the family's entry into the middle class through their occupation of their newly built house: "Cyclone à ou dehors, 'éclair à ou dehors, nous: en'dans. C'était cela bâtir" (16); or her identity as a "mixed-blood," to her, "bâtard-chinoise" (18). There are also various specifications in the text that the conversation takes place in Creole (18, for example).

13. Further discussion of the Mauritian situation follows in chapters 4 and 5.

14. See Prabhu "Mariama Bâ's" 245–46.

15. In a different way, Frantz Fanon also sees the individual's crisis as being that of Martinican society's itself. "Antillean society is a neurotic society, a society of 'comparison.' Hence we were driven from the individual back to the social structure. If there is a taint, it lies not in the 'soul' of the individual but rather in that of the environment" (*BSWM* 212).

16. The term signal indicates the type of signifying process that eschews ambiguity and has a universal currency, while a sign, especially in the formulation of Charles S. Peirce, implies interactions between the object, the representamen, and the interpretant in an ongoing process, where each of the three elements in the sign relation "shifts roles as further determinations and representations are realized" (Paramentier 29).

Chapter 3

1. All translations of the novel are my own.

2. Interestingly, the term "noir" at this time suggests any racial group that was not white.

3. A number of my former graduate colleagues, now Francophone scholars "at large" in the U.S. academy, will recall this ambiguity as having been presented and discussed through an excellent history of progressive French thinkers from Montesquieu to André Gide by Elisabeth Mudimbé-Boyi in her seminar on Francophone Studies at Duke University in the mid-1990s.

4. It is significant that Jameson chooses the term "antinomy" rather than "contradiction" because for him, contradiction can be resolved. An antinomy remains a parallel reality that cannot even be brought into dialogue with its other (see *Seeds of Time* see 1–8). Antinomy, as a textual articulation of social contradiction demands a more narrative process for its reformulation, if its resolution remains impossible. The identification of antinomy in cultural objects is seen, in Jameson's dialectical criticism, as a symptom of social contradiction (see "On Interpretation" in *Political Unconscious* 15–102).

5. My translation, based on Gauvin's French translation.

6. In the first group he names: "le prolétariat réunionnnais, les colons (dans le sens de métayers), les petits propriétaires, les petits commerçants, etc."[1] and in the second: "les fonctionnaires, les cadres des entreprises métropolitaines, les importateurs, les usiniers, les membres des 'professions libérales'"[2] (Gauvin *Du créole opprimé* 68). [1. The réunionese proletariat, the colonizers (in the sense of farmers), small proprietors, small merchants, etc. 2. The functionaries, employees of metropolitan businesses, importers, factory owners, members o the "liberal professions."]

Chapter 4

1. In the colonial period the term "Creole" first meant whites born in the colony and later came to encompass all aspects of culture and society taking root in the colony. However, reference to "Creoles" as individuals or the group means for colonial reference, whites of the colony, as in the novel treated in chapter 3. Closer to independence, the notion of the Creole population whose votes were being vied for from different factions includes the lighter skinned *mulâtres* and the darker skinned *créoles*. What seems like such a crude descriptor was used commonly and is understood in Mauritian culture even today. Although the term *morisyen* has been proposed to replace Creole (language) in this chapter I retain the use of Creole because it is the collusion between language and ethnicity/race that I am treating and it is in this complicity that I examine this term. Each use is specified by the context in which it is evoked and clarifications are provided when needed.

2. For a detailed historical introduction to the area, see Dieter Braun.

3. On language competence in Mauritius, see Peter Stein.

4. For a more general statement that linguistic antagonisms represent conflicts of interests among different groups of people in the African and Caribbean contexts see Nzepa.

5. For a more detailed discussion of the introduction of "Oriental" languages in the Mauritian school curriculum, see Hookoomsing and Rughoonundun "Les langues."

6. Regarding non-African slaves in the Mascarenes, see Gerbeau.

7. For a discussion of this comparative aspect, see Nathalie Melas especially 277–78.

8. See Boisson and Louit.

9. The term "public discourse" encompasses speeches and other pronouncements made by government officials (some examples are Ministers, Members of Parliament, or the lawyer for the indentured Indian laborers) as well as individuals who have some connection with the administration of the island (for example, Bernadin de Saint-Pierre, a high-profile French visitor introduced to the colonial administrators upon his arrival). The point is that this excludes less formal but no less important milieus from where one might examine other types of representation of the same questions, such as jokes, proverbs, music, or dance. This is not an exhaustive examination of any particular source of public discourse. However, the examples studied are emblematic of the tendencies in official language that is intrinsically related to the administration, be it colonial or postcolonial.

10. An anthropological analysis of these groups is provided in Ericksen *Communicating*.

11. For more details on the electoral process in general, see Centre d'études et de recherches sur les sociétés de l'océan indien (1984).

12. The creation of an independent organization, *Ledikasyon pu Travayer*, in 1975 and its ongoing activities are still important steps in acknowledging Mauritian Creole and its valorization in the daily life of monolingual Creole speakers. This organization works with adults and is committed to rendering all Mauritians literate.

13. See Alladin 110.

14. See, for example, the Mauritius Legislative Council Debates No: 46 of the year 1948–49: 24 June and 19 July 1949 for strong speeches by Ramgoolam in favor of the government adjudicating the sale of farmland and the fixing of prices of such sales. Needless to say, the bulk of such sales were occurring between the whites who owned the land and Indians who had toiled over it for generations.

15. These three texts have been recently published together as *Ile de France: voyages et controverses*.

16. Most recently, and after submission of this manuscript, Megan Vaughan's very welcome *Creating the Creole Island* sheds light on slavery in Mauritius in the eighteenth century.

17. However, the performance of séga music and dance at five-star hotels, although attracting some "locals" as well, becomes primarily a showcasing of Mauritian culture for tourists and tends to be closer to what Edouard Glissant might disapprovingly call "folklore" or an artificial reproduction of an aspect of culture that is not naturally created from within it as he cautions against the revival of Creole language in Martinique that he observed (*Caribbean Discourse* xxv).

18. Since writing this piece, Bérenger's coalition lost the 2005 elections to Navin Ramgoolam's Alliance-Sociale.

Chapter 5

1. In this chapter the term "Creole" is used to indicate all parts of what we have understood to be the "general population" except whites. I have chosen to use Creole rather than distinguish métis or mulâtre, which are the terms used for those of lighter skin, because my aim is to consider the ways in which precisely the distinction works against any kind of solidarity of all those of light and dark skin whose efforts to enter white culture are barred even if differentially. Solidarity within this group and between this group and Indians becomes impossible when the distinction between lighter and darker nonwhites is upheld. Terms such as métis or mulâtre are used when required due to their use in the literary texts or when the distinction is being discussed. Unless otherwise specified, Creole refers to all those not considered white or Asian (Chinese or Indian). I have also capitalized the "c" to match terms such as Indian or Chinese rather than white, thus setting up a Creole ethnicity or cultural group rather than a racial combination. While the reach of such an effort remains quite evidently tied to this academic discussion, I hope to show that the type of thinking it allows might in fact have greater scope.

2. All translations of Humbert's and de Souza's novels that follow are my own.

3. The relationship of Yolande with André functions much like that described in *Métisse*; André, however, is able to "pass" while Lucien does not have this possibility.

4. Lionnet makes a comparison between Sassita and Mme Morin on the basis of passivity (see *Autobiographical Voices* 214).

5. See Joubert and Joubert and Raminadrasoa for references to the history of the literature of this region. More recently, see the edited volume by Issur and Hookoomsing.

6. In 1807, the British Parliament's Abolition of the Slave Trade Act posed a threat to the French colonialists in Mauritius. The planters rebelled and there were periods when there was no British ship allowed into Mauritius during this period. However, in 1835 the act came into effect; slaves were forced to work for four years as paid laborers. In the mean time, labor was being imported primarily from India.

7. Unlike La Réunion, there is no hilly retreat for many maroons to have survived. The hilly regions are far more easily accessible on Mauritius.

8. The "monstrousness" of the mixed-blood has been studied (see Stepan, for example), although this is less of an issue in the Mauritian context. I am referring more to how this group began to be seen, and could see itself, in a new *role* in the colonial framework as the educated (and thus privileged) intermediary group that would enter the administration in large numbers.

9. See, for example, Wallerstein's discussion of this in "The Bourgeois(ie) as concept and Reality." in *Race, Nation, Class* (especially 138–39).

10. This negative view of the intermediary is echoed not only in postcolonial theory but also by various writers, notably Morocco's Driss Chraïbi. See my "Theorizing" on this subject.

11. It is true that old ethnic alliances are gradually coming to be seen as insufficient. But a more sustained and overt recognition of this fact would radically change the very availability of both the older racial and newer ethnic classifications.

12. This is a citation from the novel.

13. Parallel to the French (to French language and France), Biharis (to Bhojpuri/Hindi and India), Muslims (mostly to Urdu or Gujerati and India), Tamils (Tamil and India), Telugus (Telugu and India), Chinese (Mandarin or Hakka and China).

14. "[J]e m'habillais plus sagement de jupes et de chemisiers bien fermés, je renonçais à la verroterie et aux rubans de couleur vive. Je copiais les petites jeunes filles de bonne famille" (113) [I dressed more appropriately in skirts and blouses that were well closed, I gave up costume jewelry and brightly colored ribbons. I copied the little girls from good families].

15. See also p. 453 for a similar interrogation of Anne.

16. Although Lionnet remarks that this moment of the denunciation of the fetus "is the immolation of the métis, the créole, as symbol, product and (pro)creation of Western colonialism . . ." the thrust of the moment, for her, is that Anne "aim[s] the insult at her sister but thereby amputating herself, depriviledging otherness as radically *other* in order to co-opt it, to abort it" (*Autobiographical Voices* 212). In her larger framework, Lionnet is concerned with the move to claim "specificity," especially by the woman (writer). In this novel, she reads the portrait as undermining the traditional "heroine" to reconstruct that of the female writer (see especially *Autobiographical Voices* 221–22).

17. See especially Ahmad; also, more recently Bensmaïa.

18. Originally a dance of the dead performed by Africans.

19. Referring quite simply to those who wanted it and those who did not.

20. "Should the study of race relations, in this meaning of the word, be distinguished from the study of ethnicity or ethnic relations? Pierre van den Berghe [. . .] does not think so, but would rather regard 'race' relations as a special case of ethnicity. Others, among them Michael Banton [. . .], have argued the need to distinguish between race and ethnicity. In Banton's view, race refers to the categorization of

'them' [. . .]. However, ethnicity can assume many forms, and since ethnic ideologies tend to stress common descent among their members, their distinction between race and ethnicity is a problematic one, even if Banton's distinction between groups and categories can be useful [. . .]. I shall not, therefore, distinguish between race relations and ethnicity" (Eriksen *Ethnicity and Nationalism* 5).

21. Wallerstein is talking of the period following World War II, and referring less to "Third World" areas here. I should qualify that in using this terminology in the context of Mauritius, the "placement" of this new bourgeoisie would still be intermediate rather than top level. This would still be reserved for the small minority of whites who today have diversified from sugar to include such institutions as banks, for example.

22. Religion is not an entirely distinct category from ethnicity. The languages spoken/claimed also are able to communicate religion. For example, Bhojpuri, Tamil, Telegu, and Hindi speakers are Hindus; Gujarati speakers and claimers of Urdu (Arab in early census) tend to be Muslim; Tamils who claim French tend to be converted Christians.

23. Most actions relating to Africa have been actions of the State: through delegations, organization of the African Unity Conference (1976). Ramgoolam was notably Chairman of the Organisation of African Unity in 1976. Far more recently, writers, for example, Ananden's *Rue la Poudrière*, look to African publishers as well.

24. Personal communication, Dev Virahsawmy, August 1999. Dev Virahsawmy is Mauritius' famous playwright (in Creole), whose most recent international success was *Toufann*. Once a prominent member of the radical MMM discussed in chapter 4, Virahsawmy has turned more toward artistic production.

25. Maunick, the poet who overtly paid homage to the négritude movement. Léopold Senghor wrote the preface to his *Ensoleillé vif*.

26. Wallerstein notes concerning this group that "these civil servants were not bourgeois at all in the sense of playing any of the traditional economic roles of the bourgeois as entrepreneur, employer of wage labor, innovator, risk taker, profit maximizer. Well, that is not quite correct. Administrative bourgeois often played these classic economic roles, but when they did, they were not celebrated for it, but rather denounced for corruption!" (140).

Chapter 6

1. In the francophone context, both Chris Bongie and H. Adlai Murdoch draw substantially from Glissant's work. In tracking Edouard Glissant's work, primarily from his fiction but also through his theoretical texts, Celia Britton, more recently, provides us with various points of contact between this Caribbean and French theorist and other influential theorists of postcoloniality. The authoritative work of Glissant's first translator, J. Michael Dash, addresses the difficulty of Glissant's early reception and the coming of his later accolades in an historical view of this intellectual's long career. Few working outside the field of "French studies" turn to his work in much detail.

2. Nick Nesbitt makes a cogent connection between historical experience and dialectical relation in Glissant (see 175), concentrating on Glissant's novel *Malemort* and citing his *Traitée du Tout-monde*. I am interested in pursuing, here, the definition and processes quite specific to *Relation*, which are laid out in *Poétique*. In the end, I find Nesbitt's conclusion that Glissant's call for biological ecologism for Martinique is really based in the logic of the Enlightenment (186) less convincing (at least in the way he presents it) in that this logic is not really pursued nor explicated in the analyses of Glissant's work. If a specific reference were being made to Horkheimer and Adorno's *Dialectic of Enlightenment*, it did not become obvious to me.

3. Although there are various differences among these theories, I will restrict my comparison to Homi K. Bhabha's theory of hybridity discussed in the introduction.

4. See Prabhu and Quayson for a discussion of these Glissantian terms.

5. When Chris Bongie writes that he will be (even if "strategically") "isolating some of [Glissant's] political conjectures in 'Discours antillais' from the context of his work as a whole and putting them into question from the perspective of a postmodernism that can no longer credit the imperative of self-possessions that undergrids them" (354), it is to undo the very basic characteristic of his writing—the circularity, the nonexplosive quality, the repetitiveness . . . the whole *story* of his work, which I believe, at this point, cannot be understood outside the postcolonial. What I am pointing to as the inscription of the functional/instrumental and utopian impulses in Glissant's work are rendered impossible within Bongie's assessment of so-called progressive and regressive tendencies. A similar type of separation is suggested by Peter Hallward's reading of Glissant.

6. This aspect is eloquently considered in Cailler (especially 104).

7. See, for example, the early *Marxism and Form* 383, 385. Jameson's writing consistently seeks to chart the theoretical with and through the social. This is evident in his ideas about the national allegory in third world literary texts through to his analyses of cinema or architecture.

8. One cannot fail to be struck by the similarity between progression from métissage to *Relation* with the following formulation: "When we turn now to a properly Marxist literary criticism, it will be through a similar *epistemological shock* that we will be able to identify its presence: for such a shock is constitutive of and inseparable from dialectical thinking, as the mark of an abrupt shift to a higher level of consciousness, to a larger context of being" (Jameson *Marxism and Form* 375).

9. See *Caribbean Discourse* 187–91. When the push to standardize and make official creole language as a more authentic alternative to French for Martinique came from Martinican intellectuals Glissant was strongly opposed to it. The créolité movement, spearheaded by Jean Bernabé, Patrick Chamomiseau, and Raphaël Confiant, had its own influential manifesto entitled *Eloge de la créolité* [*In Praise of Creoleness*].

10. On the other hand, for one critic, "[. . .] Glissant's work is, from start to finish, committed to any number of ideological errors made in the name of structuring

resistance; these errors stem, for instance from a questionable (which is certainly not to say wrongheaded) belief in the reality of such things as national identity and cultural alienation . . ." (Bongie 143).

11. Dash notes that Glissant, early on, identified Césaire's work as being of a particular moment and therefore foresaw a datedness that it was bound to acquire (Dash 31, 36). In fact, Dash remarks that "already one has the feeling in Glissant's work that negritude would one day be little more than a period style" (38), recording the distance he explicitly takes from his Martinican compatriots and other African francophone poets.

12. See Kojève especially 227–33.

13. Glissant himself comments that "[i]t is difficult for a French Caribbean individual to be the brother, the friend, or quite simply the associate or fellow countryman of Fanon. Because, of all the French Caribbean intellectuals, he is the only one to have *acted on his ideas*, through his involvement in the Algerian struggle" (*Caribbean Discourse* 25). Glissant sees both Fanon's revolutionary work and Césaire's revolution in/through poetry as forms of "diversion" which for him are "versions of the return to Africa" (*Caribbean Discourse* 24). But for him, this act of diversion is necessary before a return to what he calls "the point of entanglement" (*Caribbean Discourse* 26), which perhaps neither of his compatriots accomplished—Fanon owing to his early death, and Césaire due to the decisions made in his political career.

14. For Marx: "The philosophers have only interpreted the world, in various ways; the point is to change it" (in Marx and Engels 145).

15. "Cultural diversity is an epistemological object—culture as an object of empirical knowledge—whereas cultural difference is the process of the *enunciation* of culture as 'knowledge*able*' authoritative, adequate to the construction of systems of cultural identification. If cultural diversity is a category of comparative ethics, aesthetics or ethnology, cultural difference is a process of signification through which statements *of* culture or *on* culture differentiate, discriminate and authorize the production of fields of force, reference, applicability and capacity. Cultural diversity is the recognition of pre-given cultural contents and customs; held in a time-frame of relativism it gives rise to liberal notions of multiculturalism, cultural exchange or the culture of humanity. Cultural diversity is also the representation of a radical rhetoric of the separation of totalized cultures that live unsullied by the intertextuality of their historical locations, safe in the utopianism of a mythic memory of a unique collective identity. Cultural diversity may even emerge as a system of the articulation and exchange of cultural signs in certain early structuralist accounts of anthropology" (*Location* 34).

16. Glissant's belief in, indeed requirement of, an ethical engagement at the level of the individual echoes Sartre's call for responsibility. The idea that a productive encounter with otherness implies action, and that the terms of such action cannot be given in advance would certainly be in keeping with Sartre's notion of existence preceding essence, even if Glissant does not cite Sartre. These moments in Glissant reveal him to be a radical thinker who nevertheless drew heavily from the tendencies and intellectual climate of his formative years.

17. Murdoch notes the parallel discontinuity Glissant "draws between the verbal act of expression and the physical act of marronnage," and which "demonstrates the simultaneous importance of rupture and of the transmission and transformation of tradition" (202) characteristic of the Caribbean from its very conception in the slave ship. Such discontinuity transforms the time itself of political action that cannot, then, be pinpointed in a narrative moment precisely because its time is not linear.

18. Young defends Bhabha against critics who find the latter's theory to be nonmaterialist. When he asserts that Bhabha's work is not incompatible with a less restrictively "textual" criticism (163) in effect he affirms that the theory itself remains most appropriate for textual criticism despite its more ambitious aims.

Chapter 7

1. Among others, Gautam Premanth has noted that in glossing the importance of nationalism and national consciousness to Fanon's theoretical endeavors, especially in his later work, the notion of struggle becomes decontextualized into a principle of negotiation rather than retaining any connection to organized movement in the process of decolonization (see especially 65). See also Parry's criticism of this tendency in postcolonial criticism (especially "Problems" 35).

2. Ato Sekyi-Otu, for example, takes to task Christopher Miller's reading of *Wretched of the Earth*, and shows that Miller quotes Fanon too simplistically. He argues that Miller lifts sentences on violence out of context, thereby losing the subtlety with which Fanon analyzes the new national culture and lodges his criticism of its darker side (42–43).

3. See especially Bhabha "Interrogating Identity" 40–65 in *Location* and Hall "The After-life."

4. See *Location* 176–177 for a discussion of the language metaphor. The lack of analytical distinction between interpretation and other forms of agency is suggested in a sentence such as: "There is the more complex possibility of *negotiating meaning and agency* through the time-lag in-between the sign [. . .] and its initiation of a discourse or narrative [. . .]" [my emphasis] (183). But the idea that "the question of agency [. . .] emerges" (182) rather than that agency itself is created through individual struggle does not help to illuminate how something located outside the sentence, and which is "not quite experience, not yet concept" (181) becomes translated into action by sentient human actors.

5. The translation reads "will erect a value-making superstructure on my whole vision of the world." Rather, I want to emphasize here that this superstructure cradles, validates, and gives coherence to every moment of a particular vision of the world and that it sanctions the two movements of aggression and love.

6. Fanon's ironic lack of attention to such a totality in his vituperative arguments against Mayotte Capécia in this chapter can be seen as a demonstration of an improperly conducted analysis as per his own indications, which we have just examined. What played out there methodologically, as well, was the erasure of the black woman as a

complete sensuous subjectivity in that it is only an amputated version of the black woman as well as one severed from an engagement with a larger reality that are framed in Fanon's analyses of Capécia.

7. For David Macey, this unfortunate translation betrays Fanon's text, by mistaking a lived experience for a fact, "to such an extent as to make it almost incomprehensible" (29). While it is evident that the translator has taken some liberty in changing the title of the chapter, I found it quite persuasive in following this narrative. In this chapter, Fanon illustrates how, through the black man's lived experience, he is historically faced with his blackness, which is presented to him as a "fact," by white culture and eventually becomes validated by his own internalization of white culture.

8. Fanon's remarks, although made here on heterosexual love between a man and a woman, will be taken up in the context of a wider sense of love, one for which Bhabha feels called upon to apologize for its humanist tendency. Fanon's version of love between "men" is not a bland love of easy brotherhood. Like all Fanonian affect, it is demanding and ethical. His essay, The North African Syndrome" that was published in *Esprit* and then included by Maspero in *Pour une révolution africaine* ends with: "If YOU do not demand the man, if YOU do not sacrifice the man that is in you so that the man who is on this earth shall be more than a body, more than a Mohammed, by what conjurer's trick will I have to acquire the certainty that you, too, are worthy of my love?" (*Toward the African Revolution* 16).

9. Other examples of the narrator's preoccupation with an historical account can be evoked: "With enthusiasm, I set to cataloguing . . ." "As times changed . . ." "After much reluctance, scientists had conceded. . . ." "I put all the parts back together. But I had to change my tune" "That victory played cat and mouse; it made a fool of me." "But on certain points the white man remained intractable" (see 119–120). This is followed by a quotation taken from Alan Burns who quotes a certain Jon Alfred Mjoen's presentation on Race Crossing at the Second International Congress of Eugenics. At this point, the historical-universal black narrator is able to anticipate what the strategy was to such a discourse.

10. Although J. P. Riquelme tries to resuscitate this remark of Bhabha's that has been critiqued by E. San Juan Jr. through a proper resituation of the remark within Bhabha's *Location of Culture* (see Riquelme 566), I remain unconvinced of the mindfulness of Bhabha's reading. "Fanon is not principally posing the question [What does a black man want?] of political oppression as the violation of a human essence, although he lapses into such a lament in his more existential moments. He is not raising the question of colonial man in the universalist terms of the liberal-humanist. [. . .] Fanon's question is addressed not to such a unified notion of history nor to such a unitary concept of man. It is one of the original and disturbing qualities of *Black Skin White Masks* that it rarely historicizes the colonial experience. There is no master narrative or realist perspective that provides a background of social and historical facts against which emerge the problems of the individual or collective psyche" (*Location* 42). First, it is not *Fanon* who lapses into lamenting the violation of a human essence. However, in narrating the history of "the" black man, this narrator is confronted by this phase in the black man's tactics, a tactic his narrator assumes in dramatizing the

anguish of the black man of his day in the face of white culture. It is clear that Fanon does not believe in the existence or the unquestioned need for the idea of "the" black man—yet, his historical narrator assumes such an entity as it has been created through the unfortunate reality of colonialism. What is disturbing is that a critic of the sophisticated intelligence of Homi Bhabha fails to note the "historicity," which has been bequeathed to the black narrator and that Fanon has the courage to assume, with the idea of changing it. There *is* a master narrative into which Fanon's narrator is forced to enter. *Black Skin, White Masks* is all about reclaiming the right to enter the field of discourse created by colonial culture in the era in which he writes, and which was constructed as History even before the height of the colonial period. Such entry is complicated by the desire of the narrator as an individual black subject to forsake this collective narrative position for a properly individual "I." The hybridity of the text, as we have seen, arises, in part, due to the tension between such an idiosyncratic, personal, unique narrative position, and one that is already oriented, making it respond to a unitary, stifling reality in which the black man can be nothing but a generic nigger.

11. In his later writing (and, no doubt, referring specifically to négritude), Fanon writes: "No neologism can mask the new certainty: the plunge into the chasm of the past is the condition and the source of freedom" (*Towards* 43).

12. Of the various comments upon Fanon's critique of Sartre, I found most persuasive Sonia Kruk's subtle analysis.

13. "The racist in a culture with racism is therefore normal. The idea that one forms of man, to be sure, is never totally dependent on economic relations, in other words—and this must not be forgotten—on relations existing historically and geographically among men and groups. And even greater number of members belonging to racist societies are taking a position. They are dedicating themselves to a world in which racism would be impossible. But everyone is not up to this kind of commitment. One cannot with impunity require of a man that he be against 'the prejudices of his group.' And, we repeat, every colonialist group is racist" (*Towards* 40).

14. "Psychologists, who tend to explain everything by movements of the psyche, claim to discover [racist] behavior on the level of contacts between individuals: the criticism of an original hat, of a way of speaking, of walking . . . Such attempts deliberately leave out of account the special character of the colonial situation" (*Towards* 33).

Works Cited

Adorno, Theodor W. *Negative Dialectics*. New York: Continuum, 2000.

Agenor, Monique. *Bé-Maho: chroniques sous le vent*. Paris: Serpent à plumes, 1996.

Ahmad, Aijaz. *In Theory: Classes, Nations, Litaratures*. London: Verso, 1992.

Alexander, N. "An African Renaissance without African Languages?" *Social Dynamics* 25 (1999): 11–12.

Alladin, K. *President for the People*. Rose Hill, Mauritius: The Mauritius Printing, 1988.

Ananden, Andanda Devi. *Rue la Poudrière*. Abidjan: Nouvelles editions africaines, 1989.

Appiah, Kwame Anthony. "Is the Post—in Postmodernism the Post—in Postcolonial." *Critical Inquiry* 17 (1991): 336–57.

Archives coloniales. *Constitutions de l'Ile Maurice*. Port Louis: Colonial Archives printing, n.d.

Armand, Alain, Gérard Chopinet. *Littérature réunionnaise d'expression créole*: 1828–1982. Paris: Harmattan, 1983.

Bahri, Deepika. "Once More with Feeling: What is Postcolonialism?" *Ariel* 26.1 (1995): 51–82.

Baker, Phillip and Chris Corne. *Isle de France Creole: Affinities and Origins*. Ann Arbor: Karoma, 1982.

Balibar, Etienne, Immanuel Wallerstein. *Race, Nation, Class: Ambiguous Identities*. Trans. of Etienne Balibar by Chris Turner. London: Verso, 1991.

Barber, Karin. "African Language Literatures and Postcolonial Criticism." *Research in African Literatures* 26 (1995): 3–30.

Baucom, Ian. "Frantz Fanon's Radio: Solidarity, Diaspora, and the Tactics of Listening." *Contemporary Literature* 42.1 (2001): 33–41, 45, 48.

Beaton, Patrick. *Creoles and Coolies: Five Years in Mauritius*. London: James Nisbet, n.d.

Benjamin, Walter. *Illuminations: Essays and Reflections*. Ed. and intro. Hannah Arendt. Trans. Harry Zohn. New York: Schocken, 1969.

Bensmaïa, Réda. "Postcolonial Nations: Political or Poetic Allegories? (On Tahar Djaout's 'L'invention du désert')." *Research in African Literatures* 30.2 (1999): 151–63.

Bentolila, Alain. "Réflexions sur le problème de l'alphabétisation à Sainte-Lucie." *Créole et Education*. Spec. issue of *Espace Créole* 7(1990): 9–30.

Bérenger Paul. "Statement by the Honorable Prime Minister." http://pm.gov.mu/pqpm/pq150205.htm. Accessed 05 March 2005.

Bernabé, Jean, Patrick Chamoiseau, Raphaël Confiant. *Eloge de la Créolité/ In Praise of Creoleness*. Trans. M. B. Taleb-Khyar. Paris: Gallimard, 1989, 1993.

Bhabha, Homi K. *Location of Culture*. London: Routledge, 1994.

———. *Nation and Narration*. London: Routledge, 1990.

———. "Remembering Fanon: Self, Psyche, and the colonial Condition." In Patrick Williams and Laura Chrisman. Colonial Discourse and Postcolonial Theory: A Reader. New York: Columbia University Press, 1994. 112–23. First Printed as Foreword. Frantz Fanon *Black Skin, White Masks*. London: Pluto, 1986. vi–xxvi.

Bhasin, V. K. *Super Power Rivalry in the Indian Ocean*. New Delhi: C. Chand, 1981.

Blankaert. "Of Monstrous Métis? Hybridity, Fear of Miscegenation, and Patriotism from Buffon to Paul Broca." In eds. Sue Peabody and Tyler Stovall. *Color of Liberty: Histories of Race in France*. Durham: Duke University Press, 2003. 29–42.

Boisson, J.-M, M. Louit. "Les Elections législatives du 20 décembre 1976 à l'île Maurice: l'enjeu économique et politique." In *Ile Maurice: sociale économique et politique (1974–1980)*. Aix-en-Provence: U d'Aix-Marseille, 1984. 13–66.

Bongie, Chris. *Islands and Exiles: The Creole Identities of Post-Colonial Literature*. Stanford: Stanford University Press, 1998.

Boyer, Monique. *Métisse*. Paris: Harmattan, 1994.

Braun, Dieter. *Indian Ocean: Region of Conflict or 'Peace Zone'?* Trans. C. Geldart and K. Llanwarne, London, C. Hurst, Canberra, Croom-Helm, 1983.

Britton, Celia M. *Edouard Glissant and Postcolonial Theory: Strategies of Language and Resistance*. Charlottesville: University of Virginia Press, 1999.

Cailler, Bernadette. *Conquérants de la nuit nue: Edouard Glissant et l'Histoire antillaise*. Tübingen: Gunter Narr Verlag, 1988.

Callikan-Proag, Ashlaka. Preface. *Namaste*. Rose-Hill (Mauritius): Océan indien, 1981.

Canclini, Néstor García. "The State of War and the State of Hybridization." In eds. Paul Gilroy, Lawrence Grossberg, Angela McRobbie. *Without Guarantees: In Honour of Stuart Hall*. 38–52.

Capécia, Mayotte. *Je suis martiniquaise*. Paris: Correa, 1948.

Centre d'études et de recherches sur les sociétés de l'océan indien. *Ile Maurice: sociale économique et politique (1974–1980)*. Aix-en-Provence: U d'Aix-Marseille, 1984.

Chakrabarty, Dipesh. "Postcoloniality and the Artifice of History: Who speaks for 'Indian' Pasts?" *Representations* 37 (1992): 1–26.

Champdemerle, Paul. *Le problème de la main-dœuvre à l'île de la réunion*. Diss. University of Paris, 1929. Paris: Raoul Hugnin, 1929.

Chane-Kune, Sonia. *Aux Origines de l'identité réunionnaise*. Paris: Harmattan, 1993.

Chaudenson, Robert. *Créoles et enseignements*. Espaces francophones 3. Paris: Harmattan, 1989.

Damoiseau, Robert. "Aspect et temps en créole haïtien et en français, problèmes pédagogiques." *Créole et Education*. Spec. issue of *Espace Créole* 7(1990): 65–97.

Dash, Michael. *Edouard Glissant*. Cambridge, U.K.: Cambridge University Press, 1994. Cambridge Series in African and Caribbean Literature Vol. 3.

Deleuze, Gilles, Félix Guattari. *Anti-Oedipus: Capitalism and Schizophrenia*. Trans. Robert Hurley, Mark Seem, Helen Lane. Pref. Michel Foucault. Minneapolis: Minnesota University Press, 1983.

Depestre, René. *Bonjour et adieu à la negritude*. Paris: Seghers, 1980.

de Souza, Carl. *La maison qui marchait vers le large*. Paris: Serpent à plume, 1995.

Dirlik, Arif. "The Postcolonial Aura: Third World Criticism in the Age of Global Capitalism." *Critical Inquiry* 20.2 (1994): 328–56.

Dubois, Laurent. "Inscribing Race in the Revolutionary French Antilles." In eds. Sue Peabody and Tyler Stovall. *Color of Liberty: Histories of Race in France*. Durham: Duke University Press, 2003. 95–107.

Eriksen, Thomas Hylland. *Ethnicity and Nationalism: Anthropological Perspectives*. Anthropology, Culture and Society 1. London: Pluto, 1993.

———. *Us and Them in Modern Societies: Ethnicity and Nationalism in Mauritius, Trinidad and Beyond*. Oslo: Scandinavian University Press, 1992.

———. *Communicating Cultural Difference and Identity: Ethnicity and Nationalism in Mauritius*. Oslo Occasional Papers in Social Anthropology 16. Blindern: University of Oslo, 1988.

Etienne, Pauline. 'Adding Insult to injury.' *Express* (2005) http://www.lexpress.mu/display_article_sup.php?news_id=38291. Accessed 06 June 2005.

Fanon, Frantz. Peau noire masques blancs. Paris: Seuil, 1952.

———. *Black Skin, White Masks*. Trans. Charles Lam Markmann. New York: Grove, 1967.

———. *Wretched of the Earth*. Trans. Constance Farrington. New York: Grove Weidenfeld, 1991.

———. *Toward the African Revolution*. Trans. Haakon Chevalier. New York: Grove, 1967.

Fludernik, Monika. "The Constitution of Hybridity: Postcolonial Interventions." *Hybridity and Postcolonialism: Twentieth-Century Indian Literature*. Tübingen: Verlag, 1998. 19–53.

Fuma, Sudel. *Esclaves et citoyens: le destin de 62.000 réunionnais—histoire de l'insertion des affranchis de 1848 dans la société réunionnaise.* St-Denis (La Réunion): Fondation pour la recherche et le développement dans l'océan indien, 1982.

Fuss, Diana. *Identification Papers.* London: Routledge, 1995.

Gates, Henry Louis. "Critical Fanonism." *Critical Inquiry* 17.3 (1991): 457–70.

Gauvin, Axel. *Du creole opprimé au creole libéré: défense de la langue réunionnaise.* Paris: Harmattan, 1977.

Gerbeau, M. "Des Minorités mal connues: esclaves indiens et malais des mascareignes au XIXe siècle." Table ronde: Migrations, Minorités et échanges en océan indien, XIXe-XXe siècle. University of Provence, Aix-en-Provence, 1978. 160–206.

Ghosh, Amitav. *Glass Palace.* New York: Random House, 2001.

Gilroy, Paul. *Between Camps: Race, Identity and Nationalism at the End of the Colour Line.* London: Penguin, 2000.

———. *Black Atlantic: Modernity and Double-Consciousness.* Cambridge, MA: Harvard University Press, 1993.

———. *Small Acts: Thoughts on the Politics of Black Cultures.* London: Serpent's Tail, 1993.

Giraud, Michel, Danièle Manesse. "Contribution à l'analyse des échecs scolaires: compétences des élèves en lecture et en expression écrite et représentations sociales de l'école aux Antilles françaises." *Créole et Education.* Spec. issue of *Espace Créole* 7 (1990): 31–48.

Glissant, Edouard. *Caribbean Discourse.* Trans. J. Michael Dash. Charlottesville: University of Virginia Press, 1989. Caraf 7.

———. *Poétique de la Relation.* Paris: Gallimard, 1990.

———. *Poetics of Relation.* Trans. Betsy Wing. Ann Arbor: University of Michigan Press, 1997.

Graham, Gerald. *Great Britain in the Indian Ocean: A Study of Maritime Enterprise: 1810–1850.* London: Oxford University Press, 1967.

Gramsci, Antonio. *Selections from the prison Notebooks.* Eds. and Trans. Quintin Hoare and Geoffrey Nowell Smith. New York: International Publishers, 1971.

Guha, Ranajit. "Dominance without Hegemonry and Its Historiography" *Subaltern Studies VI.* New Delhi: Oxford University Press, 1989. 210–301.

Hall, Stuart. "Deviance, politics, and the media." In eds. Paul Rock and Mary McIntosh. Deviance and Social Control. London: Tavistock, 1974. 261–305.

———. "The After-life of Frantz Fanon: Why Fanon? Why Now? Why 'Black Skin, White Masks?" in ed. Alan Read. *Fact of Blackness: Frantz Fanon and visual Representation.* London: Institute of Contemporary Arts, 1996. 12–37.

———. "Cultural Identity and Diaspora." In ed. and intro. Patrick Willimans, Laura Chrisman. *Colonial Discourse and Post-Colonial Theory: A Reader.* New York: Columbia University Press, 1994.

Hallward, Peter. "Edouard Glissant between the Singular and the Specific." *Yale Journal of Criticism* 11.2 (1998): 441–64.

Hazareesingh, R. *History of Indians in Mauritius*. London: MacMillan, 1975.

Hegel, Georg W. F. *Science of Logic*. Trans. A.V. Miller. London: Allen and Unwin, 1969.

Henry, Paget. "Fanon, African and Afro-Caribbean Philosophy." in eds. Lewis R. Gordon, Tracy D. Sharpley-Whiting, Renée White. *Fanon: A Critical Reader*. Oxford: Blackwell, 1996. 220–43.

Higgins, John. Ed. *Raymond Williams Reader*. Oxford: Blackwell, 2001.

Hookoomsing, Vinesh. "L'Ile Maurice et ses langues." *Notre Librairie* 114 (1993): 26–31.

hooks, bell. "Feminism as a persistent critique of history: What's love got to do with it?" *Fact of Blackness: Frantz Fanon and Visual Representation*. Ed. Alan Read. London: Bay Press, 1996. 76–85.

Humbert, Marie-Thérèse. *A l'autre bout de moi*. Paris: Stock, 1982.

Inhabitants of Mauritius. *Memorial in support of their Petition to his Majesty*. London: Effingham Wilsom,1833.

Irele, Abiola. *African Experience in Theory and Ideology*. Bloomington: Indiana University Press, 1990.

Issur, Kumari R. Vinesh Y. Hookoomsing. *L'Océan indien dans les literatures francophones*. Paris: Karthala, 2001.

Ithier, J.J. W. *Littérature de langue française à l'ile Maurice*. Paris: Slatkine, 1930. Geneva: Slatkine, 1981.

Jameson, Fredric. "Globalization and Political Strategy." *New Left Review* 4 (2000): 49–68.

———. "Third-World Literature in the Era of Multinational Capitalism." *Social Text* (1996): 65–88.

———. *Political Unconscious: Narrative as a Socially Symbolic Act*. Ithaca: Cornell University Press, 1981.

———. *Marxism and Form: Twentieth Century Dialectical Theories of Literature*. Princeton: Princeton University Press, 1971.

———. *Seeds of Time*. New York: Columbia University Press, 1994.

———. "Criticism in History." *Ideologies of Theory: Essays 1971–86*. Vol 1. Situations of Theory. Minneapolis: University of Minnesota Press, 1988. 119–36.

Jay, Martin. *Marxism and Totality: The Adventures of a Concept from Lukács to Habermas*. Berkeley: University of California Press, 1984.

Jordan, Z. A. *Evolution of Dialectical Materialism: A Philosophical and Sociological Analysis*. New York: St. Martin's Press, 1967.

Joubert, Jean-Louis, Jean-Irénée Raminadrasoa. *Littératures de l'océan indien.* Paris: Edicef, 1991.

Joubert, Jean-Louis. "Iles et exils (sur l'imaginaire littéraire aux Mascareignes)." *Littérature insulaires: Caraïbes et Mascareignes.* Itinéraires et Contacts de Cultures. Vol 3. Paris: Harmattan, 1983. 117–29.

Julien, Eileen. "Terrains de Rencontre: Cesaire. Fanon, and Wright on Culture and Decolonization." *Yale French Studies* 98 (2000): 149–66.

Kaul, Suvir. "Colonial Figures and Postcolonial Reading." *Diacritics* 26.1 (1996): 74–89.

Kojève, Alexandre. *Introduction to the Reading of Hegel: Lectures on the 'Phenomenology of Spirit' Assembled by Raymond Queneau.* Ed. Alan Bloom. Trans. James H. Nichols, Jr. New York: Basic, 1969.

Kruks, Sonia. "Fanon, Sartre, and Identity Politics." in eds. Lewis R. Gordon, Tracy D. Sharpley-Whiting, Renée White. *Fanon: A Critical Reader.* Oxford: Blackwell, 1996. 122–33.

Lacan, Jacques. *Ecrits: A Selection.* Trans. Alain Sheridan. London: Norton, 1977.

Laclau, Ernesto, Chantal Mouffe. *Hegemony and Socialist Strategy: Towards a Radical Democratic Politics.* London: Verso, 1985.

Lazarus, Neil. *Nationalism and Cultural Practice in the Postcolonial World.* Cultural Margins 6. Cambridge, U.K.: Cambridge University Press, 1999.

———. "Disavowing Decolonization: Fanon, Nationalism, and the Problematic of Representation in Current Theories of Colonial Desire." *Research in African Literatures* 24.3 (1993): 69–89.

LeBlond, Marius-Ary. *Miracle de la Race.* Paris: Albin-Michel, n.d.

———. *Nationalism and Cultural Practice in the Postcolonial World.* Cultural Margins 6. Cambridge, U.K.: Cambridge University Press, 1999.

Liddell, Janice L, and Yakinin Belinda Kemp, eds. *Arms Akimbo: Africana Women in Contemporary Literature.* Gainesville: University Press of Florida, 1999.

Lionnet, Françoise. *Autobiographical Voices: Race, Gender, Self-Portraiture.* Ithaca: Cornell University Press, 1989.

———. "'Créolité' in the Indian Ocean: Two Models of Cultural Diversity." *Yale French Studies* 82.2 (1993): 101–12.

———. *Postcolonial Representations: Women, Literature, Identity.* Ithaca: Cornell University Press, 1995.

Li, Victor. "Towards Articulation: Postcolonial Theory and Demotic Resistance." *Ariel* 26.1 (1995): 167–89.

Lukács, Georg. *History and Class Consciousness: Studies in Marxist Dialectics.* Trans. Rodney Livingstone. Cambridge, MA: M.I.T. Press, 1971.

Lüsebrink, Hans-Jürgen. "Métissage culturel et société coloniale: émergence et enjeux d'un débat, de la press coloniale aux premiers écrivains africains (1935–1947)." In *Métissages Littérature-Histoire.* Paris: Harmattan, 1992. Vol 1. 109–18.

Macey, David. *Frantz Fanon: A Biography.* New York: Picador, 2002.

———. Fanon, Phenomenology, Race." In *Philosophies of Race and Ethnicity.* London: Continuum, 2002. 29–39.

Marcus, George. E., Michael M.J. Fischer. *Anthropology as Cultural Critique: An Experiment in the Human Sciences.* Chicago: University of Chicago Press, 1999. First ed. 1986.

Marimoutou, Jean-Claude Carpanin. "Ecrire métis." *Métissages: Littérature-Histoire.* Cahiers CRLH-CIRAOI. Vol 7. Harmattan: Saint-Denis (La Réunion): 1992. 247–60.

Marx, Karl. *Capital: A Critique of Political Economy.* Trans. Ben Fowkes. Intro. Ernest Mandel. Vol. 1. New York: Vintage, 1972.

———. *Economic and Philosophic Manuscripts of 1844.* Trans. Martin Milligan. (Followed by Marx, Karl, Friedrich Engels, *Communist Manifesto.*) New York: Prometheus, 1988.

Marx, Karl, Friedrich Engels. Ed. Robert Tucker. *Marx/Engels Reader.* Norton: New York, 1978. First ed. 1972.

Mauritius Legislative Council. *Debates.* Port Lewis: Printed by Claude M. d'Unienville, The Mauritius Co., LTD, n.d.

Mbemebe, Achille. *On the Postcolony.* Berkeley: University of California Press, 2001.

McClintock, Anne. "The Angels of Progress: Pitfalls of the Term Post-Colonialism." *Social Text* 10.3 (1992): 84–98.

Michel, Martina. "Positioning the Subject: Locating Postcolonial Studies." *Ariel* 26.1 (1995): 83–99.

Moore-Gilbert, Bart. *Postcolonial Theory: Contexts, Practices, Politics.* London: Verso, 1997.

———. "Frantz Fanon: En-gendering Nationalist Discourse." *Women's Cultural Review* 7.2 (1996): 125–35.

Murdoch, Adlai H. *Creole Identity in the French Caribbean Novel.* Gainesville: University Press of Florida, 2001.

Nancy, Jean-Luc. "Cut-Throat Sun." in Ed. Alfred Artega. *An Other Tongue.* Durham: Duke University Press, 1994.

Nesbitt, Nick. *Voicing Memory: History and Subjectivity in French Caribbean Literature.* New World Studies. 13. Charlottesville: University of Virginia Press, 2003.

Nietzsche, Friedrich. "On the Utility and Liability of history for Life." in *Unfashionable Observations.* Trans. and afterword. Richard T. Gray. Ed. Ernst Behler. Complete Works of Friedrich Nietzsche. Vol. 2. Stanford: Stanford University Press, 1995. 83–168.

Noel, Karl. *Esclavage à l'Ile de France. (Ile Maurice) de 1715 à 1810.* Paris: Two Cities, 1991.

Nzepa, Zacharie Petnkeu. "Espace francophone et politiques linguistiques: glottophagie ou diversité culturelle?" *Presence francophone* 60 (2003): 80–97.

Olaniyan, Tejumola. *Scars of Conquest / Masks of Resistance*. New York: Oxford University Press, 1995.

Parmentier, Richard. "Signs' Place in *Median Res*: Peirce's Concept of Semiotic Mediation." In eds. Mertz, Elizabeth, Richard Parmentier. *Semiotic Mediation: Sociolcultural and Psychological Perspectives.* Language, Thought, and Culture: Advances in the Study of Cognition. Orlando: Academic Press, 1985.

Parry, Benita. "Problems in Current Theories of Colonial Discourse." *Oxford Literary Review* 9.12 (1987): 27–58.

———. "Signs of Our Times: A Discussion of Homi Bhabha's 'The Location of Culture.'" in eds. Miyoshi, Masao, Harry Harootunian. *Learning Places: The Afterlives of Area Studies*. Durham: Duke University Press, 2002. 119–49.

———. *Postcolonial Studies: A Materialist Critique*. London: Routledge, 2004.

Plevitz, Adolphe de. Presenter. *Petition of the Old Immigrants of Mauritius*. Np: Port Louis, 1871.

Prabhu, Anjali. "Creolization in Process: Languages, Literatures, Nationalisms." Dissertation. Duke University, 1999.

———. "Theorizing the Role of the Intermediary in Postcolonial (Con)text:Driss Chraibi's 'Une enquête au pays.'" *Studies in Twentieth-Century Literature* 27.1 (2003): 167–90.

———. "Mariama Bâ's 'So long a letter': 'Women, Culture and Development' from a Francophone/Postcolonial Perspective." In eds. Kum-Kum Bhavnani, John Foran, Priya Kurian. *Feminist Futures: Re-Imagining Women, Culture, and Development*. London: Zed, 2003. 239–55.

Prabhu, Anjali, Ato Quayson. "Francophone Studies / Postcolonial Studies: 'Postcolonializing' through 'Relation.'" In eds. H. Adlai Murdoch and Anne Donadey. *Postcolonial Studies in a Francophone Frame: Intersections and Re-visions*. Gainesville: University Press of Florida, 2004. 224–34.

Prabhu, Anjali. "Representation in Mauritius: Who Speaks for African Pasts?" *International Journal of Francophone Studies* 8.2 (2005): 183–97.

———. "Narration in Frantz Fanon's 'Peau noire masques blancs': Some Reconsiderations." *Research in African Literatures* 37.4 (2006): 189–210.

———. "Interrogating Hybridity: Subaltern Agency and Totality in Postcolonial Theory." *Diacritics* 35.2 (2005).

Premnath, Gautam. "Remembering Fanon: Decolonizing Diaspora." In eds. Chrisman, Laura, Benita Parry. *Postcolonial Theory and Criticism*. Brewer: Cambridge. 57–73.

Prosper, Jean-Georges. *Histoire de la littérature mauriuenne de langue française*. Rose Hill (Mauritius): Océan indien, 1994. Second ed.

———. "La place de Maurice daus la créolie de l'Océan indien." *Notre Librairie* 114 (1993): 84–87.

Radhakrishnan, R. *Diasporic Mediations: Between Home and Location*. Minneapolis: University of Minnesota Press, 1996.

Ramaseshan, Radhika. "PM walks into Mauritius poll—Singh pays tribute to island 'Gandhi,' party sees politics" *Telegraph* 2005. http://www.telegraphindia.com/1050401/asp/nation/story_4560336.asp. Accessed 06 June 2005.

Ramgoolam, Seewoosagar. *Selected Speeches*. London: Macmillan, 1979.

Rano, Jonas. *Créolitude: silences et cicatrices pour seuls témoins*. Paris: Harmattan, 1997.

Rassool, N. "Literacy and Social Development in the Information Age: Redefining Possibilities in Sub-Saharan Africa." *Social Dynamics* 25 (1999): 130–49.

Renan, Ernest. Trans. Martin Thom. "What is a Nation?" in *Nation and Narration*. London: Routledge, 1990.

Riquelme, J. P. "Location and Home in Beckett, Bhabha, Fanon, and Heidigger." *Centennial Review*. 42.3 (1998): 541–68.

Robillard, D. "Les spécificités du créole mauricien sur le plan sociolinguistique." *Notre Librairie* 114 (1993): 123–38.

Rughoonundun, Nita. "Les langues à l'´école mauricienne." *Notre Librairie* 114 (1993): 32–37.

———. "Créolophonie et Education à Maurice." *Créole et Education*. Spec. issue of *Espace Créole* 7 (1990): 49–64.

Said, Edward. "Reflections on Exile." In *Reflections on Exile and Other Essays*. Cambridge: Harvard University Press, 2000. 357–66.

———. "The Future of Criticism." *Modern Language Notes*. 99.4 (1984): 951–58.

Saint-Pierre, Bernadin de., Thomi Pitot, Abbé Ducrocq. *Ile de France: Voyage et Controverses*. Alma: Mauritius, 1996.

Sartre, Jean-Paul. *Being and Nothingness*. Trans. Hazel E. Barnes. New York: Washington Square Press, 1956.

———. *L'Existentialisme est un humanisme*. Paris: Nagel, 1970.

Sedinger, Tracey. "Nation and Identification: Psychoanalysis, Race, and Sexual Difference." *Cultural Critique* 50 (2002): 40–73.

Sekyi-Otu, Ato. *Fanon's Dialectic of Experience*. Cambridge: Harvard University Press, 1996.

Shohat, Ella, Robert Stam. "From Eurocentrismto Polycentrism." *Unthinking Eurocentrism*. London: Routledge, 1994. 13–54.

Spivak, Gayatri Chakravorty. "Thinking Cultural Questions in 'Pure' Literary Terms." In Eds. Paul Gilroy, Lawrence Grossberg, Angela McRobbie. *Without Guarantees: In Honour of Stuart Hall*. London: Verso, 2000. 335–57.

Stein, Peter. "Connaissance et emploi des langues à l'Ile Maurice." Diss. University Regensburg, 1981. Kreolische Bibliothek 2. Helmut Buske: Hamburg, 1982.

Stewart, Charles. "Syncretism and its Synonyms: Reflections on Cultural Mixture." *Diacritics* 29.3 (1999): 40–62.

Stoler, Laura Ann. *Race and the Education of Desire: Foucault's History of Sexuality and the Colonial Order of Things*. Durham: Duke University Press, 1995.

Suk, Jeannie. "Glissant, 'Détour,' and History." In *Postcolonial Paradoxes in French Caribbean Writing: Césaire, Glissant, Condé*. Oxford: Clarendon, 2001. 56–83.

Trigo, Abril. "Shifting Paradigms: From Transculturation to Hybridity: A Theoretcial Critique." *Critical studies*. Special Issue: Eds. De Grandis, Rita, Zilà Bernd Unforseeable Americas.13 (1999): 85–111.

Vaughan, Megan. *Creating the Creole Island: Slavery in Eighteenth-Century Mauritius*. Durham: Duke University Press, 2005.

Venugopal, K. "A Non-Partisan Visit to Mauritius." *Hindu*. (2005). http://www.hindu.com/2005/03/30/stories/2005033003841100.htm. Accessed 06 June 2005.

Vergès, Françoise. *Monsters and Revolutionaries: Colonial Family Romance and Métissage*. Durham: Duke University Press, 1999.

——— . "Post-Scriptum." In eds. David Theo Goldberg, Ato Quayson. *Relocating Postcolonialism*. Oxford: Blackwell, 2002. 349–58.

Virahsawmy, Dev. *Toufann*. Rose Hill (Mauritius): Bukié Banane, 1991.

Wevers, Lydia. "The Fact of the Matter: History, Narrative and Record in 'The Singing Whakapapa' and 'Tasman's Lay.'" *Southerly* 59.2 (1999): 65–73.

Williams, Raymond. *Culture and Society 1780–1950*. London: Chatto and Windus, 1960.

——— . *Marxism and Literature*. Oxford: Oxford University Press, 1977.

——— . "Film and the Dramatic Tradition." In ed. John Higgins. *Raymond Williams Reader*. Oxford: Blackwell, 2001. 25–41.

——— . "Thomas Hardy." In Ed. John Higgins. *Raymond Williams Reader*. Oxford: Blackwell, 2001. 119–40.

Yiddel, Janice, Belinda Kemp. *Arms Akimbo: Africana Women in Contemporary Literature*. Gainesville: University of Florida Press, 1999.

Young, Robert. *Colonial Desire: Hybridity in Theory, Culture, and Race*. London: Routledge, 1995.

Index

Abolition, 32, 36, 38, 40, 58, 89, 157n6 (Boyer on), 23
Administration, xv, 32, 37, 40, 57, 59, 68, 75, 77, 90, 101, 102, 103, 156n9, 158n8
Administrator(s), 16, 90, 156n9
Adorno, Theodor, 109–110
Affect, xv, 12, 34, 124, 163n8 (ive), 141
Africa (includes Madagascar), 30, 61, 63, 64, 67, 81, 137, 142 (-n[s], *see also* Creole[s], Black[s]), 3, 35, 51, 60, 67, 68, 69, 70, 71, 79, 80, 84, 90, 91, 101, 103, 142, 152n10, 156n4, 158n17, 159n23, 161n11 (non-), 156n6 (-n diaspora), 3 (-n continent), 3, 56, 63, 68 (s), 3, 5, 13, 63, 82 (-ness), 15, 51, 52, 66, 69, 70, 71, 77, 82, 84, 91
Agency, xi, xiii, xiv, xv, 1, 2, 3, 7, 8, 9, 12, 13, 15, 17, 19, 20, 43, 45, 47, 69, 104, 105, 106, 111, 117, 118, 119, 122, 124, 130, 134, 135, 137, 138, 139, 141, 144, 145 (Bhabha on), 69, 162n4
Agenor, Monique, 154n8
Ahmad, Aijaz, 17, 158n17
Alienation, 110, 111, 112, 113, 115, 119, 141, 161n10
Alladin, K., 156n13
Allegorical, 93, 98
Allegory, 31, 98–99, 160n7
Althusser, Louis, 114, 120
Ambiguity/ambivalence, 37, 38, 45, 51, 59, 130, 140, 152n15, 154n16, 155n3 (Bhabha on), 43

Ambiguous, 43, 98 (un-), 93
Ananden, Ananda Devi, 159n23
Antagonism/antagonistic, 3, 52, 111, 117 (Lacalu and Mouffe on), 112 (Bhabha on), 121
Anthropology, 6, 40, 161n15
Anthropological, 14, 16, 90, 99, 104, 156n10
Appiah, Anthony K., 151n1
Armand, Alain and Gérard Chopinet, 47
Assimilate, 85
Assimilation, 4, 7, 12, 18, 38, 39, 42, 68, 93, 127, 131
Assimilatory, 20, 92

Bâ, Mariama, 33
Bahri, Deepika, 151n1
Balibar, Etienne, 59, 70
Barber, Karin, 113
Baucom, Ian, 7, 10
Beaton, Patrick, 54, 57, 61, 103–104
Benjamin, Walter, 84
Bentolila, Alain, 153n1
Bensmaïa, Réda, 98–99, 158n17
Bérenger, Paul, 71, 72, 74, 81, 83, 157n18
Bernabé, Jean, Patrick Chamoiseau, and Raphaël Confiant, 4, 30, 160n9
Bhabha, Homi K., xiii, 4, 5, 10, 13, 17, 45, 52, 116, 117, 118, 122, 124, 130, 152n12, 160n3, 163n8 (Riquelme on), 163n10 (Young on), 125, 162n18 (on Hall), 43 (on

175

Bhabha, Homi K. *(continued)*
Fanon's *BSWM*), 136, 138
(*Location*), 6, 9, 10, 11, 12, 14, 43, 44, 47, 69, 119, 121, 125, 130, 136, 153n20, 161n15, 162n2, 162n3, 162n4, 163–164n1 (*Nation and Narration*), 68, 99
Bhojpuri, 32, 54, 55, 56, 79, 158n13, 159n22
Bihari, 90, 101, 102, 158n13
Black(s), xiii, 20, 22, 24, 26, 29, 33, 36, 39, 45, 67, 69, 71, 77, 79, 83, 123, 124, 126, 127, 128, 129, 130, 131, 132, 133, 134, 135, 136, 137, 138, 139, 140, 141, 142, 143, 144, 145, 154n8, 155n1, 162–163n6, 163n7, 163n9
Blackness, 25, 27, 29, 32, 52, 132, 138, 143, 163n7 (Gilroy on), 11
Blanckaert, Claude, 40–42
Boisson, J-M, M. Louit, 58–59, 61, 67, 156n8
Bongie, Chris, 159n1, 160n5, 160–161n10
Bourbon. *See* La Réunion.
Bourdieu, Pierre, 19, 48, 49 (on education), 32
Bourgeois (-ie), 6, 17, 21, 25, 28, 29, 90, 91, 95, 102, 159n21, 159n26 (-ification), 26
Boyer, Monique, 15–34, 36, 42, 43, 44, 97, 153n3, 157n3
Braun, Dieter, 155n2
Britain, 1, 75, 90
British, 10, 53, 54, 57, 61, 67, 75, 77, 81, 89, 90, 101, 102, 157n6 (colonialism), xi, xii, 17
Britton, Celia, 159n1

Cabon, Marcel, 64, 65
Cailler, Bernadette, 160n6
Callikan-Proag, Aslakha, 64 (on Cabon), 65
Canclini, Nestór García, 147–148
Capécia, Mayotte, 33, 129, 162–163n6 (Fanon on), 25–26, 154n8

Capital, 2, 5, 18, 57, 92, 111, 113, 120 (-ist/istic), 18, 91, 108, 112, 113 (-ization), 109 (Bourdieu on), 49 (Fanon on), 92
Capitalism, xii, 120, 123 (global), xv, 2, 8, 9, 42
Césaire, Aimé, 4, 114, 115, 136, 137, 143, 144, 153n18, 161n11, 161n13 (Fanon on), 142
Centre d'études et de recherches sur les sociétés de l'océan indien, 156n11
Champdemerle, Paul, 60
Chane-Kune, Sonia, 54, 153n6
Chaudenson, Robert, 153n1
China/Chinese (includes Mauritian Chinese/Sinomauritian), 16, 23, 24, 31, 34, 35, 36, 54, 57, 58, 60, 61, 63, 66, 67, 69, 70, 72, 90, 99, 101, 103, 153n6, 157n1, 158n13
Citizenship, 25, 27, 29 (French), 31, 46
Civil service, 32
Claim (to hybridity), xv (to agency), 7 (s/ed), 1, 9
Class(es), 20, 30, 33, 36, 40, 42, 52, 56, 58, 71, 89, 90, 91, 103, 109, 110, 112, 115, 117, 120 (middle-), 29, 36, 46, 92, 154n12 (working-/proletariat), 5, 20, 21, 24, 25, 29, 33, 109, 139, 155n6 (-less), 139
Code noir. *See* slave.
Colonial, xii, xiv, xv, 14, 16, 26, 28, 31, 35, 43, 44, 47, 57, 59, 60, 62, 67, 77, 79, 92, 102, 124, 125, 127, 130, 137, 142, 144, 155n1, 163–164n10, 164n14 (Bhabha on), 9 (administration), xv, 37, 40, 59, 90, 158n8 (culture), xv, 127, 143, 145 (enterprise), 15 (exploitation), 3 (hybridity), 15, 38, 41 (novel), 34, 35, 37, 41, 42, 43, 44, 46, 89 (system), 88, 90 (world), 41 (pre-), 136 (anti-), 145 (-ist), 18, 67, 157n6, 164n13 (-ism), xii, xiv, 1, 3, 13, 16, 17, 18, 19, 23, 27, 30, 32, 35, 42, 46, 51, 59, 65, 92, 115, 126, 133, 134, 135, 138, 139, 140, 141, 142, 151n1, 158n13

Index

Colonization, xiii, 47, 109 (de-), 149, 162n1
Colonized (ex-colonized), xii (colonizer-colonized), xiii (world), 6
Colonizer/colonialist, xii, 57, 58, 62, 90, 124 (ex-colonizer), xi (colonizer-colonized), xiii
Colony/colonies, xii, 6, 37, 38, 39, 40, 41, 71, 75, 81, 90, 101, 102, 124, 154n8 (post-), 52, 79
Collective, 31, 89, 120, 130, 132, 138, 139, 147, 149
Collectivity/collectivities, 47, 59, 60, 119, 133
Communist, 5, 10, 86 (Manifesto), 5 (Party), 114
Confiant, Raphaël, 115
Conflict/conflictual/conflicting, xiv, 156n4 (confrontation), 145, 147
Contradiction, xv, 11, 13, 15, 17, 34, 35, 109, 110, 111, 112, 115, 117, 120, 122, 140, 148, 149, 153n15 (Jameson on), 155n3 (contradictory), 14, 104, 108, 110, 151n3
Coolie(s), (*see also* indenture[d]), 54, 90
Creole(s), xii, 16, 17, 18, 19, 36, 37, 38, 39, 44, 54, 58, 60, 61, 64, 67, 68, 71, 72, 79, 80, 85, 87, 91, 92, 95, 97, 98, 100, 102, 152n13, 155n1 (islands), xi (language/morisyen), ix, x, 15, 19, 21, 29, 31, 32, 34, 43, 45, 46, 48, 54, 55, 56, 57, 60, 61, 66, 68, 69, 73, 80, 101, 112, 154n11, 154n12, 155n1, 156n12, 159n24 (Gauvin on), 49, 153n1 (Rasool, Alexander, Chaudenson, Rughoonundun, Giraud, Manesse, Bentolila, Damoiseau on), 15n1(specificity), xi
Créolie, 48
Creolist(s), 5, 30
Creolité, 2, 4, 48 (*Eloge de la-*), 4, 30, 160n9
Créolitude, 151n6
Creolization, 1, 2, 3, 4, 5, 7, 9, 10, 13, 14, 18, 20, 22, 25, 27, 34, 42, 52, 70, 71, 84, 92, 104, 105, 106, 108, 110, 116, 117, 121, 122, 147, 151n3, 151n4, 151–152n7, 152n10
Creolizing, 91
Critical, 22, 23, 25, 29, 98 (history), 20, 26, 27, 30
Critique/criticism, 27, 112, 124, 139, 164n12 (of new theories of hyridity), xv (of capitalism), 2, 98 (of modernization /development), 6
Culture(s), xi, 11, 16, 17, 18, 31, 34, 35, 46, 52, 67, 73, 79, 80, 104, 112, 113, 115, 132, 139, 142, 145, 147, 148, 151n1, 157n17, 157n1, 163n7 (Lionnet on), 152n9 (Williams on), 20 (hybrid), xiii (colonial/white), xv, 2, 130, 137, 139, 143, 145
Cultural, 7, 12, 31, 41, 42, 44, 46, 57, 65, 68, 71, 73, 90, 99, 102, 104, 121 115, 119, 123, 129, 133, 142, 145, 152n13, 154n11, 157n1 (-ally), 129
Curriculum (*see* education)

Damoiseau, Robert, 153n1
Dash, Michael, 8, 106, 115, 159n1, 161n11
Deleuze, Gilles, 114
Deleuze Gilles and Félix Guattari, 152n11
Depestre, Rene, 152n10
Derivative(s), xii, xiii, xiv, 1, 15, 16, 17
De Mann, Paul, 99
De Souza, Carl, 61, 87, 88, 157n2
Department, 1, 17, 19, 30, 51, 112 (-al), 29, 47 (-alization), 27, 45, 46
Diachronic, 4 (-ally), 26
Diachrony, 5
Dialectic(s), 5, 52, 106, 109, 122, 148 (Fanon on), 133 (-al), 73, 107, 108, 114, 119, 120, 144, 160n2, 160n8
Dialogue, xii, 4
Diaspora, 1, 2, 3, 4, 5, 13, 18, 34, 42, 70, 71, 83, 84, 105, 147, 149, 151n3, 151n4, 152n10 (Hall on), 4 (African), 3, 5, 70, 84 (Indian), 5 Chinese), 5 (Hall on), 9 (Gilroy on), 11, 70, 151–152n7

Diasporic, 10, 83, 84, 91 (discourse[s]), 3, 5, 10, 52, 73 (-s), 4
Difference(s), xiv, 2, 4, 6, 7, 17, 29, 30, 31, 40, 41, 43, 44, 52, 90, 99, 101, 104, 106, 109, 111, 116, 117, 120, 122, 125, 127, 139, 142, 147, 152n7, 152n9, 152n15 (alterity), 116 (diversity), 116, 125 (heterogeneity), 108 (otherness), 117, 118, 125, 127, 148 (Bhabha on), 43, 68, 161n15 (Hall on), 153n15 (Melas on), 62
Dirlik, Arif, 151n1
Discourse(s), 5, 12, 30, 37, 41, 46, 49, 54, 64, 80, 81, 84, 99, 124, 134, 140, 141, 162n4, 163n9 (communist), 10 (diasporic), 3, 10 (of hybridity), 3, 147 (political), 4, 66, 68 (public), 52, 71, 73, 74, 77, 80, 91, 156n9 (postcolonial), 11 (theoretical), 4 (national[ist]), 62, 70, 81
Dominance, 115
Dominant, 11, 52, 109, 121, 145
Dominating, 151n1
Domination, 5, 6, 125, 135, 137, 153n15
Dubois, Laurent, 40, 124
Ducroq (abbé), 78, 79

Economic(s), 7, 16, 92, 151n1, 154n8, 159n26 (crisis), 35
Economistically, 25
Economy, 72, 91, 119
Education, xii, 19, 20, 36, 48, 67, 91, 102, 103, 112, 154n11 (Bourdieu on), 32 (school/curriculum), 32, 36, 57, 73, 156n4
Edwards, Brent Hayes, 151n4
English, 53, 68, 131 (language), x, 17 56, 57, 73, 79 (translation), 127, 133, 134, 135
Eriksen, Thomas Hylland, 16, 99 (*Communicating*), 65, 91, 156n11 (*Ethnicity and Nationalism*), 100, 101, 102, 103, 158–159n20 (*Us and Them*), 104
Ethic(s)/ethical, 45, 47, 96, 107, 109, 117, 118, 119, 120, 126, 127, 130, 133, 139, 142, 144, 145, 149, 161n15, 161n16, 163n8 (Glissant on), 116 (Fanon on), 126
Ethnic, 52, 55, 57, 59, 60, 70, 73, 74, 75, 92, 102, 139, 147, 158n11 (-ity), x, 16, 18, 24, 66, 71, 74, 85, 90, 99, 100, 101, 104, 123, 148, 155n1, 157n1, 159n22 (Eriksen on), 158–159n20
Ethnified, 95
Etienne, Pauline, 72

Fanon, Frantz, xii, xiii, 12, 13, 97, 98, 114, 123, 126, 127, 130, 134, 148 (Baucom on), 7 (Bhabha on), 162n3 (Hall on), 162n3 (Kruks on), 164n12 (Melas on), 62 (Premnath on), 162n1 (Sekyi-Otu on), 162n2 (Glissant on), 161n103 (on Capécia), 25–26, 154n8 (*BSWM*), xiii, xiv, xv, 25–26, 27, 62, 95, 123, 124, 125, 126, 128–129, 131, 132, 133, 134, 135, 136, 137, 139, 142, 144, 148, 149, 152n12, 153n18, 154n8, 153n20, 162–163n6 (*Wretched of the Earth*), 92, 141 (*Towards*), 138, 142, 143, 144, 145, 164n11, 164n13, 164n14
Fonctionnaire/functionary, 25, 29, 40, 155n6
France, 19, 39, 41, 48, 115, 124, 158n13
Francophone, xi, 2, 4, 48 152n10, 154n12, 155n3, 159n21, 161n11
French, 18, 19 22, 24, 25, 26, 27, 29, 30, 34, 35, 41, 42, 43, 44, 48, 49, 51, 53, 57, 59, 60, 62, 69, 72, 73, 74, 77, 80, 81, 89, 90, 91, 101, 107, 112, 113, 114, 127, 142, 156n9, 157n6, 158n13, 159n1 (language), x, 20, 31, 32, 49, 68, 69, 72, 73, 79, 112, 113, 129, 155n3, 159n22, 160n9 (colonialism), xi, xii, 17, 22, 32 (citizenship), 31 (theories), 2
Fludernik, Monika, 151n2

Gandhi, Indira, 62, 63
Gandhi, Mohandas Karamchand (Mahatma), 63, 68 (Institute), 61, 62–63, 64

Index

Gates, Henry Louis, Jr., 134
Gauvin, Axel, 20, 48 (*Du créole opprimé*), 31, 48, 49, 153n1, 155n5
Gellner, Ernest, 99
Gerbeau, M., 156n6
Gilroy, Paul, 4, 10, 71, 151n4, 152n8, 152n10 (*Small Acts*), 11, 123 (*Between Camps*), 70, 72–72 (*Black Atlantic*), 71, 80, 83, 84, 151–152n7
Giraud, Michel and Danièle Manèse, 153n1
Glissant, Edouard, xii, xiv xv, 12, 13, 17, 33, 44, 96, 97, 113, 116, 119, 120, 121, 148, 149, 152n12, 153n18, 154n10, 159n1, 160n2, 161n16 (Dash on), 115 (Murdoch on), 162n17 (Nesbitt on), 160n2 (on Fanon), 161n13 ('s conception of *Relation*), xiv, 8 17, 105, 106, 107, 108, 109, 110, 111, 112, 116, 117, 120, 121, 122, 148, 154n10, 157n17, 160n2, 160n8 (*Caribbean Discourse*), 34, 119, 152n10, 160n9, 161n13 (*Poétique de la Relation/Poetics of Relation*), 105–122
Global (-ized), 2 (-ism), 16 (-ization), 16, 17, 18, 147, 149 (capitalism), xv
Goa, 53
Goldmann, Lucien, 111
Graham, Gerald, 53, 54

Hall, Stuart, 10, 12, 13, 124 (Bhabha on), 43 ("Cultural Identity and Diaspora"), 4, 5, 6, 9, 152n9, 153n16 ("Deviance"), 9 ("The After-Life"), 162n3
Hallward, Peter, 160n5
Hazareesingh, K., 61, 102
Hegel, Georg W., 17, 105, 107, 108, 109, 114, 117, 121 (-ian), 116
Hegemonic, 66, 118, 121
Hegemony, 7, 8, 43, 56, 112, 115, 121, 133, 153n17
Heterogeneity. *See* difference.
Hierarchy, 32, 41, 61, 85 (Dubois on), 40

Hierarchical, 14, 28, 138 (non-), 8, 112
Hindi, x, 54, 65, 66, 79, 85, 158n13, 159n22
Hindu(s), 59, 67, 71, 74, 75, 93, 100, 101, 102, 159n22
History (histories), xii, xiii, 5, 6, 10, 11, 14, 20, 21, 22–23, 24, 26, 27, 30, 31, 33, 42, 43, 44, 47, 51, 52, 60, 63, 65, 68, 69, 77, 79, 80, 82, 87, 91, 98, 99, 104, 105, 112, 113, 119, 134, 135, 136, 137, 139, 140, 141, 147, 148, 163–164n10 (Bhabha on), 6, 125 (Hall on), 152n9 (Lionnet on), 152n9 (Fanon on), 140 (Ramgoolam on), 62 (critical-), 20, 26, 27, 30
Historical, xv, 13, 22, 27, 74, 102, 104, 111, 115, 117, 136, 140, 159n1, 163–164n10 (-universal), 130, 134, 135, 138, 140, 141, 144, 148, 163n9 (-ly), xiv, 26, 27, 28, 30, 42, 43, 57, 77, 88, 89, 113, 132, 137, 139, 145, 155n2
Homogenize, 111, 152n11
Homogenizing, xii
Homogenization, xiii, 12, 101
Hookoomsing, Vinesh, 156n5
Horkheimer, Max and Theodor Adorno, 160n2
Humbert, Marie-Thérèse, 58, 85, 86, 87, 93, 94, 95, 96, 97, 98, 157n1 (Lionnet on), 92, 157n4
Hybrid, 2, 9, 10, 17, 22, 104, 105, 113, 119, 121, 124, 138, 139, 147, 148 (location), xv (nation), xi (culture), xiii (occurrence), xv (non-), 117
Hybridity, x, xi, xii, xiii, xiv, xv, 1, 2, 6, 7, 8, 9, 10, 11, 12, 13, 15, 17, 18, 19, 20, 22, 24, 25, 27, 34, 35, 38, 40, 41, 42, 43, 44, 51, 52, 60, 71, 91, 96, 104, 106, 117, 118, 120, 122, 123, 124, 125, 126, 127, 129, 130, 138, 139, 143, 145, 147, 148, 149, 151n3, 160n3, 164n10 (Fludernik on), 151n2, 153n17 (Stewart on), 151n2 (Trigo on), 152n14 (avatars of), 3 (postcolonial theories of), xiii, xiv, xv,

Hybridity *(continued)*
   113, 117, 119 (new theories of), xiv, xv, 7, 35 (versions of), xv (related terms), 1, 2, 5, 152n2, 152n14
Hybridizing/hybridization, 2, 33, 145, 147
Hyppolite, Jean, 114

Identification, 83, 93, 110, 126, 127, 147, 161n15
Identity/identities, 5, 23, 28, 29, 32, 46, 56, 59, 61, 65, 69, 79, 82, 89, 90, 92, 93, 95, 97, 103, 108, 113, 138, 141, 152n7, 161n10 (Lionnet on), 152n9 (Hall on), 4, 5, 152n9 (Nancy on), 70
Ile-de-France. *See* Mauritius.
Immigrant(s), 23, 28, 42, 57, 59, 60, 68, 71, 101, 102
Immigration, 4, 10, 16, 23, 42, 58, 71, 90, 101, 153n6 (Balibar on), 59
Indenture(d), 6, 16, 17, 23, 27, 42, 58, 67, 69, 77, 102, 156n9 (coolie), 54, 90
Independent/independence, 1, 49, 52, 55, 59, 67, 71, 74, 79, 80, 100, 155n1
India, x, 10, 53, 56, 70, 72, 81, 90, 102, 157n6, 158n13
Indian(s) (includes Mauritian Indians, Indo-Mauritians), ix, x, xi, 5 16, 32, 35, 36, 55, 56, 57, 58, 59, 60, 61, 63, 64, 66, 66, 67, 69, 71, 72, 73, 75, 77, 79, 80, 81, 82, 85, 87, 90, 91, 100, 101, 102, 156n9 156n14
Indianness, ix, x, 71, 73, 91
Indian Ocean, xi, xii, 12, 54
Indo-Mauritians. *See* Indian[s].
Inequality/inequalities, xiv, 1, 2, 12, 13, 120, 123, 147
Irele, Abiola, 152
Island/islands, xi, xv, 1, 15, 16, 18, 25, 28, 30, 32, 51, 55, 62, 84, 97, 112, 154n8 (Mascerenes), 53, 156n6
Issur, Kumari and Vinesh Hookoomsing, 157n5
Ithier, J., 32

Jameson, Fredric, ix, 111, 119, 120 ("Cultural Logic"), 120–121 ("Globalization and Political"), 13, 45 (*Marxism and Form*), 107, 108, 160n7, 160n8 (*Political Unconscious*), 44, 112, 155n4 (*Seeds of Time*), 155n4 ("Third World Literature"), 98, 99, 153n18
Jordan, Z. A., 108
Joubert, Jean-Louis, 157n5
Joubert, Jean-Louis and Jean-Irénée Raminadrasoa, 157n5
Julien, Eileen, 139

Kaul, Suvir, 31
Kojève, Alexandre, 114, 153n18, 161n12

Labor, 27, 42, 54, 58, 69, 80, 90, 102, 103, 108, 110, 111, 113, 119, 157n6 (work), 112 (slave-), 6, 10 (-er/worker), 23, 58, 74, 75, 80, 90, 91, 101, 102, 108, 109, 110, 111, 113, 156n9, 157n6, 159n26
Labourdonnais, Mahé de (Hazareesingh on), 61, 102
Lacan, Jacques, 46, 114, 118, 119
Laclau, Ernesto and Chantal Mouffe, 112
Language(s)/idiom[s], 19, 21, 27, 29, 31, 32, 34, 43, 44, 45, 46, 47, 48, 52, 54, 55, 56, 61, 65, 66, 68, 70, 73, 79, 80, 85, 91, 100, 101, 102, 103, 106, 112, 113, 116, 119, 124, 148, 156n3, 156n5, 156n9, 159n22, 160n9 (Gauvin on), 49 (Spivak on), 33 (Williams on), 20 (Bhabha on), 44 (Lionnet on), 57, 66, 152n15 (Rughoonundun on), (Ramgoolam on), 55 (-metaphor), 47, 125, 162n4
La Réunion, xi, xiv, 1, 17, 19, 23, 25, 26, 28, 30, 32, 33, 34, 35, 39, 42, 45, 46, 47, 48, 51, 52, 53, 53, 148, 154n8, 155n6, 157n7
Lazarus, Neil (*Nationalism*), 122 ("Disavowing Decolonization"), 123

Index

Leblond, Marius-Ary, 34, 35, 36, 37, 38, 39
Li, David, 151n1
Lionnet, Françoise, 5, 10, 11, 13 (on history), 152n9 (on language), 57 (*Autobiographical Voices*), 8, 9, 92, 152n9, 152–153n15, 157n4, 158n16 (Créolité in the Indian Ocean"), ix, xi, 57, 66 (*Postcolonial Representations*), 5, 6, 152n9
Lukácks, Georg, 119–120
Lüsebrink, Hans-Jürgen, 152n10

Macey, David, 163n7
Madagascar. *See* Africa.
Mahatma. *See* Gandhi.
Mahatma Gandhi Institute, ix
Marcus, George E. and Michael M. J. Fischer, 6, 7
Marimoutou, Jean-Claude Carpanin, 153n2
Markman, Charles (*see also* Fanon *BSWM*), 162n4
Maroon(s). *See* slave(s).
Martinican(s), 33, 112, 113, 114, 129, 141, 142, 154n15, 161n11
Martinique, 33, 112, 114, 115, 127, 160n9
Marx, Karl, 14, 112, 113, 153n18 (-ian/-ist), xiii, xiv, 3, 12, 17, 105, 106, 107, 108, 110, 111, 112, 114, 115, 116, 117, 120, 121, 122, 160n8 (-ism), 3, 17, 105, 115, 117, 122 (*Capital*), 108–109, 110, 111, 112–113 (Economic and Philosophical Manuscripts), 111
Marx, Karl and Friedrich Engels, 105, 107, 115, 161n14 (*Communist Manifesto*), 5, 6
Mascarenes, 53, 156n6
Masson, Loys, 53–54
Maunick, Edouard, 68, 103, 159n25
Mauritian, 73, 79, 154n13, 156n12, 157n17 (context), 54, 58, 70, 74, 158n8 (exceptionalism), ix (Indian[s]), ix, x, xi, 5 16, 32, 35, 36, 55, 56, 57, 58, 59, 60, 61, 63, 64, 66, 66, 67, 69, 71, 72, 73, 75, 77, 79, 80, 81, 82, 85, 87, 90, 91, 100, 101, 102, 156n9 156n14 (Indianness), xi, 91 (Mauritians/Mauritian people), x, 67, 71, 72, 100 (politics), xv, 60, 65, 75, 77 (society), 52, 70, 73, 83, 84, 87, 88, 91, 93, 97 (-ness), xi, 99
Mauritius, ix, x, xi, xiv, xv, 1, 15, 16, 17, 42, 49, 52, 53, 54, 55, 57, 61, 62, 63, 64, 65, 66, 68, 70, 71, 72, 73, 74, 79, 80, 81, 82, 84, 85, 89, 90, 99, 100, 101, 103, 148, 156n3, 156n16, 157n6, 157n7
Mauritius Legislative Council, 75, 76, 80, 156n14
Mbembe, Achille, 13, 104
McClintock, Ann, 151n1
Melas, Nathalie, 62, 156n7
Memory/memories, 10, 21, 58, 67, 102, 118
Métissage, xiv, 1, 2, 9, 15, 20, 21, 22, 24, 25, 26, 27, 29, 31, 34, 42, 43, 45, 46, 52, 105, 106, 108, 110, 111, 116, 117, 119, 122, 152n10 (Lionnet on), 9
Métis(se), 19, 20, 22, 67, 68, 70, 71, 72, 85, 92, 101, 103, 130, 152n13, 153n15, 155n1, 157n1, 158n16 (mulatto/mixed-blood), 37, 38, 87, 91, 158n8 (Lionnet on), 158n16
Michel, Martina, 151n1
Minh-Ha, Trinh T., 99
Minority, 4, 11, 79, 104, 159n21
Modern, 80 (-ity), 12
Moore-Gilbert, Bart, 7
Morisyen. *See* Creole language.
Motherland/mother country, 4, 5, 10, 89
Mother tongue, 31, 56
Mouvement Militant Mauricien (MMM), 66, 73, 76, 81, 82, 159n24
Mudimbé-Boyi, Elisabeth, 155n3
Mulatto. *See* Métis/se.
Murdoch, H. Adlai, 159n1, 162n17
Muslim(s), 59, 67, 71, 73, 101, 159n22

Index

Nancy, Jean-Luc, 70
Nation, xv, 17, 22, 26, 29, 30, 31, 32, 33, 34, 43, 46, 52, 58, 62, 63, 68, 71, 72, 73, 74, 80, 81, 83, 84, 85, 90, 91, 92, 99, 102, 103, 104, 153n15 (Bhabha on), 68 (postcolonial), xi, 65, 123 (hybrid), xi (-al), 4, 17, 59, 66, 90, 98, 99, 103, 139, 147, 160n7, 161n10, 162n1 (-alism), 15, 16, 19, 21, 89, 90, 99, 100, 102, 104, 123 (-alist/-alistic), 49, 62, 70, 81 (-hood), 19, 29, 46, 51
Native, xii, 31, 124
Négritude, 4, 134, 136, 137, 138, 139, 140, 141 (Dash on), 115, 161n11 (Fanon on), 164n11 (post-), 152n10
Nesbitt, Nick, 153n18, 160n2
Nietzsche, Friedrich, 20, 21, 24, 153n4, 153n5, 154n7
Nigger (/ Negro/cafre/nègre), 40, 44, 45, 46, 47, 97, 127, 129, 132, 134, 136, 138, 139, 140, 142, 143, 144, 164n10 (Boyer on), 27, 30, 32 (Fanon on), 127, 128, 131, 140
Noël, Karl, 79
Nzepa, Zacharie Petnkeu, 156n4

Olaniyan, Tejumola, 151n4
Opacity, 108, 109
Opposing, 3
Opposite, 108, 110
Opposition, 108, 125

Parry, Benita, 12, 119, 162n1
Particular, xv, 3, 4, 55, 100, 109, 110, 111, 115, 117, 119, 121, 133, 147, 151n3 (-ity), 134
Peirce, Charles S., 154n16
Pitot, Thomi, 78, 89
Plevitz, Adolphe de, 74, 75
Plural, xv, 71, 72, 83 (-istic), 73 (-ity), 99, 115
Politics, 2, 3 12, 16, 27, 31, 38, 43, 49, 52, 70, 92, 97, 103, 115, 125, 134, 151n1 (radical), xiv (Mauritian), xv, 60, 65, 70, 73, 75, 77

Political, xv, 2, 13, 14, 16, 30, 31, 48, 54, 59, 61, 66, 68, 102, 104, 115, 126, 130, 133, 139, 148,
Pondichéry, 53, 102
Population(s), 2, 4, 11, 34, 54, 56, 59, 60, 61, 66, 68, 69, 75, 77, 79, 89, 90, 91, 97, 101, 102, 104, 155n1 ("general"), 56, 58, 59, 60, 67, 72, 79, 80, 85 (immigrant), 28 (subaltern), xv
Portugese, 53
Postcolonial, xv, 17, 35, 43, 95, 113, 119, 120, 122, 123, 124, 157n1, 158n10, 160n5 (Michel, Bahri, Li, Appiah, Dirlik, McClintock, Shohat and Stam on), 151n1 (canon), xi (context), 14, 16 (discourse[s]), 11, 13, 14, 26 (hybridity), xii, xiii, 15, 42, 104 (locations), xiv, 7, 13 (nation), xi, 65 (praxis), 14 (regions), 7, 98 (societies), xiv (studies), xi, xii, xiii, xiv, 1, 2, 4, 6, 13, 113, 126, 145 (texts), xiii (theories of hybridity), xiii, xiv, xv, 14, 17, 27, 47, 108, 113, 117, 119 (women), 33 (world), xiv, 114
Postcoloniality, xii, 13, 17, 70, 159n1
Power, 1, 9, 17, 27, 28, 30, 65, 94, 99, 111 (Bhabha on), 43
Prabhu, Anjali ("Creolization"), ix ("Interrogating Hybridity"), viii ("Mariama Bâ"), 155n14 ("Narration"), xviii ("Representation"), xviii ("Theorizing"), 158n10
Prabhu, Anjali and Ato Quayson, 106, 153n19, 160n4
Premnath, Gautam, 162n1
Proletariat. *See* class, working-.
Prosper, Jean-Georges ("La place"), 48 (*Histoire*), 62 (*Histoire*), 89
Purity, 37, 38

Queneu, Raymond, 114

Race, xii, xiii, 16, 18, 21, 25, 27, 29, 30, 31, 35, 36, 37, 38, 39, 46, 52, 90, 117, 124, 130, 135, 139, 155n1,

Index

158–159n20, 163n9 (Blanckaert on), 40–41, 124
Racial, x, xii, xiii, 25, 40, 42, 43, 66, 68, 73, 100, 134, 155n2, 157n1 (inter-), 28 (multi-), xv (-izing), 28
Racism, 45, 123, 142, 164n13
Racist, 59, 92, 142 (Fanon on), 164n13, 164n14 (ideologies), 3 (remark), 28 (signs), 43 (tendencies), 20 Radical 47, 115, 158n11, 161n15, 161n16 (agency), 104 (conception), 2 (difference/otherness), 111, 116, 117, 127 (hybridity), 60 (métissage), 24, 26 (politics), xiv (-ly), xiv, 106, 158n11, 158n16
Ramasehsan, Radhika, 71
Ramgoolam, Navin, 74, 157n17
Ramgoolam, Seewoosagar, 51, 52, 55, 61, 62, 63, 66, 67, 68, 73, 75, 80, 99, 100, 103, 156n14, 159n23
Rano, Jonas, 151n6
Real reality/realities, xv, 1, 2, 14, 17, 20, 23, 24, 31, 34, 37, 44, 55, 56, 64, 73, 76, 102, 103, 104, 106, 108, 109, 110, 115, 116, 118, 119, 120, 131, 140, 141, 144, 148, 163n6, 164n10
Relation, xiv, 17, 29, 97, 106, 115
Renan, Ernest, 85
Réunion/Réunionness/Réunionese, Bourbon. *See* La Réunion.
Revolution, 12, 92, 109, 117, 119, 120, 122, 127 (Jameson on), 44 (ary), xiv, 41, 92, 107, 111, 114, 122, 145, 147, 161n13
Riquelme, J. P., 163n10
Robillard, D., 56
Rughoonundun, Nita ("Créolophonie"), 57 ("Les langues"), 153n1, 156n5

Said, Edward, 31, 125
Saint-Pierre, Bernadin de, 77 (Pitot on), 78
San Juan, E. Jr., 163n10
Sartre, Jean-Paul, 115, 128, 131, 132, 139, 140, 143, 144, 161n16 (Fanon on), 140

Séga, 67, 80, 99, 157n17
Sekyi-Otu, Ato, 162n2
Self, 126, 127, 134, 135, 138, 139 (individual[s]), 127, 138, 139, 141, 142, 144, 147, 148, 149, 154n15, 155n1, 156n9, 164n10
Selfhood, 31, 97, 128, 134, 138
Senghor, Léopold Sédar, 136, 137, 139, 159n25
Shohat, Ella and Robert Stam, 151n1
Singh, Manmohan (or Indian Prime Minister), 71, 72, 83
Sino-Mauritian. *See* Chinese.
Skepticism, 2, 31
Slave(s)/maroon, 22, 57, 61, 67, 70, 77, 78, 79, 80, 82, 83, 90, 101, 103, 115, 119, 157n6, 90, 154n8, 154n11, 156n6, 157n7, 162n17 (labor), 6, 11, 69, 71, 81, 82 (-ry), 3, 17, 22, 23, 27, 41, 42, 52, 58, 62, 64, 66, 71, 77, 79, 80, 82, 84, 89, 124, 136, 140, 154n8, 156n16 (Code Noir), 77, 78, 79
Social, xii, xiii, xiv, xv, 2, 7, 8, 18, 27, 95, 97, 111, 113, 115, 117, 118, 119, 120, 148, 153n20, 154n15, 155n4, 160n7 (equality), 61 (-ly), 95
Societal, 1, 119
Society/societies, xi, xv, 2, 14, 22, 25, 26, 28, 30, 37, 52, 60, 53, 69, 70, 82, 83, 84, 87, 88, 91, 92, 93, 95, 97, 103, 104, 110, 111, 112, 115, 139, 142, 154n15, 155n1
Solidarity, 3, 4, 10, 42, 91, 139, 151n7 (Baucom on), 7 (Lionnet on), 8
Specific, xv, 3, 5, 99, 105, 125, 138, 147 (-ation[s]), 15, 124, 147 (-ity/-ities), xi, 2, 51, 82, 107, 129, 145, 158n16
Spivak, Gayatri Chakravorty, 14, 125 ("Thinking Cultural"), 33 (Gates on), 134
Stein, Peter, 156n3
Stepan, Nancy, 158n8
Stereotype(s)/stereotyping/stereotyped, 130, 132, 133, 137, 140, 148
Stereotypical, 138
Stewart, Charles, 151n2

Stoler, Anne, 26
Structure(s), 26, 29, 59, 79, 83, 85, 87, 100, 102, 104, 113, 116, 144, 45 (Fanon on), 145, 153n20, 154n15 (of feeling), 12, 15, 19, 21, 29, 31, 34 (of structures), 120 (-al), 28, 37, 38, 49, 104, 153n1 (-ed), 60, 131 (-ing/re—ing), 46, 99, 133, 134, 139 (sub-), 20, 125 (super-), 162n5
Subaltern, 121, 122, 153n17 (agency), xiii, 1, 7, 9, 12, 105, 117 (populations), xv (subject[s]), xii, xiii, 3, 8, 126 (ity), 11, 121
Subject(s), 14, 46, 108, 110, 113, 117, 119, 124, 125, 134, 136, 138, 141, 143, 144, 148, 164n10 (Lionnet on), 6 (Bhabha on), 6, 43, 125 (Hall on), 9 (Jameson on), 120 (Lacan on), 118 (subaltern), xii, xiii, 3, 8, 126 (-hood), 128, 129, 130, 134, 137, 139, 141 (-ive), 33, 108, 111, 119 (-ivity), 4, 31, 44, 106, 109, 112, 113, 125, 129, 130, 131, 142 (inter-ive), 126 (de-ification), 130
Suez Canal, 36
Sugar, 35, 57, 71, 75, 90 (-cane), 35
Swahili, 103
Synchronic, 21, 22 (-ally), 26
Synchrony, 5
Synthesis, 22, 106, 116 (Glissant on), 106
Synthesized, 30

Tamil, x, 32, 54, 55, 66, 79, 90, 101, 102, 158n13, 159n22
Telugu, 54, 55, 66, 79, 101, 158n13, 159n22
Theoretical, 111, 117, 124, 135, 138, 148 (concept), 2 (evaluation), 84 (formulation), 4 (framework), 10 (need), 4, 5 (positioning), 15 (project), 121 (process), 116
Theorist(s)/theoretician(s), xi, xiii, 2, 4, 6, 7, 9, 123
Theorize(d), 96, 105, 134, 144
Theorizing, xi, 35, 125, 139 (theorization), 122

Theory, xi, xiii, 2, 7, 8, 17, 18, 43, 95, 106, 107, 111, 115, 120, 145, 158n10, 162n18 (Lacan on), 118 (of hybridity), 10, 14, 125, 128, 130, 160n3
Theories, 10, 16, 43, 105, 112, 122, 135 (of hybridity), xiv, 2, 7 (postcolonial theories of hybridity), xiii, xiv, xv, 17, 27, 47, 117, 119
Tosquelles, François, 114
Totality, xiii, xiv, xv, 11, 15, 17, 20, 26, 29, 34, 46, 84, 99, 100, 104, 105, 108, 109, 110, 115, 118, 119, 120, 121, 122, 125, 126, 127, 134, 139, 143, 145, 147, 148, 149, 162n6 (Bhabha on), 121 (Fanon on), 127
Transculturation, 1, 2
Transnational, 4
Trauma, 5, 10, 13, 91, 147 (-tic), 22, 118
Trigo, Abril, 152n14

United Nations, 70
Universal, 100, 109, 110, 138, 140, 141, 154n16 (-historical), 130, 134, 135, 138, 140, 141, 144, 148 (-ism), xiii (-ity), 70, 115 (-izing), 17, 137 (-ly), 60
Universal suffrage, 75, 81
Unnuth, Abhimanyu, 65
Utopia, xv, 34, 106, 122, 140, 142, 148 (-n), x, 2, 20, 29, 10, 111, 115, 119, 122, 152–153n15, 160n5 (-nism), 14

Vaughan, Meghan, 156n16
Venugopal, K., 72
Vergès, Francoise, xiv, 12, 13, 22, 28 ("Post-Scriptum"), xiv–xv (*Monsters and Revolutionaries*), 15, 27, 42
Virahsawmy, Dev, 159n24

Wallerstein, Emmanuel, 102, 103, 158n9, 159n21, 159n26
Williams, Raymond, 12, 15, 19, 111 (*Culture and Society*), 20 ("Film..."), 34 (*Marxism*), 26, 29, 34 ("Thomas Hardy"), 29

Index

White/whites/whiteness, x, xi, xii, xiii, 24, 2. 38, 42, 46, 56, 58, 59, 67, 68, 71, 72, 74, 76, 77, 79, 85, 87, 89, 92, 93, 94, 95, 97, 103, 123, 124, 126, 127, 128, 129, 131, 132, 133, 134, 135, 136, 137, 138, 139, 140, 141, 142, 143, 144, 154n8, 156n14, 163n7, 163n9 (race), xii, 16, 35, 36, 46

Worker. *See* laborer.

Yiddel, Janice and Belinda Kemp, 151n5
Young, Robert J. C., 124–125, 130, 162n18

**SUNY series,
Explorations in Postcolonial Studies**

Emmanuel C. Eze and Arif Dirlik, editors

Natascha Gentz and Stefan Kramer (eds.), *Globalization, Cultural Identities, and Media Representations*

Sandra Ponzanesi, *Paradoxes of Postcolonial Culture: Contemporary Women Writers of the Indian and Afro-Italian Diaspora*

Sam Durrant, *Postcolonial Narrative and the Work of Mourning: J.M. Coetzee, Wilson Harris, and Toni Morrison*

Patrick Colm Hogan, *Empire and Poetic Voice: Cognitive and Cultural Studies of Literary Tradition and Colonialism*

Olakunle George, *Relocating Agency: Modernity and African Letters*

Elisabeth Mudimbe-Boyi (ed.), *Beyond Dichotomies: Histories, Identities, Cultures, and the Challenge of Globalization*

John C. Hawley (ed.), *Postcolonial, Queer: Theoretical Intersections*

Alfred J. Lopez, *Posts and Pasts: A Theory of Postcolonialism*

S. Shankar, *Textual Traffic: Colonialism, Modernity, and the Economy of the Text*

Patrick Colm Hogan, *Colonialism and Cultural Identity: Crises of Tradition in the Anglophone Literatures of India, Africa, and the Caribbean*

M. T. Kato, *From Kung Fu to Hip Hop: Globalization, Revolution, and Popular Culture*